LOTS MORE
Tell Me Why

What is the Sphinx?

What city is really a country?

Who was Booker T. Washington?

How much does the earth weigh?

LOTS MORE
Tell Me Why

By ARKADY LEOKUM

Illustrations by
CYNTHIA ILIFF KOEHLER
and ALVIN KOEHLER

**Answers to
hundreds
of questions
children ask**

GROSSET & DUNLAP · PUBLISHERS · NEW YORK

A NATIONAL GENERAL COMPANY

For My Wife, Mae,
Without Whose Help This Book
Would Have Been Finished Much Sooner

Library of Congress Catalog Card Number: 71-158763
ISBN: 0-448-02463-2 (Trade Edition)
ISBN: 0-448-03333-x (Library Edition)

1978 PRINTING

CONTENTS

Chapter 2
How It Began

Chapter 3
The Human Body

Chapter 4
How Other Creatures Live

Chapter 5
How Things Are Made

Chapter 1

The World Around Us

What Is Radiation?

Looking at it very simply, radiation is the sending out of waves of energy. You have known about it since you were a baby—though you didn't know what it was. When you held your hand in front of a hot stove or radiator, or a light bulb, you felt radiant heat. When you sat in the warm sun, a type of radiation called ultraviolet rays was striking your skin.

All these are examples of electromagnetic radiation. The other major type of radiation is called radioactive radiation, and it comes from either radioactive material or nuclear reactions. In radioactive radiation, particles, as well as waves of energy, are given off.

Since electromagnetic radiation is the sending out of waves of energy, we should know something about those waves. The distance between the waves is called the wavelength. The number of waves passing a given point each second is the frequency. And when all the waves within a certain range of wavelengths are grouped together, we call them the spectrum.

The group with the shortest wavelength is the X-ray spectrum. Next comes the ultraviolet spectrum. Then comes the visible-light spectrum; we can see these waves. The waves get still longer, and we can no longer see them. This is the infrared spectrum. Even longer waves (Hertzian waves) are used for radio, television, and radar.

What produces all these waves? In some cases machines are required; in others they are produced naturally. Naturally made waves come from the sun. To produce any radiation requires energy. In the case of the sun, atomic energy is produced by a reaction called fusion. In the case of X-rays, a target must be bombarded with particles.

Radioactive radiation is the process of change or decay that certain elements undergo. Such elements are radioactive. They radiate particles (and waves, too) as the nuclei of their atoms break up.

13

What Are UFO's?

The popular name for them is "flying saucers." UFO stands for "unidentified flying object."

Do they really exist? Many books have been written about them and thousands of people claim they have seen them; some even claim they have photographed them. And no matter what scientific investigations reveal, there will still be people who believe they exist.

Studies of saucer reports show that UFO's are very different from one another. Some people report having seen flat saucers; others see saucers shaped like spheres, cigars, or doughnuts.

The colors of saucers seem to be as different as their sizes. Saucers of nearly all colors have been reported. Some seem to change color as they are being watched.

Saucers have been seen to move in every direction and at nearly every speed. They can turn at right angles, move straight up or straight down, or travel in a zigzag path. They can hang motionless in the air, and make either a hissing noise or a roar.

When the United States Air Force started to investigate the reports about flying saucers, it discovered that people weren't "imagining" what they saw. Everyone who reported a flying saucer had seen something. But what?

In some cases, the "something" was actually a weather balloon. In other cases, it was a satellite, a cloud, a meteor, a star, a bird, a comet, a planet, or fireworks. It was also what are called sun dogs. These are images of the sun reflected through ice crystals. Many flying-saucer stories have been traced to fireballs, which are formed by lightning.

If saucers were really spaceships, there would be a certain pattern in the reports about them. But there is no such pattern. The reason is that people are not seeing spaceships but many other things. So scientists believe that there is no evidence that we are being visited, watched, or invaded by intelligent beings from other worlds.

FIREWORKS

WEATHER BALLOON

SILVER INSTRUMENTATION BALLOON

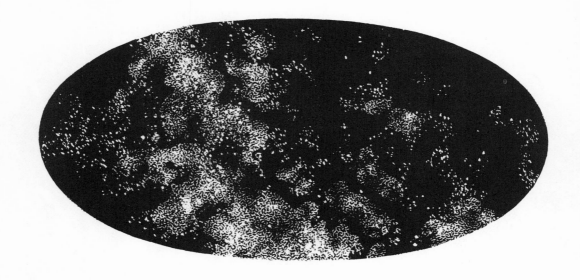

How Many Galaxies Are There?

Scattered throughout the universe are vast islands of stars, called galaxies. Our sun is a star in the Milky Way galaxy. This is our galaxy, too, and it has billions of stars in it. It takes light about one hundred thousand years to go from one end of our galaxy to the other (and light travels about six trillion miles in one year!).

Astronomers have discovered through the use of telescopes that there are millions of galaxies beyond our own. There are basically three types of galaxies that we know about. Those that have a spiral shape (like our own Milky Way) are called spiral galaxies. The one nearest to us is about two million light-years away. It is the great spiral galaxy in the constellation Andromeda.

About 17 percent of the brightest galaxies that have been observed are called elliptical galaxies. (An ellipse is like a stretched-out circle.) These galaxies contain mostly stars and seem to have little or no dust and gas.

Some galaxies are called irregular galaxies because they appear to have no special shape. These galaxies contain stars, dust, and gas. The two galaxies nearest the Milky Way are irregular galaxies.

There are also some small galaxies that are called dwarf galaxies. The smallest are only a few hundred light-years across and contain only a few thousand stars. There may be more dwarf galaxies in the universe than larger ones.

Galaxies are separated from one another by hundreds of thousands of light-years. They usually occur in groups or clusters, each group containing ten or more large galaxies and some dwarfs.

The most distant clusters of galaxies so far observed lie billions of light-years from our Milky Way. And there are galaxies so far away from us that it is almost impossible for us to imagine the vastness of the distance. So the answer to the question of how many galaxies there are in the universe will probably always remain a mystery.

Why Do All the Planets Look Different?

The reason each of the planets looks different to us is that each one seems to be made up of different substances. Even though they are all planets revolving around the sun and part of the solar system, their composition varies.

We actually know very little about what the planets are made of, and this is one of the questions man hopes to answer with the space explorations that are presently going on and those that are being planned for the future.

Let's take a brief look at each of the other planets and see what is known of their make-up. Mercury is a small, rocky world. It has some dark areas on its surface, and has a very thin atmosphere of carbon dioxide.

Venus is a white globe with some hazy markings. It is completely covered by a layer of white clouds. The clouds contain carbon-dioxide gas, and some nitrogen and oxygen may also be present. We still don't know whether the surface of Venus is very hot or not. If it is not hot, there may be oceans on Venus. If it is very hot, then it is probably a vast and lifeless desert.

Mars is a small, rocky world. Parts of Mars are darker than others, but we still don't know whether these markings are canals or not. Mars has little if any oxygen, so the question about life on Mars is still a mystery.

Jupiter appears as a yellowish globe with darker bands of color crossing it. Jupiter is covered by a layer of clouds that may be thousands of miles deep. We still don't know whether Jupiter has a rocky core or whether the main body of the planet is made up of solid hydrogen.

Saturn is also covered by clouds. It has bands of color—yellowish at the equator, greenish at the poles. It may have a small, rocky core. Uranus looks slightly green with a band of silvery color. Neptune is a dim greenish object, with a few bands of color. Very little is known about Pluto. It may be a small, rocky planet like the earth. It is so cold that any atmosphere it has must be frozen.

As you can see, man still has a great deal to find out about the other members of the solar system.

What Are the Sizes of the Planets?

A planet is very different from a star. A star is a huge ball of hot gases that gives off heat and light. A planet is a much smaller body that shines by reflected light.

Let's start with the planet nearest to the sun and move outward. The first one is Mercury. Mercury's diameter is 2,900 miles—about the width of the Atlantic Ocean. So it's only a fraction of the earth's size.

The next planet we meet is Venus. It is very nearly the same size as the earth. Its diameter is 7,600 miles, while that of the earth is 7,913 miles. By the way, an odd fact about Venus is that it rotates backward; that is, from east to west. The next planet is our earth, and then comes Mars.

Mars shines in the sky with a reddish color. It has a diameter of 4,200 miles, a little more than half that of the earth. Mars has interested scientists more than most planets because of its markings that look like channels or canals. It seems the most likely planet other than ours to have life on it, perhaps some kind of plant life.

Jupiter, the next planet, is far away from the sun. It takes about 11.9 years to complete one orbit. Jupiter is the largest of the planets. It has a diameter of 86,800 miles, nearly 11 times the diameter of the earth.

18

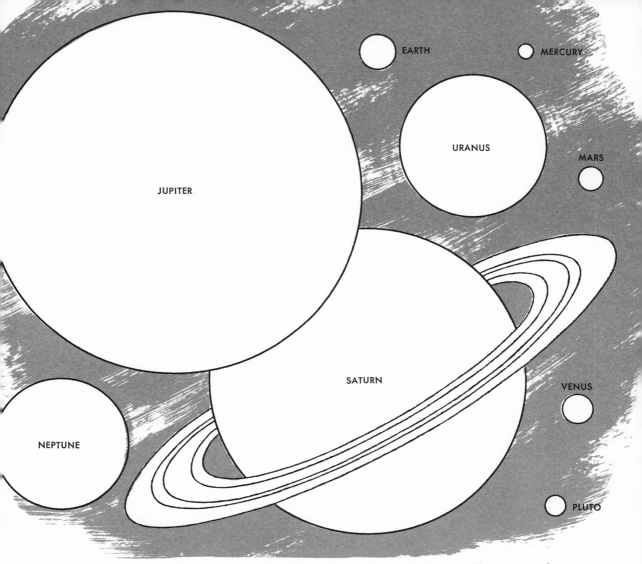

Saturn, the next planet, is another giant. It has a diameter of 71,500 miles, which is about nine times that of the earth. An unusual thing about Saturn is the group of flat rings that circle it. These rings are made up of billions of tiny particles.

Uranus, the next planet, is much larger than the earth. It has a diameter of 29,400 miles. Uranus is tilted over on its side. Its axis is tilted over at an angle of 98 degrees. (The earth tilts at an angle of 23½ degrees.) Neptune, the next planet, is 28,000 miles in diameter. And finally, the last known planet, Pluto, is believed to have a diameter of about 3,600 miles. It is so far from the sun that the sun appears to it as only a bright star in the sky.

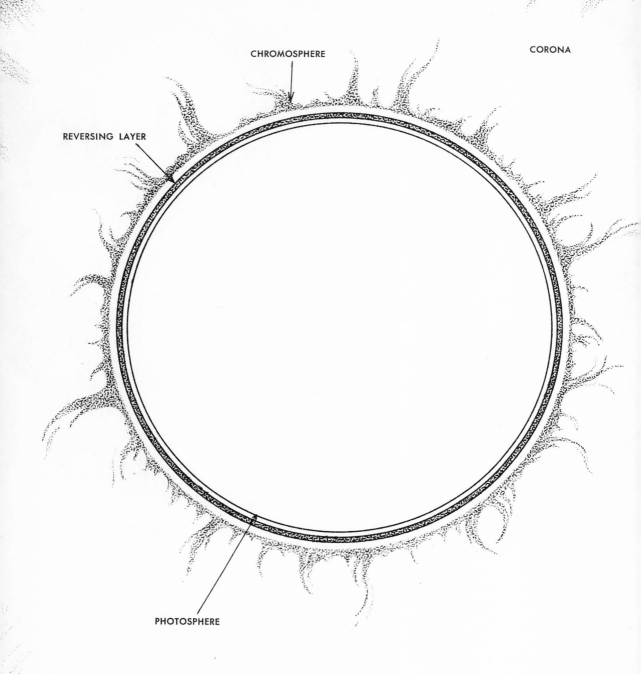

What Is the Corona of the Sun?

Have you ever seen photographs of a total eclipse of the sun? All around the dark sun, there is an uneven glow of light, and this light is called the corona.

To understand what the corona is, we have to know some things about the sun. To begin with, the sun, at least at its surface, is not a solid like the earth. This surface, which is all that we can observe of the sun, is composed of gases.

In fact, the sun is surrounded by four layers of gaseous matter that hide what is underneath. The innermost of these layers is called the photosphere. The next two layers are known as the reversing layer and the chromosphere. Together they form the sun's atmosphere. The outermost layer is the corona.

Let's see what each of these layers of gas is. The photosphere (or "light sphere") is what we see when we look toward the sun. Most of the time, dark sunspots can be seen on this bright surface.

The "reversing layer," which is made of gaseous vapors, extends several hundred miles out from the photosphere of the sun. This layer is never seen, but it can be studied by an instrument called the spectrograph.

Outside the reversing layer is the chromosphere, or color sphere. It is about nine thousand miles thick and is made up mostly of hydrogen and helium gases. At the time of a total eclipse, it shines out around the dark disk with a brilliant scarlet light. From this red border, flame-colored clouds of the same material shoot out to great heights, sometimes even as much as one million miles! They are called prominences, and they look like great flames of fire.

Then comes the outer layer, which is called the corona. It is composed of light, gaseous matter, and has two parts. The inner corona, lying next to the red chromosphere, is a band of pale yellow. The outer corona is white, with streamers extending out millions of miles from the edge of the sun.

All of this describes only the layers that surround the sun. What is beneath them still remains a mystery!

What Are Ultraviolet Rays?

Light rays, heat rays, X-rays, and ultraviolet rays are all forms of radiation. Radiation wavelengths have an amazingly large span. The longest are radio waves; the shortest, gamma rays. About halfway between the longest and shortest wavelengths are light waves, or visible radiation.

Light waves themselves have a great variety of wavelengths. Each color is a different wavelength. Red light is the longest wavelength visible to man. Next is orange, followed by yellow, green, blue, and violet, which is the shortest wavelength radiation that can be seen.

Just past the violet-light wavelength are the radiations in what scientists call the ultraviolet range. The sun emits these rays, as do certain man-made lamps specially produced for this purpose. Ultraviolet wavelengths range from just above those of violet light to more than 2,500,000 waves per inch.

Because ultraviolet rays are shorter than other rays, they are penetrating. From the sun these rays, along with heat, reach the nerves in your skin. Still, only about half the ultraviolet rays from the sun ever reach the ground. Many are absorbed high up in the earth's atmosphere.

Is the Earth Always the Same Distance from the Sun?

Do you know why it's hot in summer and cold in winter? It's because the position of the earth's axis with respect to the sun changes as the earth revolves around the sun. Now, this change is very slight, when you consider the great distance of the earth from the sun. Yet that small change is enough to make us broil in summer and freeze in winter!

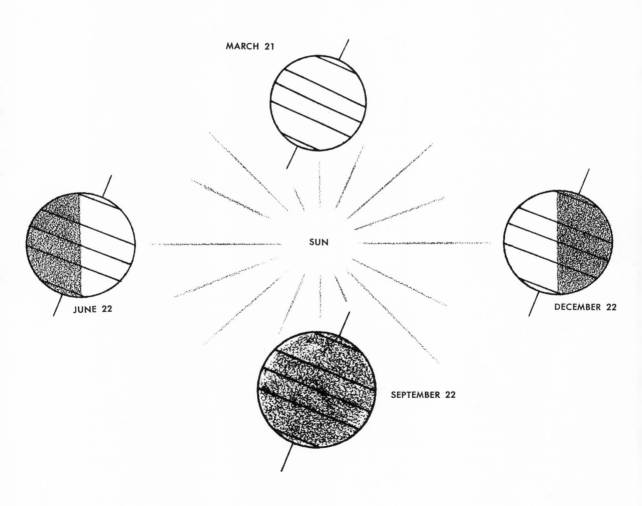

MARCH 21

SUN

JUNE 22

DECEMBER 22

SEPTEMBER 22

Can you imagine then what life would be like if the distance of the earth from the sun were to change a great deal? If we wandered farther away, life might become impossible because of the cold. If we came much nearer, we might all burn up in the heat! So the distance from the earth to the sun remains pretty much the same at all times, and that distance is, in round numbers, ninety-three million miles.

But the orbits of the planets around the sun are not quite circular, and in the case of many other planets the distance from the sun does change quite a bit during the year.

For example, the planet Mercury, nearest the sun, has an orbit that is less like a circle than the path of any other planet. The planet Venus varies in its distance from the sun from sixty-seven million to sixty-eight million miles.

Mars, the first planet beyond the earth, takes 687 days for its journey around the sun. During this trip its distance from the sun varies, but it averages about 141,700,000 miles.

Jupiter, the next planet away from the sun, provides an example of a planet whose distance from the sun varies a great deal. So we find that in discussing distance from the sun, an "average" figure is given for all the planets, including the earth. The reason for the variations is the pull on each planet by the others in our solar system.

Why Don't We Feel the Rotation of the Earth?

Until a few hundred years ago, men believed that the earth stood still; that the sun, the moon, and the stars went around it. It's easy to understand why this was so. After all, that's the way it looked. And nobody could feel the earth moving. If the earth moved, why didn't objects fly off it, including the water in the oceans?

Today, of course, we know that the earth is moving constantly in two ways. It is going around the sun, and it is rotating on its axis. The reason we don't feel it is that we go along with the surface as it moves, and so does the air that surrounds us. Gravity holds everything on earth down, including the water in the oceans.

But the rotation of the earth is known to us from many things that we observe and feel. It is this rotation that causes day and night. If the earth didn't rotate, the side facing the sun would always have daylight, and the side facing away from the sun would be in darkness. But every point on the earth is carried around to the light side and then the dark side every twenty-four hours.

Another important motion of the earth that we can't "feel," but that makes a difference in our lives, is the trip the earth takes around the sun. It is this motion that causes the change of seasons, and you know how different our life becomes with each changing season. In fact, this trip around the sun, which takes about 365¼ days, and which we call a year, is the way we measure history, the length of our lives, and so on.

The change of seasons is caused by the slant of the earth's axis. This slant or tilt is 23½ degrees from the vertical. Each pole leans toward the sun half the year and away from the sun the other half. So for six months the northern part of the earth receives more sunlight and thus more heat (summer), and during the other months it receives less sunlight and has its cooler season.

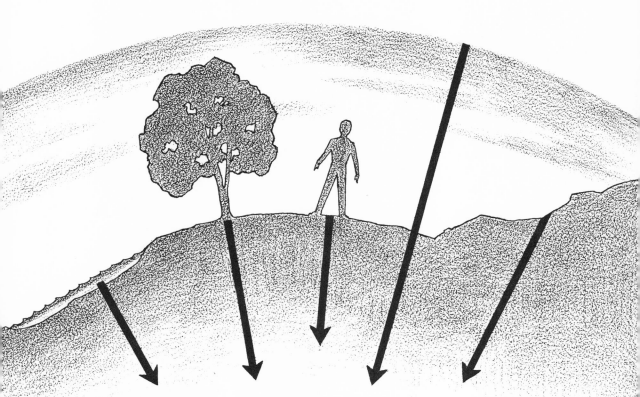

Do Other Planets Rotate?

Let's consider them one by one and see what happens in each case.

Mercury goes around the sun in an orbit that takes 88 days to complete. Scientists now believe that Mercury rotates once every 58 or 59 days. This means that Mercury has a solar day (a period of day and night) that is about 180 earth days long.

Venus, it has recently been discovered, rotates once about every 243 days. Mars rotates nearly as fast as the earth. And because it is also tilted on its axis, it has seasons like the earth's. Jupiter, which is the largest of the planets, spins very quickly. It takes less than 10 hours to rotate once. Saturn also rotates very quickly. It takes only 10 hours and 2 minutes to turn once on its axis. Uranus rotates in a very odd way because it is practically lying on its side.

Neptune and Pluto are the planets farthest away, and less is known about them than about the others. It is assumed they both rotate. Neptune's orbit around the sun takes almost 165 earth years to complete. And Pluto takes almost 249 earth years to go once around the sun.

Now that we are in the age of space exploration, scientists are learning more about the rest of the solar system than man ever knew before, and we may soon have more specific knowledge about the motions of the other planets.

How Much Does the Earth Weigh?

Since the earth is suspended in space, "weighing" it is not the same thing as putting an object on a scale. When we speak of the weight of the earth, we mean the amount of matter that makes it up. This is called its mass.

The earth's mass is about 6.6 sextillion tons. To give you an idea of how that number looks, here it is: 6,600,000,000,000,000,000,000. How did scientists find out that this was the mass of the earth?

To do this, they used a principle based on the fact that any two objects attract each other. This is what the force of gravity depends on. Put in simple terms, the law of gravity states that two objects are attracted by a force that depends on their mass and their distance apart. The bigger the objects, the greater the force that pulls them together. The farther apart they are, the smaller the force.

To measure the weight of the earth, the following is done: A small weight is suspended from a string. The exact position of that weight is measured. Now a ton of lead is brought near the hanging weight. There is an attraction between the weight and the lead, and this causes the weight to be pulled just a tiny bit out of line. (Actually, it is less than one-millionth of an inch, so you can see how carefully the measuring must be done.)

After this is measured, scientists can use mathematics to figure out the weight of the earth. They have measured the power of the earth's attraction on the weight, and they have measured the power of the one-ton lead's attraction on the suspended weight. The relative difference can be calculated and tells them the mass of the earth.

What is this mass made of? There is the crust of solid rock; then a layer called the mantle, which is also solid rock and goes down about one thousand eight hundred miles; and then the innermost part, which is the core and is about two thousand one hundred miles in radius. The material of the core is liquid because of the great heat at the center of the earth.

How Do We Know What Is at the Center of the Earth?

Since scientists, and even instruments, are unable to go down very far into the earth, they have to use other means to find out about its interior.

One of these methods is the study of volcanic eruptions. These eruptions bring up hot gases and molten rock, indicating that the interior of the earth is hot. Another method is the study of earthquakes. Earthquake waves give us a kind of X-ray picture of the earth's interior.

When an earthquake occurs, different types of vibrations spread out in all directions through the rocks. These waves are called seismic waves. They travel at different speeds in different kinds of material. And their direction changes as they go from one kind of rock to another. By studying these waves with very delicate instruments, scientists can learn about the interior of the earth.

Scientists have noticed that at a depth of one thousand eight hundred miles, there is a sudden change in the way seismic waves travel. One kind of wave changes direction and another stops entirely. So there must be a great change in the material of the earth at that depth.

The shock waves from an earthquake reach different seismic stations at different times. This is caused partly by the material through which the waves travel. So here is another clue to what material is inside the earth.

Here is a brief idea of what is in the interior of the earth. The topmost layer, the crust, is made of solid rock. It is about twenty to thirty miles thick under the continents, and about three miles thick under the oceans.

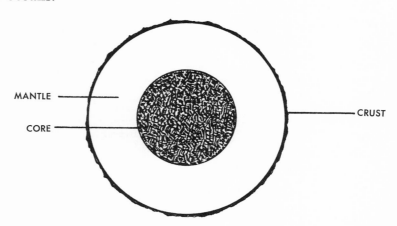

MANTLE

CORE

CRUST

Underneath the crust is the mantle, which is also made of solid rock. It goes down about one thousand eight hundred miles. The innermost part of the earth is the core. There is an outer liquid core, mostly made up of iron and nickel. Inside that, there is an inner core of solid metal about one thousand six hundred miles in diameter.

What Was the Greatest Earthquake?

If the crust of the earth were not pretty solid, it would be shaking about and moving up and down constantly. But there are places in the rocks of the earth's crust where it isn't strongly held together—where "faults" exist. Along this break one rock mass might rub against another with very great force and friction. The energy of this rubbing is changed to vibration in the rocks—and we have an earthquake!

There are two ways we can describe an earthquake in terms of size: one is in the force of the earthquake itself, and the other is in the damage it does. Since the loss of human lives and the destruction of property interest people more than technical measurements, the "great earthquakes" people remember are those in which many lives were lost.

The most famous one in North America was the San Francisco earthquake of 1906. A great fire followed this quake. Seven hundred people died and property damage amounted to about $425,000,000.

More recently, in February, 1971, a heavy quake in the Los Angeles area caused more than a billion dollars in damage to homes, businesses and roadways.

One of the most famous earthquakes in Europe took place in Lisbon, Portugal, in 1755. The city was destroyed and at least thirty thousand people were killed. In 1908, in Calabria and Sicily, Italy, a quake killed about seventy-five thousand people; and in 1915, in central Italy, hundreds of towns and villages were damaged and thirty thousand people were killed.

Two great earthquakes that caused enormous damage took place in Tokyo, Japan, and in the Kansu Province in China. The Tokyo Quake of 1923 killed more than one hundred thousand persons and destroyed this city and the city of Yokohama, too. The Chinese Quake in 1920 covered more than three hundred square miles and killed about two hundred thousand people.

An earthquake may be a great earthquake and do very little damage. For example, the greatest earthquake on record in the United States is hardly known to most people. It took place near the town of New Madrid, Missouri, in 1811 and 1812. There were 1,874 separate earthquake shocks felt and some of the shocks were felt four hundred miles away! But this area was sparsely settled, so not much damage was done.

What Is St. Elmo's Fire?

St. Elmo's fire is one of the many interesting phenomena connected with lightning, and to understand it we must review what takes place when lightning occurs.

All matter is made up of two kinds of particles, positive and negative. The two kinds of particles strongly attract each other, and if they are separated, they have a great tendency to reunite.

When a strong negative or positive charge is built up in the base of a cloud, it induces an opposite charge below it on the earth. Electrons start moving from the region of the negative charge to the positive. They gradually build up a channel or channels of charged particles between the earth and the cloud, and when there is a great surge of electrons, a lightning flash occurs.

Now suppose that instead of allowing the charges to build up until the strain is too great and must be broken, there were some way of enabling the charge from the earth below to "leak off." Instead of a lightning stroke, the charge would leak off in the form of a "brush discharge." This, by the way, is exactly the way a lightning rod works. The point of the lightning rod enables the electrons to leak off.

St. Elmo's fire is the glow that accompanies such a "brush discharge" of atmospheric electricity. It appears as a tip of light on the ends of pointed objects, such as church towers or the masts of ships during stormy weather. We usually hear a crackling or fizzing noise at the same time.

Another place St. Elmo's fire is commonly observed is on the edge of propellers, and along the wing tips, windshields, and noses of airplanes when they are flying in dry snow or in the vicinity of thunderstorms. This discharge may sometimes be strong enough to cause static in the radio of the airplane.

Is the Equator the Hottest Place on Earth?

When we talk about places on earth being "hot" or "cold," we are talking about "climate." And in a general way all climate is determined by the heat of the sun.

It is the heat of the sun that warms the land, the oceans, and the atmosphere. The heat of the sun draws moisture into the atmosphere, and thus makes rain possible. The sun's heat causes differences in air pressure, which creates winds, and together the sun's heat and the winds produce ocean currents. So, in discussing the climate of a particular location, it is important to consider the sun's heating effect on that area.

31

Now, because the surface of the earth is curved, the heating effect of the sun is greatest at the Equator and least at the Poles. At the Equator, the rays from the sun strike the earth vertically. Above and below the equatorial region, the rays strike the earth at an angle, or slant. This means that the regions above and below the Equator, the Temperate Zones, receive fewer rays from the sun than the areas in the region of the Equator, the Tropical Zone. The regions of the earth farthest from the Equator, in other words, receive the least amount of heat.

When a ray of sunlight strikes the earth at an angle, it has to pass through more atmosphere, and so some of its heat is absorbed by the air—and that's another reason the other zones receive less heat.

All of this makes the region of the Equator the hottest region on earth. But we have been talking about what is called solar climate, climate depending only on the sun's heat. There are many other factors, however, that enter into the picture to determine what is called physical climate, the actual climates found on the earth.

The most important of these other factors are water, land, and altitude. The waters of the oceans and ocean currents, the existence of large land areas, and the altitude of the land all can combine to create different climates regardless of the location on earth. That's why, at any particular time, it may be hotter at a point far from the Equator than it is at the Equator itself, although the equatorial region is the hottest on earth.

JUNGLE IN BORNEO NEAR THE EQUATOR   SNOW-COVERED PEAK NEAR THE EQUATOR IN AFRICA

Was the Sahara Always a Desert?

The Sahara desert is the world's hottest region in summer and the world's largest desert. It is bigger than the United States and has an area of over 3,500,000 square miles.

Yet at one time most of the Sahara was under water! In ages gone by, there were rivers and valleys and gorges. In fact, some people believe that the sand of the Sahara comes from the time when it was the bottom of a great sea. But this theory is not accepted by most authorities.

We do know that at one time the Sahara had the climate of a moist temperate or subtropical region. There were probably grass and trees growing there. But gradually the vegetation disappeared and the region became arid. This dried out the soil, and wind erosion broke up the particles until the sand was formed. There are still some patches of oases, however, where trees and grasses grow, and where springs and natural wells may be found.

The Sahara is kept dry by the winds in the region. They are northeast trade winds that blow steadily toward the Equator. As the air moves toward the Equator, it gets hotter and is able to hold more moisture. So the air takes up moisture like blotting paper and keeps the desert dry and hot.

In July, there are many places in the Sahara where the average temperature is 100 degrees Fahrenheit. At a place called Azizia near Tripoli, the world's record heat was recorded in 1922. It was 136.4 degrees! When the sun goes down, however, the land cools very quickly. The temperature may drop 30 to 50 degrees, and in some oases in winter, there is even frost at night!

Despite the dryness of the land, there is some animal life there, such as the desert antelope, which carries a water supply in a special sac in its body.

33

What Is an Oasis?

We all have an image of a traveler lost in the hot desert who finally comes to a spot where there is water. A fertile area with green plants or crops is naturally a welcome sight to a desert traveler. Desert land that receives enough water to allow plants and crops to grow is called an oasis.

All the world's major deserts contain oases, either natural or man-made. They vary greatly in size. They may be large areas with enough water to support a settlement or even a city. Smaller oases are places for rest where the desert traveler and his animals find food and water. Larger oases are busy marketplaces and centers for amusement.

Natural oases are found along rivers and streams that flow into deserts and where underground springs are close to the surface. In a natural oasis the brief periods of rain also help nourish plants and grasses.

In the western Sahara there are two busy oases called Laghouat and In-Salah. The water for these oases comes from rain that falls on the Atlas Mountains and collects in valleys to form small streams. In the Libyan Desert, there are few visible streams, and the oases are fed chiefly by underground water.

But an oasis may also be created by man. Today machinery drills wells thousands of feet deep. These wells provide water to support whole settlements. In fact, there is a great project being carried on in the Sahara to increase the size of the oases there and to create new ones so that settlements can be established.

Sometimes an irrigation project will bring water to what otherwise might be desert land. For example, canals built from the Colorado River across the Colorado Desert irrigate the once dry Imperial Valley in southern California. This valley is really a vast oasis and has become one of the world's most productive desert lands.

Did you know that Cairo, the largest city in Africa, began as an oasis? Phoenix, Arizona, and Salt Lake City are other examples of oasis cities.

CRATER LAKE

How Are Lakes Formed?

Lakes are inland bodies of water that occupy depressions in the surface of the land. These depressions are called basins.

Lakes result from the flow of water into low areas. Lake water comes largely from rainfall and melting snow. The water enters a lake basin through brooks, streams, rivers, underground springs, and ground water.

The lake basins themselves are formed in several ways. Many lakes are the result of faulting or warping in the earth's crust. Lake Superior in North America is an example of such a lake.

Sometimes lakes are created by volcanoes. A lava flow may block the outlet of a valley and form a lake basin. Sometimes the crater of an extinct volcano fills with water. Crater Lake in southern Oregon is an example of this.

Many lakes occupy basins formed by glacial erosion. All the Great Lakes (except Lake Superior) and Lake Winnipeg in Canada are examples of lakes that were formed by glaciers.

Along coastal areas, waves and shore currents sometimes close inlets and temporarily create lakes out of bays and estuaries. Sometimes the main stream of a river may build up its flood plain by depositing silt (mud and soil) when the river overflows. As a result, tributary valleys are flooded and lakes are formed.

In places where limestone underlies the land, ground water may dissolve and remove enough limestone to produce great sinkholes that form lake basins. Florida contains many lakes of this type.

Lakes may also be artificially made. When a dam is built across a river valley, it will block the flow of water and form a lake. Lake Mead was formed when Hoover Dam was built on the Colorado River.

What Are the Largest Waterfalls in the World?

A waterfall is any stream of water which descends suddenly from a higher to a lower level. If the volume of water is small, it is called a cascade; if large, it is called a cataract.

Some falls plunge hundreds of feet in a single narrow stream of water. Others are famous for their breadth and for the immense volume of water that pours over their ledges. Here are some of the great waterfalls of the world:

Angel Falls, in the Guiana Highlands of Venezuela, are the world's highest falls (3,212 feet), with the longest uninterrupted drop (2,648 feet). The falls were discovered in 1935 by an American aviator, James Angel.

The longest waterfall in Asia is the Gersoppa Falls in India. It is a cataract that falls in four sections for a total of 830 feet. The falls that discharge the largest volume of water of any waterfall are the Guaira Falls, which are on the border of Brazil and Paraguay. They discharge over 470,000 cubic feet of water per second. There are 18 falls, but the total drop is only about 200 feet.

One of the world's highest single waterfalls is Ribbon Falls in Yosemite National Park. It is a narrow stream that drops 1,612 feet down a cliff into the Merced River.

The second highest falls in the world are found in South Africa. They are the Tugela Falls. The falls plunge 2,800 feet in five jumps.

NIAGARA FALLS

And then, of course, there are Niagara Falls, among the most famous in the world. They are located in the Niagara River, about 16 miles northwest of Buffalo, New York. Actually, Niagara Falls consist of two cataracts—the Horseshoe (or Canadian) Falls and the American Falls. The international boundary line between Canada and the United States passes through the center of Horseshoe Falls.

About 94 percent of Niagara's waters, or some 84,000,000 gallons, flows over the Horseshoe Falls every minute.

What Is Hard Water?

Water is a tasteless, odorless, colorless compound of two gases: hydrogen, a very light gas, and oxygen, a heavier, active gas. Water exists in three states: as a liquid; as a solid, called ice; and as a gas, called water vapor.

But when we discuss the various properties of water, we discover that water as it occurs in nature is never pure in the true sense. It contains dissolved mineral material, dissolved gases, and living organisms. So it is very seldom that we are dealing with just "water."

For example, chemically pure water is tasteless. But we all know there often is a slight taste to water. Part of this taste comes from the presence of certain impurities in the water. Raindrops falling through the atmosphere absorb some of the gases through which they pass.

Most important of these gases is oxygen, which makes it possible for living things to exist under water. Carbon dioxide is another important gas in water. Its presence in a water solution (carbonic acid) makes water capable of eroding limestone rocks and forming caves and sinkholes.

The action of this carbonic acid in water dissolves lime and magnesium carbonates, and this is what makes water "hard." Hard water does not produce a soap lather easily. If boiled, it leaves a lime coating on the inside of kettles.

Besides gases, natural waters contain dissolved salts. And river and lake water is also likely to contain inorganic particles that simply float in the water.

Water is distributed over the earth in a great "energy cycle." The sun draws up water into the air by evaporation from the seas and oceans. In the air, water vapor gathers into clouds and falls as rain, hail, snow, or dew, and works its way back to the sea.

Does Water Have Taste?

Did you ever drink water from a well and say, "My, that tastes good"? Or perhaps you've heard people who live in certain cities say, "Our water tastes awful!" This might give you the idea that water itself does have a taste. But the fact is that water is actually tasteless. (It is also odorless and colorless.) We will see later why water seems to us to have a taste.

Water does not resemble either of the elements that compose it, hydrogen and oxygen. It has a set of properties all its own.

Water as it occurs in nature is never pure in the true sense. In the laboratory, the chemist can create chemically pure water. But in nature, water always contains dissolved mineral material, dissolved gases, and living organisms. These impurities give our drinking water its very slight but pleasant taste.

The reason water sometimes comes out "white" from a tap is the presence of these gases and other substances in water.

We might say then that the water we drink always does have a taste—simply because it is not chemically pure water.

What Causes a Water Shortage?

Because of a water shortage in the 1960's, New York City was declared a disaster area. People were asked not to drink too much water, or to bathe too often, and they were urged to save water in every way. Considering that five hundred million gallons of fresh water are fed into New York City every day of the year, how could there be a water shortage?

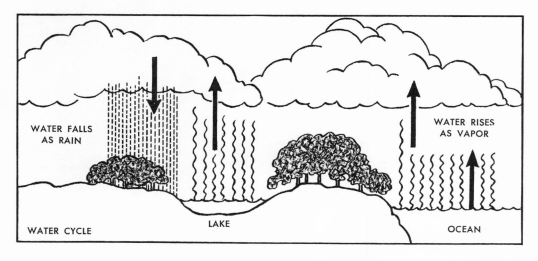

WATER FALLS
AS RAIN

WATER RISES
AS VAPOR

WATER CYCLE

LAKE

OCEAN

Let's see what a water supply system is. All the fresh water in the world adds up to only about one-thirtieth of the water there is in the salty ocean. And one-third of that fresh water is locked up in snow and ice. Much of the rest is too far underground, or too loaded with minerals, to be usable. So all the fresh water needed by man and life on earth, must come from other sources.

Where does it come from? It is supplied by the "water cycle." Each year about thirty inches of water rises as vapor into the air. It falls again as snow or rain, runs to the sea, and then evaporates again into the air. It is a process that is a cycle, repeating itself over and over again. Man uses the water as it flows by in this never-ending process.

Since nature distributes water very unevenly, with some regions getting a lot of rain and others very little, a steady supply of water must be brought to all regions where people live. This is done through a water-supply system, and some cities bring water hundreds of miles through long and costly systems of canals, reservoirs, conduits, and pipes.

For very large cities, huge reservoirs are built and the water is stored in them. But suppose there is a dry spell with very little rain? The water in the reservoir is not replenished as it is used, and the reservoir gets lower and lower. From time to time in various parts of the country, there are long periods during which no continuous, heavy rain falls. Then a water shortage is declared, and people have to be careful about using water. By the way, the average person in the United States uses from one hundred to one hundred and fifty gallons of water every day!

Why Does It Rain on Certain Days and Not on Others?

When you look up at the sky and see some big, heavy clouds, you might think it looks like rain. And we tend to think that this is all it takes to produce rain. But actually rain is the result of a long and complicated process

It takes the combined influences of the sun, the earth, and the atmosphere to produce rain. The process starts when the earth is heated by the sun. This causes the water in the earth's oceans, lakes, and streams, and in damp soil, to turn into water vapor. The water vapor then mixes with the air. This process is called evaporation.

Now rising warm air carries the water vapor up into the atmosphere. Here it expands and cools. As this happens, the warm air gives up some of its load of invisible water vapor, and this forms clouds. This process is called condensation.

Inside the cloud, the tiny droplets gradually become larger and larger as they collect more moisture. Finally the drops become so large that they can no longer be held up by the air currents, and they fall to the ground as rain.

Now let's see why this process of forming rain only happens at certain times and not at others. The first step in the process, evaporation, is going on practically all the time during the day. Water vapor is rising into the atmosphere. But this invisible water vapor does not change into visible cloud droplets every day. And this is because the water vapor has to have a surface on which to condense. If there are very few or no dust particles in the air, condensation is not likely to take place. Also, small ice and snow crystals high up in the air help droplets to form.

What is usually needed for rain is the movement of a warm air mass against a cold air mass, or a cold air mass against a warm air mass. The warm air mass contains clouds and moisture, and when this warm air mass is cooled by the cold air mass, drops of water form and fall as rain. That's why weather predictions always mention movements of air masses. They give us an idea as to whether there will be rain or not.

Where Does It Rain the Most?

Many things determine how much rain or snow any area of the world receives. These include temperature, height above sea level, location of mountain ranges, and so on.

Probably the rainiest place in the world is Mount Waialeale, Hawaii, on the island of Kauai. It has an average yearly rainfall of 471.68 inches. Cherrapunji, India, might be the next rainiest place, with its yearly average of 425 to 450 inches. At one time 150 inches of rain fell on Cherrapunji in a period of 5 days. And in one year, 1861, its rainfall added up to 905 inches.

To give you an idea of how much rain this is, let's note the rainfall in a number of cities around the world. New York City gets about 40 inches a year; San Francisco, about 20 inches; Boston, 42 inches; Chicago gets 30 inches; Ottawa in Canada gets 34 inches; Madrid, about 17 inches; and Paris, 22 inches. So you see what a contrast 450 inches in Cherrapunji is.

The driest place in the world is probably Arica, Chile. It averages only 0.02 inches of rain a year! The driest area in the United States is Greenland Ranch, Death Valley. There the average yearly rainfall is less than 1.5 inches.

Some large regions of the earth have heavy rainfall throughout the year. For example, almost every point along the Equator receives 60 inches or more of rain every year. The Equator is the meeting point of two large streams of air. All along the Equator, air moving down from the north meets air moving up from the south. There is a general upward movement of hot air laden with water vapor. As the air rises to colder heights, large amounts of water vapor condense and fall as rain.

A great deal of rain falls on the windward side of mountain ranges. The other side, called the lee, receives much less rain. An example is the Cascade Range of California. Westerly winds laden with water vapor sweep in from the Pacific Ocean. After striking the coast, the air rides up the western slopes of the mountains, cooling as it climbs higher. The cooling causes the water vapor to condense and fall as rain or snow.

What Is a Stalactite?

Stalactites appear in many caves or caverns. To see how they are formed, let us examine one such cave, the Carlsbad Caverns in New Mexico.

The special kind of rock in Carlsbad is limestone. Limestone is a fairly soft rock that can be dissolved by a weak acid. The acid that dissolves limestone comes from rainwater. Falling drops of rain pick up carbon dioxide from the air and from the soil. This carbon dioxide changes the rainwater into carbonic acid.

About one million years ago a single drop of rainwater clung to the ceiling of the cave. As the water dripped, a tiny ring of lime crystallized on the ceiling. A second drop, and a third, fourth, and fifth left lime in the same place. As time passed, the rings of lime formed a little stone "icicle." It kept on growing.

Another drop of water dripped to the floor of the cave. Again the lime was left behind. As time passed, thousands of drops fell on the same spot. The specks of lime formed what looked like a stubby stone candle. The "candle" kept on growing.

The icicle of stone on the ceiling is called a stalactite. The stubby candle on the floor is a stalagmite. Each stalactite and stalagmite grows at a different rate, depending on the wetness of the cave, the temperature of the room, and the thickness of the limestone bed above it. Some stalactites grow an inch a year, others take one hundred years or so to grow that much.

Often the stalagmites growing upward meet the stalactites growing down and form columns. The largest column in Carlsbad is one hundred feet high. The ceilings of some caves are covered with short, hollow stalactites that look like soda straws. Others have glittering stone needles on their walls, or stone pincushions bristling from the floor. Some stalactites grow sideways and up as well as down.

When water stops reaching the underground caves, the stalactites stop growing, and the cave is considered "dead."

What Is a Quarry?

Quarrying is the process by which rock materials are removed from the ground. The rocks may be quarried as solid blocks or slabs, or as crushed and broken stone. The block or slab rock is usually used for building. Crushed rock is most often used for roadbeds.

There are different types of quarries. In some, the rock is in a huge, solid mass. In others, the rock forms layers of different thicknesses. A pit quarry is actually a big hole in the ground. Sometimes it's wide and shallow, and sometimes it's a deep, narrow hole. Workers in pit quarries have to use ladders or stairs, or they may have to be lowered into the quarry by mechanical devices.

In pit quarries, there is often a water problem. This is because the quarry is like a big stone bowl, collecting and holding all the rainwater that pours into it. When this happens, the water has to be pumped out.

Sometimes rock suitable for quarrying is found above the ground. This is called a shelf quarry. In such a quarry, machines can be moved right up to the face of the quarry, and the rock can be hauled away directly.

How is it decided where to establish a quarry? Tests must be made first. Geologists can tell where the chances of finding a high grade of rock are good. Then the rock itself must be tested.

In testing, a number of holes are drilled at various spots in the area. Special drills are used that can cut a core of rock about two inches in diameter. This core is brought up to the surface and analyzed. Some drills can go down as far as two thousand eight hundred feet, or more than half a mile. The test indicates whether there is enough good stone available to make quarrying profitable.

How Many Types of Climate Are There?

There are many different types of climate on earth. Climate, by the way, is the combination of temperature, moisture, wind, and sunshine at a place over a period of many years. Climates of the world can be classified according to their latitudes and the plants that grow there. Different kinds of plants need different amounts of moisture and heat to grow. So the vegetation of a place tells us about temperature and rainfall conditions over a long period of time.

Basically, there are five major classifications of climates, with many subdivisions in each class. There are tropical climates, subtropical climates, mid-latitude climates, high-latitude climates, and high-altitude climates.

Tropical climates are found in regions between 350° North and 350° South latitude. In the tropical rain forests (nearest the Equator), conditions are warm and rainy all year long, and there is a thick cover of trees. In this tropical area there are also tropical wet-and-dry climates; tropical savannas, where the climate is too dry for forests; tropical steppes (still drier); and the tropical desert climate.

Subtropical climates prevail in 30° and 40° North and South latitudes. In these areas there is a Mediterranean climate of hot, dry summers and mild, wet winters and a humid subtropical climate of hot summers and mild winters, with enough rainfall in all seasons to sustain forests.

Mid-latitude climates occur between 40° and 60° North and South latitudes. Included in this area are a marine west coast climate (west coast of North America); cool steppe or cool desert climates; and humid continental climates—each with different vegetation and rainfall patterns.

High-latitude climates are characteristic of from 60° North and South latitudes to the Poles. Here temperatures are very cold in winter and cool in summer. Within this area is a taiga climate (very cold in winter); a tundra climate, where only grasses, mosses and lichens can grow; and the polar climate, where great ice caps exist.

High-altitude climates, or highland climates, are found on the high mountains of the world, even at the Equator.

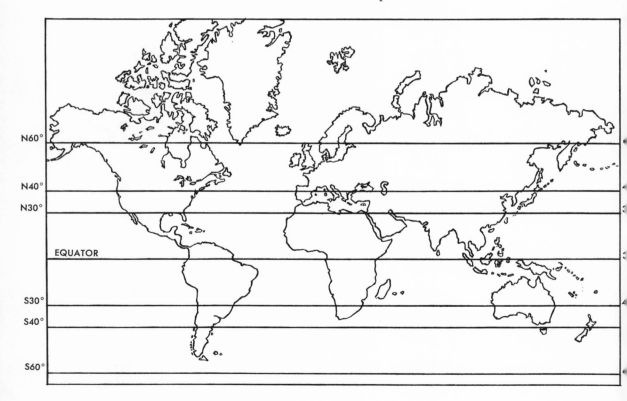

What Is the Tundra?

The term "tundra" comes from a Finnish word that means "barren land" or "hostile territory." It is generally used to refer to the treeless zone of the Arctic.

The tundra is certainly not a very pleasant place to live. It has no trees. It has very low temperatures in winter, and in summer the average is only 50 degrees Fahrenheit. There is very little rain, and the winds are generally strong all year.

Despite these conditions, various forms of life do exist in the tundra, and it might be interesting to see which life forms can survive such conditions. Tundra plants include lichens, which form crusts on the surface of rocks; mosses, which fill cracks in the rocks and are embedded in the coarse gravel; some grasses and grasslike herbs; and some low shrubs. Most of the plants in the tundra are not annuals, and there are very few species in any one region.

Animals are also few in number. Lemmings live in the tundra, and the musk ox and the polar bear are strictly tundra animals. A large number of birds have their breeding ground in the tundra. This is because there are long light hours in the summer, so food can be gathered for a long time and large flocks of young can be fed. There are a great many ducks, geese, and plovers in the tundra.

Tundra soil is very shallow. It lies over a permanently frozen substratum called the permafrost. During the summer, the top layer thaws out, and plant roots and bacterial life take hold.

The tundra zone does not begin as an even line at a certain latitude. It varies from continent to continent. But once you're in the tundra, you will know you're in one of the bleakest regions on earth.

How Is Snow Beneficial to Crops?

We all know how too much snow can disrupt the life of a community. But snow can be beneficial, especially to crops.

If crops are to grow, they must have water. Where does the water come from that flows in springs or streams? And how about the water that is in the ground? It is now known that all of this water (except for a very minor part) comes from rain and snow. The water from falling rain and melting snow filters down from the surface of the earth and supplies and feeds all the rivers, streams, and springs.

Water is always present in the atmosphere as an invisible gas—water vapor. Under favorable conditions this vapor condenses into droplets of water, or forms ice crystals, which become clouds and finally turn into rain or snow.

In most parts of the world, rain is the chief form of precipitation, and thus the chief source of water. But in frigid zones and at high altitudes, snow may be the most common form of precipitation. In fact the snow that accumulates in mountains near dry regions may form a natural reservoir of water far larger than any built by man.

When this snow melts during spring and early summer, it becomes a source of water for irrigation. In some areas this melting snow may supply the only water available for crops. In the mountains of Western United States, snow surveys are made to determine how much water will be available for crops during the dry season.

What Are Oats?

Oats are the seeds of a plant belonging to the grass family. When you think of oats, you probably think of the breakfast cereal called oatmeal or of oatmeal cookies. These are the only forms in which most people eat oats. What happens to the rest of the huge crop of oats? Most of it is used for animal food.

The first oats probably originated in the cool, moist areas of eastern Europe. For centuries men considered oats to be a weed. Some experts believe that the early Greeks and Romans cultivated oats for animal food. But it wasn't until the thirteenth century that peasants began to depend on oats as one of the most important foods for people.

Oats were brought to some small islands off New England in 1602 and spread rapidly as a crop in North America during the next fifty years. Today the United States is the biggest producer of oats, with Canada, the Soviet Union, and countries of northern Europe also producing great quantities.

Oat plants grow from two to five feet tall. The leaves are long and slender. Each stem has a head with many small, delicate branches. The branches end with little spikes on which the flowers blossom and the grains later form.

The plants grow in cool, moist climates. Oats do not need special soils, and as long as the land is not too wet, will often grow in places where other crops cannot be grown at all.

More than other cereal crops, oats are used as a general-purpose feed for animals. Harvested oats, mixed with other cereal grains, are used for all livestock and poultry.

When oats are milled for people to eat, the hard outer covering, or hull, and its parts are removed. The germ and other parts that are very rich in vitamins and minerals are left in.

What Is the Difference Between Fruits and Vegetables?

The word "fruit" usually describes any fleshy part of a plant that has developed from a flower and has seeds. Vegetables are herbaceous plants. An herbaceous plant is one that has a soft stem and little or no woody tissue.

According to botanists, the part of a plant that carries seeds is its fruit. They divide fruits into three main classes: fleshy fruits with seeds in the flesh, such as oranges, melons, berries, and apples; fruits containing pits or stones, such as cherries, plums, and peaches; and dry fruits, such as nuts, grains, beans, and peas.

If it surprises you to learn that botanists consider beans and peas fruits (because they contain seeds), you will be even more surprised to learn that cucumbers and squash can be called fruits also! It all depends on how technical we want to be. In addition, because eating customs vary in different parts of the world, the same edible part of a plant may be considered a fruit in one place and a vegetable in another.

Just as there are "families" of related creatures in the animal kingdom, so many vegetables are related. Did you know, for example, that the cabbage, turnip, radish, broccoli, and cauliflower all belong to one family of vegetables?

Lettuce, chicory, and artichokes belong to another vegetable family. The gourd family includes cucumbers, melons, pumpkins, and squash. The pea family consists of peas, all kinds of beans, peanuts, and soybeans.

Asparagus is related to the common onion, leek, garlic, chive and shallot. Beets, spinach, and Swiss chard all belong to one family. And here is an interesting one: the nightshade family. It includes potatoes, eggplants, peppers, and tobacco!

Fruits and vegetables are alike in that they supply us with the vitamins and minerals that help to keep us healthy.

Is the Tomato a Fruit or Vegetable?

Of course, it doesn't really matter very much which it is, since we use it in this country as a vegetable. A fascinating thing about this question is that the Supreme Court of the United States actually had to decide what the tomato is!

Botanically, the tomato is a fruit. There can be no question about that. But it is used in soups, sauces, ketchup, and in many other ways in the main part of the meal. So, for purposes of trade, the Supreme Court in 1893 classified the tomato as a vegetable!

The tomato originated in its wild form in South America in Peru, Ecuador, and Bolivia. Long before Columbus came to the new world, cultivated forms of the tomato had already been developed in Mexico. And it is probable that tomatoes from Mexico were the first ones ever seen by people in Europe.

The first definite description of the tomato in Europe was in Italy in 1554, where it was called *pomi d'oro,* or "apple of gold." This means that a yellow type of tomato was the first kind known in Europe. Before the end of the sixteenth century, tomatoes were being grown in the gardens of England, Spain, Italy, France and the countries of mid-Europe. But they were considered a sort of curiosity.

By the mid-1700's people in several countries of Europe were using the tomato as food, and the first person to grow it in the United States was Thomas Jefferson, in 1781. But a great many people considered the tomato to be poisonous. It wasn't until about 1900 that it became popular for eating.

The tomato plant is a relative of the potato and tobacco plants. It needs a long growing season and light, rich, well-drained soil. In northern Europe and the northern United States it is often grown in hothouses during the winter. It is also grown in Florida, Texas, and Mexico during the winter. Winter tomatoes are picked while green and shipped to northern markets. They ripen on the way to market.

How Many Kinds of Oranges Are There?

Nobody knows exactly where the orange originated. Though it is grown today in most of the warmer parts of the world, it was not until recently that the crop became so widespread.

The Greeks and Romans knew about the orange, and it probably was carried from India to western Asia and then to all of Europe. The Spanish colonists brought the sour orange to the West Indies, and from there to Florida soon after the first settlement there in 1565.

The three most important species of oranges are the sweet or common orange, the mandarin orange, and the sour orange. But as many as ninety-seven varieties of sweet and mandarin oranges alone have been counted!

Different varieties of oranges are grown in different parts of the country and the world. For example, of the sweet oranges, California and Arizona grow the Washington Navel and the Valencia. In Florida there is quite a variety of sweet oranges grown: the Hamlin, Pineapple, Parson Brown, Homosassa, and Valencia. Texas also grows the Valencia and the Hamlin.

An interesting type of sweet orange is called the blood orange. It has a pulp with a deep-red tint. It is grown extensively in the Mediter-ranean region, but has not become popular in the United States.

The mandarin oranges, which include the tangerines, are grown mostly in Florida. The Temple, which is a loose, thin-skinned orange, is a hybrid of the mandarin and the sweet orange.

The sour orange is grown to some extent everywhere, but Spain produces most of the sour oranges used for commercial purposes. The chief use of this orange is in making marmalade, since it is too acid and bitter to be eaten as a fruit. But there are many other interesting uses, ranging from medicines to perfume!

Is All Milk the Same?

People have used milk as a food since very ancient times. Yet in different parts of the world, different animals have been the source of its supply.

In the United States and among other English-speaking people, the cow furnishes most of the milk supply. In Spain, a great deal of the milk comes from sheep. The desert tribes of Arabia get milk from the camel. In Egypt, the water buffalo is a source of milk. In Lapland, reindeer furnish milk to the people. In Peru, the llama is a milk-pro-ducing animal. In Tibet, the people get milk from the yak. And in many countries, the goat is an important supplier of milk.

GOAT ON MILKING STAND

Is all this milk the same? The answer is no. Each animal produces milk especially suited for its own young. Cow's milk is intended for a calf and not for a human baby. Since a calf is a much coarser creature than a baby, cow's milk is much coarser than human milk.

But cow's milk is enough like human milk so that a baby can drink it and grow strong and healthy. Cow's milk has less sugar, more salts, and four times as much casein, an important protein substance, as human milk.

While milk differs a great deal, depending on the species of animal, it always contains fat, protein, carbohydrate, and minerals. No matter which milk people drink in different parts of the world, they obtain these vital substances for nourishment.

Just to see how different milks compare, let's look at cow's milk and reindeer milk. Cow's milk contains about 87 per cent water; reindeer milk, only about 68 per cent. Cow's milk has about 4 per cent fat; reindeer milk, about 17 per cent. Reindeer milk has half the amount of sugar of cow's milk, three times as much casein, and about five times as much other protein. So you see, it's quite different from cow's milk, and yet the people of Lapland get along on it very well indeed!

Even cow's milk may vary greatly, depending on the breed, the health of the individual cow, and the time between milkings. The last milk to be drawn at each milking is richer in fat than the rest, so a good job of milking can produce richer milk from the same cow than a poor job!

Why Doesn't All Coffee Taste Alike?

Coffee has been one of the favorite drinks of man for about a thousand years. It was first discovered and became popular among the people of Arabia, and didn't reach Europe until about the sixteenth century.

The introduction of coffee into Europe caused quite a commotion. At times it was banned; at other times it was used as a medicine! Finally the coffeehouses of England established it as a popular beverage.

When you buy a can of coffee, there is nothing in it but coffee. Yet different brands of coffee have different tastes. The reason for this may be in the manner of preparation, the method of roasting, and so on. But the most important reason for differences in taste has to do with the blend of the beans.

Coffees grown in the various countries differ in type as well as grade. For example, coffee is grown at altitudes of from one thousand five hundred to six thousand feet. It is generally agreed that the finest coffees come from the higher elevations—three thousand to six thousand feet.

But this isn't the only difference in coffees. Coffees from different plantations in the same section of the country may have a whole variety of different characteristics.

In the coffee business, coffees are divided into two general groups. One is the coffee grown in Brazil, which is called Brazils. The other is coffee grown in other countries, which is called Milds.

In a general sense, the Milds coffees are considered superior to the Brazils, but many of the Brazils are actually finer than many Milds. Every brand of coffee you buy has its own blend, its own combination of coffees. The job of coffee tasting and blending requires great skill. But you can see how various combinations will produce different tastes.

Other important reasons for different tastes are the skill in roasting (not to over-roast or under-roast) and the method of grinding. Nature makes coffee—but man makes it taste good.

How Is Tobacco Grown?

The tobacco plant usually grows four to six feet high. The leaves are large, about two or three feet in length. They are covered with many long, soft hairs that hold a gummy juice.

There are many ways in which this plant is grown, but all commercial tobacco needs a lot of care. Tobacco seed is mixed with fertilizer and corn or cottonseed meal before it is sown. In warm areas, the seedbeds are covered with cotton cloth. In colder areas the covering is usually glass.

In six to ten weeks in most areas, the plants grow six to eight inches. They develop four to six leaves, and are now ready to be set into fields that have been carefully prepared and fertilized.

As the plants begin to flower, each is topped, which means that the budding seed head is removed. This is done so that the leaves will be stronger and have a deeper color.

Three or four months after the seedlings have been placed in the growing field, the plants are ready for harvesting. Two methods are used: priming and stalk cutting.

In priming tobacco, each leaf is pulled separately as it ripens. Two to four leaves are removed from a plant each week. This process takes five to eight weeks. In stalk-cut tobacco, the whole plant is cut down.

After harvesting, the tobacco must be cured. The purpose of this is to dry the leaf and bring out the proper color. A tobacco leaf is cured by heat, air, or sun. In flue-curing, green leaves are hung in small insulated barns that are heated by flues. Stalk-cut tobacco is air cured. Other types of tobacco are strung together on sticks and hung in the sun.

The final stage in the care of tobacco is aging. This is done to mellow the leaf and improve its flavor.

What is Paprika?

True pepper is made from the pepper plant, which has the scientific name of *Piper nigrum*. But a great many other kinds of pepper are obtained from plants of entirely different families.

For example, there are the red pepper or chilies. They belong to the genus *capsicum*. There are also cayenne peppers and tabasco peppers. Still another kind, bell peppers, are called pimientos when canned in oil. Pimientos is the Spanish name for the pepper plant. And finally there is paprika, which is a red pepper produced from the bell pepper. When these are ripe, they are red and hot, but are milder than many other kinds. That's why paprika can be used more freely than other kinds of pepper.

Pepper is considered to be the most important of all the spices in the world. After salt, it is the seasoning most used for food. In ancient times, and during the middle ages, only the rich could afford to use pepper. It had to be carried by caravan from the Far East, and this made it so expensive that a pound of pepper was considered a fitting present for a king!

In some ways pepper was like gold. People could pay taxes with pepper, and it was given as tribute to rulers by their subjects. When an army conquered an enemy and soldiers were given a share of the spoils, pepper would be one of the great rewards they would receive.

The Portuguese were so anxious to find a way of getting pepper at lower cost that they tried to find a sea route to India. After they found the way around the Cape of Good Hope, the cost of pepper in Europe dropped a great deal. Today, of course, pepper costs so little that we don't even think twice when we buy it. In the United States, more than fifteen thousand tons of pepper are used a year!

Pepper comes from the fruit or seeds of a climbing shrub. Black pepper is made by picking unripe berries and drying them until black. White pepper is made by removing the outer coat before grinding.

CRABGRASS

ORCHID

CARROT

Why Do Plants Have Roots?

A plant needs roots for two chief reasons: as a means of anchorage or support, and to absorb water and mineral salts from the soil.

The roots of most plants grow in the soil. They don't "just sit there," but seem to reach out in the soil to help the plant grow. By elongating near their tips, roots are always coming in contact with new portions of soil.

Thousands of tiny root hairs project from the surface of the young root and absorb materials from the soil. That's why when a young root is pulled from the soil, soil particles often cling to the root hairs.

Some plants have taproots. A taproot is a large, single root, much larger than any of the branch roots. It may be fleshy like a carrot, or woody like a hickory root. Other plants have not one large root, but several roots of approximately equal size. These form what is called a fibrous root system.

Grasses have fibrous root systems. Soil in which there are many fibrous roots is protected in this way from erosion. In still other plants, most of the roots grow from stems as, for example, the geranium.

As roots grow older, some of them store large quantities of sugar and starch. Beets and sweet potatoes are examples of this. A sweet potato is a root, but an Irish potato, with its eyes, is a stem.

Not all plants have roots that grow in the soil. Some tropical orchids that grow on trees have spongy roots that grow in the air and absorb moisture. Both the English ivy and poison ivy cling to walls or trees by means of tiny aerial roots.

Some plants have special roots that develop from the stem above the ground and grow down into the soil, forming props. A few roots, such as the sweet potato, form buds that grow into leafy branches and can be used to propagate the plant.

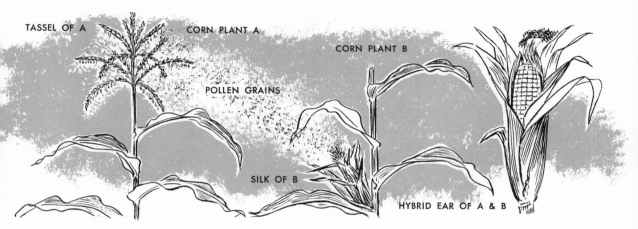

What Is a Hybrid Plant?

First of all, what is a hybrid? A hybrid is a crossbreed of a plant or animal. This means that it is the result of the union of the male of one species, race, etc., with the female of another.

This can happen in nature or among people without any deliberate plan. But in plants this is often done deliberately and for very good reasons.

Probably the best example of the advantages of hybrid plants is the case of corn. In the early days in the United States, farmers took particular care in the selection of seed ears for the next year's crop. By constant selection many varieties and strains of corn thus came into existence. These were selected because of their adaptability to different soils and climates.

But beginning about 1905, plant scientists started a new method of producing different kinds of corn. It was discovered that when the plant was self-pollinated—that is, the pollen in the tassels was applied by hand to the silks on the ear of the same plant—widely different kinds of corn plants appeared. By repeating this process and saving only the best plants for seed strains, "inbred lines" were established.

Many of these inbred lines had certain special, desirable characteristics, but all of them were lower in yield. Now came the next step. When such inbred lines were cross-pollinated, by applying the pollen of one strain to the silks of another, the kernels thus formed often gave rise to very productive hybrid plants.

And these hybrid plants were very good indeed! In many cases they were superior in disease resistance and in strength of stalks, and were very high in yield. Thus by first purifying or sorting out the most desirable characters of the old varieties, and then recombining these, very superior types of corn have been produced. In other plants, too, the same process of producing hybrids has had wonderful results!

GILLS

SPORE CAPSULES

FERN SPORE

What Is a Spore?

A flowering plant makes a new plant by means of a seed. Plants that don't have flowers make a new plant by means of a spore.

A spore is a one-celled organism. It is invisible to the eye and can only be seen under a microscope. There are spores in the air all around us. That's why when food is left exposed, and molds and mildews form on it, we know where they came from. Some types of spores that were in the air settled on the food and began to grow.

Some of the plants that reproduce by means of spores are mushrooms, ferns, and mosses. The algae that live in water also produce spores.

A plant carries its spores in cases that are called sporangia. In a mushroom, the sporangium is inside the gills beneath the mushroom cap. In mosses, the spores are carried in a capsule at the top of the stalk.

When the spore case is ripe, it opens, and the ripe spores are released. Since they are finer than dust, the wind scatters them far and wide. In the case of water plants, such as the algae, the spores can actually swim away. They have tiny tails called cilia. These spores are called zoospores, and when the ripe case opens, the zoospores swim away quickly. After a short time they come to rest and lose their tails. Then they begin to grow into new plants.

Some spores reproduce by cell division. They grow by pushing out a germ tube through a thin place in the cell wall. The germ tube branches into a mass of threads out of which the new plant grows. This is called asexual reproduction, because differentiated male and female cells are not needed for reproduction to take place.

Other spores are specialized male and female cells. In order to start a new plant, one male and one female cell must join to form a fertilized egg. Some plants alternate in the kind of spores they produce, asexual in one generation and sexual spores in the next.

How Do New Flowers Grow?

Every living thing has some means of reproducing itself. In flowers, the process takes place as follows:

A typical flower has four main parts. There is usually a green outer cup made up of leaflike sepals. Within the sepals are the petals. Within the petals are the reproductive organs necessary for producing seeds.

In the very center of the flower are one or more pistils. Around the pistils is a ring of stamens. The pistil is the female part of the flower. The bottom of it is enlarged and is called the ovary. Inside the ovary are little round ovules, which later become seeds. But they

PETAL

STAMENS
ANTHER
SEPAL
STIGMA   OVARY

POLLEN GRAINS

become seeds only if they are fertilized by the contents of a pollen grain.

Pollen grains are produced by the stamens, the male organs of the flower. If seeds are to form, the pollen grains must go through the top of the pistil and reach the ovules at the bottom. The top of the pistil is called the stigma.

Pollen grains first fall on the stigma. They absorb moisture there from the sugary liquid on the surface. Then they swell and grow. The grain pushes down and becomes a tube. The tube keeps growing down through the stalk of the pistil, then through the wall of the ovary, and then into an ovule.

The contents of the tube then empty into the ovule and fertilize it. Many pollen tubes may grow down to an ovary at the same time. Each tube will enter and fertilize a single ovule.

Only pollen from the same kind of plant will grow tubes and reach the ovules. The part of the stamen that produces pollen is called the anther. The transfer of pollen from anther to stigma is called pollination. If it takes place in the same flower, it is called self-pollination. If the pollen goes to a flower on a different plant of the same kind, it is called cross-pollination.

Cross-pollination of flowers is done by the wind, by insects, by birds, and by certain animals. Later on, the seeds that develop also have to be carried to a place where they can take root and grow into flowers.

Do Cacti Have Leaves?

A cactus (plural: cacti) is able to exist under extreme conditions because it is a plant that has adapted itself to those conditions.

Cacti have the same basic structures and processes as other plants. But the work that is done by leaves in most other plants is done by the stems and branches of the cacti. In fact, the absence of leaves and the presence of spine-covered branches and stems enable them to survive in hot, dry regions.

The leaves of other plants are thin structures and are filled with pores through which the plant breathes. During the cell-making process carried on by the plants, water is given off to the air through these pores.

A cactus plant must guard every drop of water. So the work of the leaves is taken over by the stems and branches. Their thick skins have very few pores, and the water in the cactus is retained.

The roots of cacti are spread out, close to the surface of the ground. That's why cacti can quickly absorb water from the earth after a rainfall. This water, which is taken in through the roots, is stored in the spongy or hollow stems of a cactus. The outer layer of the plant is thick and waxy, and this also prevents the escape of water.

The outer skin of a cactus is ribbed. Some cacti have ribs that fold and expand like an accordion. They expand as they fill up with water and fold together as the water in the stem is used up.

There are some members of the cactus family that do have leaves, such as the lemon vine of the West Indies. But in most cacti the leaves have developed into spines, needles, or hairs. These help protect the cacti from animals that would otherwise eat them, since they may be the only green plants in the area.

Why Do Trees Have Leaves?

Green plants and trees have to manufacture their food. The leaves are the food factories for the plants and trees.

Leaves of fruit trees manufacture the food that helps to make fruit. For example, peaches and maple sugar are sweet. So peach and maple tree leaves make sugar. They do this by taking materials from the air and the ground. One of these materials is carbon dioxide, a gas taken from the air. The other material is water, which comes from the soil. By a process called photosynthesis, the leaves manufacture sugar from the water and carbon dioxide.

Every factory must have machines and power to run the machines. The machines of the leaf are many little green bodies called chloroplasts. They are green because they have in them a green matter called chlorophyll. Sunshine is the power that runs the machines. Leaves change color in the fall when the chlorophyll disappears, and the red-and-yellow coloring matter can then be seen.

Chloroplasts work inside a leaf. The leaf is made up of cells. Some of these cells contain chloroplasts; others have few or none and do other jobs. "Guard" cells help regulate the size of the openings through which air passes. Many of these guard cells are on the underside of a leaf. A pair of guard cells and the opening between them is called a stoma (plural: stomata).

The roots of a plant or tree take water from the soil that eventually reaches the veins of the leaves. These veins carry back food the leaves have made. The air that goes into a leaf through the stomata has carbon dioxide in it. When the sun is shining, the leaves use the

SUGAR MADE HE—

VEIN

MAGNIFIE
CROSS-SEC
OF LEAF

STOMATA

UNDERSIDE OF LEAF

carbon dioxide to make sugar. The rest of the air, with additional oxygen, is given off through the stomata. But when it is dark and leaves are not making food, they do not need carbon dioxide. Then they give off air with carbon dioxide left in it.

Leaves give off water, too. Part of the water taken in through the roots is used to make sugar. The rest is given off from the leaves.

What Is a National Forest?

National forests are areas that belong to all the people of the United States. They are protected and managed, along with the national grasslands, by the Forest Service of the United States Department of Agriculture.

To most people the word "forest" means trees. And it is true that the national forests are the source of much of the nation's timber. But they are much more than this. Many of them contain grazing lands that have few trees. Some parts of the national-forest system have been set aside as wilderness areas. No cutting of trees is allowed there, there are no structures to spoil the scenery, and no machines are allowed to disturb the peace and quiet.

The national forests are also the home of more than one-third of the country's big-game animals and of many millions of smaller creatures. Lakes cover nearly two million acres. Skiing areas are used by winter-sports fans. Areas large enough for almost three hundred thousand persons to camp in at one time are maintained, and there are eighty-one thousand miles of fishing streams.

More than one hundred million people visit the national forests each year. In the 154 national forests and nineteen national grasslands, there is a total of 186,000,000 acres. Most of these lands have always been owned by the public. In the eastern United States, however, much national-forest land was specially purchased by the government to protect the watersheds of streams, to produce timber, and to provide for recreation.

National forests differ from national parks. National parks have been set aside to preserve in a natural state some outstanding examples of America's scenic and scientific treasures. In the national parks no hunting, cutting of timber, or other removal of resources is permitted.

What Is the Tallest Tree?

Trees are green plants. They have roots, stems, leaves, and seeds, just as other green plants do. Trees are also the oldest of all green plants. Some of the sequoia trees of the northwestern United States are more than four thousand years old. This means they were fully grown trees long before Columbus discovered America!

And trees are the biggest of all green plants. The tallest trees known to exist on earth are the giant redwoods of California. There is one tree there, growing in the Humboldt National Forest, that is believed to be the tallest tree in the world. It is called the Founder's Tree and is 364 feet high!

Some authorities believe that long ago the eucalyptus tree of Australia may have been as tall as these California redwoods, but those growing today average about fifty feet shorter. Two other kinds of trees that come close to the redwood are the Douglas fir and the sequoia, some of which have grown over three hundred feet tall.

The roots of a tree not only take water and mineral materials from the soil, but also hold the plant firmly in the ground. And with very large trees, it takes quite a bit of root system to hold the tree firmly. Did you know that the roots of trees take up nearly as much room under the ground as their tops or crowns do above?

Scientists have learned to tell the age of trees by counting rings in the wood. There are rings in the cross-section of most kinds of tree trunks. New wood is formed each year in a layer outside the old wood and beneath the bark. It is this layer that becomes the ring. Each ring in the wood of the trunk of a tree represents one year of the tree's life. The trunk gets bigger and bigger around as new rings or layers are added.

A tree adds rings not only to its trunk but to its branches and twigs, too. Some new length is added to the tip ends of the twigs and branches each year. Because growth in height takes place only at the tips of branches, the limbs of trees never move farther from the ground than they were in the beginning!

ANNUAL RING

CLOSE-UP OF GIANT REDWOOD
LEAVES AND CONES

MAGNIFIED WOOD FIBERS

TUBE CELLS CROSSWISE

TUBE UP AND DOWN

What Is Wood?

Wood is one of the most valuable raw materials supplied by nature. Man has used wood for thousands of years. What exactly is wood?

Wood is a strong, hard type of plant tissue. In this case the plant is a tree. It is made up of cells that are packed together something like the cells of a honeycomb. The walls of the cells are composed of cellulose, and this is the material that forms the walls of all plant cells.

The cells of wood are mostly long and narrow, like tubes or pipes, and they extend up and down the tree. Wood cells are also called fibers because of their long, narrow shape. It is this tubelike construction that gives wood fibers their great strength and springiness in proportion to their weight.

There are hollow air spaces inside the fibers, and these act as barriers to the movement of heat. This is why wood is a good heat insulator.

The strength, weight, and hardness of wood depend chiefly on the size of the fibers and the way they are arranged together. The thicker the walls of the fibers, the heavier and stronger the wood. This is simply because fibers with thick walls contain less air and more wood substance than the thin fiber walls of lighter and weaker woods.

When wood fibers lie generally straight and parallel to each other, the wood is easy to split. For example, oak splits easily because its fibers are parallel. On the other hand, elm and sycamore are very difficult to split, because their fibers are twisted and tangled together.

Wood contains a number of other substances besides cellulose. The most important of these is a substance called lignin. It cements the fibers together. Chemists have known about lignin and studied it for more than one hundred years, but they still have not discovered its exact formula!

Wood also contains various amounts of natural oils, gums, resins, and other chemicals. They give wood such properties as odor, color, resistance to decay, and ability to take a polish.

What Are Hardwoods and Softwoods?

Trees, and the woods that come from them, have been divided into two main classes. The common name for one class of trees and lumber is softwoods, and the other class is called hardwoods. The difference between them is supposed to be in their hardness or softness of texture. A harder wood, as you might imagine, doesn't scratch as easily and stands up better under wear and tear.

The most important North American softwoods are the cedar, southern cypress, Douglas fir, true fir, hemlock, western larch, northern white pine, ponderosa pine, southern pine, sugar pine, western white pine, redwood, and spruce. Softwoods are also described in terms of being evergreens, cone-bearing trees, or needle-leaved trees.

Hardwood trees generally have broad leaves and shed them in the autumn or in the spring, as some oaks do. The important North American hardwoods are the ash, aspen, basswood, beech, birch, cottonwood, elm, gum, hickory, maple, oak, black walnut, and yellow poplar.

But the terms "softwoods" and "hardwoods" are really used as names for a class of woods or trees. Some of the softwoods are really hard in texture, and some of the hardwoods are soft—softer than some of the so-called softwoods!

The "basic wood substance" of which the cell walls of all woods are made weighs about the same in all kinds of woods. But because the cells have cavities of various sizes, a greater or lesser portion of the wooden block is taken up by these cavities. The size and proportions of the openings and walls of the wood cells vary greatly. This is why there is so much difference in the weight of various woods. Oak, for example, weighs more than twice as much as basswood. The greater the weight, the stronger the wood.

What Is Gum?

Gum has a whole variety of interesting uses—many of them more important than providing you with something to chew on! And, of course, there are a great many different kinds of gums.

One gum, called gum arabic, is used in making candies, medicines, and mucilage, and in the manufacture of silks. Like most of the true gums, it comes from the plant as a thick, sticky liquid, which hardens when exposed to air and dissolves in water.

Gum arabic is produced by several varieties of acacia trees, which grow in Africa, Australia, and Asia. It is sold in the form of clear yellow or reddish lumps. Some gums, instead of dissolving in water, absorb it and make a soft, gluey, gelatin-like mass. One such gum is called gum dragon, and is used in making cough medicines and as a sizing in cloth.

Another important gum is cherry gum, which is used in stiffening straw for the manufacture of straw hats and other articles. Other common gums are plum, peach, spruce, and chicle.

Chicle is produced by the naseberry and other trees and is used in making ordinary chewing gum. All these gums are used in the manufacture of ink, cloth, paper, and medicines. Some of the finest gums are used in medical and research laboratories for work with cultures.

Most gums are gathered in the dry seasons and brought to the markets in the form of nodules or "tears." Chemically, gums consist of an acid nucleus combined with sugar molecules.

In addition to the true gums we have described above, there are gum resins. They are also produced by plants, but they differ from true gums because they contain resin, and therefore will not dissolve completely in water.

Two famous gum resins are frankincense and myrrh. They are very fragrant and are used in making perfume and incense.

CHERRY GUM

ACACIA

What Is Peat?

Peat is not coal. It might be called a step in the process of making coal.

Coal itself is made of the remains of ancient trees and plants that grew in swampy jungles in warm, moist climates hundreds of millions of years ago. These trees and plants fell into the swamp waters. Bacteria changed some parts of the wood into gases that escaped, leaving behind a black mixture, mostly carbon. In time the pressure from mud and sand above squeezed out most of the liquid, leaving behind a pasty mass that slowly hardened into coal.

This process, from beginning to end, took thousands of years. But the first stages of that process of making coal can actually be seen going on today. In the Great Dismal Swamp of Virginia and North Carolina and in thousands of swamps of the northern states and Canada, peat is being made.

In these swamps, plants are gradually decaying in a process that leaves most of the carbon in place. A few years of such action produces a brown, matted mass of twigs, branches, and leaves. This is known as peat. When the water is drained from such a swamp, the peat can be cut into blocks, set out to dry, and then burned as fuel.

Drying is important because peat in the ground may be three-fourths water. In Ireland, where peat is plentiful and the higher forms of coal are expensive, more than half of the farms depend entirely on peat for fuel.

The other forms of coal are developments from peat. If peat is allowed to remain where it forms, it gradually changes into lignite, or brown coal. It is more solid than coal, but still soft enough to crumble when shipped long distances.

71

The next form of coal is bituminous, or soft coal. It is formed from lignite by chemical change and pressure in the earth over thousands of years. This is the most important member of the coal family. It burns easily and is abundant.

If bituminous coal remains in the earth and is subjected to enough pressure, it gradually changes to hard coal or anthracite. It burns with very little smoke and for a longer time than bituminous coal.

What Is Lignite?

One of the most important searches being carried on by scientists is for new sources of energy. It's not just that they want to find cheaper and more efficient sources of energy to do the work of the world, it's also because some of the natural sources we now have will eventually be used up!

Have you ever seen an abandoned coal mine? At one time coal was being taken from there to feed huge furnaces and to heat buildings. But now there isn't enough coal left to make it worth mining.

Coal is still, however, the most important solid fuel man has. In fact, it furnishes the United States with about half of its fuel.

Let's consider the different kinds of coal. Obviously, a process that took millions upon millions of years didn't create exactly the same kind of product everywhere.

Peat, for example, is the youngest of all coals. This means the vegetation from which it came was buried a shorter time than that of other coals. Peat has the least heat value of all solid fuels, and is not used much for fuel purposes in the United States.

Lignite is sometimes called brown coal. It is a little older than peat and has more heating value. Half the lignite mined each year in the United States is used as fuel for producing electricity.

Bituminous coal has the highest heating value of all solid fuels. Finally, there is anthracite coal, which is the hardest of all coals and the oldest in nature.

What Is a Fuel?

A fuel is a material that is burned in order to get heat and light, and also to generate power. The process of burning, or combustion, is a chemical reaction. A material combines with oxygen from the air and gives off energy. The energy is given off in the form of heat and light.

The energy in fuels came originally from the sun. The plants from which fuels come trap energy from the sun's rays and use it to build their tissues. Burning wood and charcoal releases energy that has been stored up by plants in this way. When we burn coal or oil, we use energy stored up by plants that lived millions of years ago.

There are many different types of fuels, and actually anything that burns can be called a fuel. But the most common fuels are wood, coal, natural gas, and gasoline.

Fuels can also be classified as solid, liquid, or gaseous. Or they can be classified according to their origin—natural, chemical, or metal based.

Wood was one of the first fuels used by man, and was his most important one for many centuries. It was the easiest to get, and the cheapest. But during the sixteenth century, wood started to become scarce in Europe, and coal began to replace it.

Coal contains a high percentage of carbon. Carbon is the most important part of most fuels. Fuels with a high percentage of carbon burn evenly and with a hot flame. Hard coal, or anthracite, has a higher percentage of carbon than other types of coal, and so makes less smoke and ash.

The most important liquid fuels come from petroleum. They include kerosene, gasoline, and heating oils.

WOOD

PETROLEUM

ANTHRACITE

73

What Is Natural Gas?

In certain parts of Iran and India, where natural gas issued from crevices in the rocks, the natives thought their fire god was responsible for it. So they kept it burning as a tribute to him.

The curious thing is that in the United States, which seems to have the greatest accumulation of natural gas, people didn't know what it was either for a long time, and didn't know what to do with it. Since natural gas sometimes escapes from rocks or crevices without any drilling, these places were called "burning springs" in the United States as early as 1775. The first discovery of gas by drilling was made in the nineteenth century. It wasn't collected and piped on a commercial scale until 1872.

Natural gas is a mixture of combustible gases and vapors, chiefly methane. Sometimes it is found alone; sometimes it is found mixed with oil and must be extracted. At other places it is found with oil but is not mixed with it.

In nearly every oil field there is natural gas. It gathers in porous rock with a covering of heavy shale that keeps the gas in and keeps the air out. It accumulates in a kind of arched section of the stone, and sometimes there are gas beds above the oil.

When drilling is carried on at oil fields and oil is brought in, it sometimes happens that a gas bed is tapped, too, and gas begins to escape in a great flame. At one oil field in Oklahoma, about $25,000 worth of oil a day was collected, but at the same time $75,000 worth of gas escaped every day for a whole year!

Natural gas is clean and convenient to use for cooking and heating, but because of the problem of transportation it costs more than coal in most places. Today there are great pipeline systems that carry natural gas from its source to far distant places in a network that covers the country. In some cases the natural gas is carried through these pipes for more than one thousand miles!

GAS PIPELINES
IN THE EAST

What Is Neon?

When we walk down the main street of a city at night, we see all sorts of colored lights on stores and advertising signs. We think of them as neon lights.

But the fact is that not all of them are lights made by glowing neon gas. Other gases, such as helium, argon, krypton, and xenon, are also used in lights. Each gas gives out a different-colored light when electricity is sent through it.

The color of the light given out will vary, depending on such things as the temperature, pressure, and electric voltage. Neon gives out a red-orange light; argon gives out a reddish-blue light; the light from helium is white, yellow, or sometimes violet; from krypton it is yellow, green, or pale violet; and from xenon it is either blue or blue-green.

By passing electricity through neon gas, the atoms are made to give off light. What happens is that the energy of the electric current knocks electrons off some of the atoms of neon. When these electrons rejoin the neon atoms, energy in the form of light is given off.

All the gases we have mentioned here form a family of elements called the noble gases. Sometimes they are called rare gases because they are fairly scarce. All of these gases are relatively inactive chemically. This means they do not burn, and they form no chemical compounds under normal conditions.

The chief source of these gases is ordinary air (except for helium, which is obtained from natural gas). The gases are mixed together in the air with oxygen, nitrogen, carbon dioxide, and other substances.

To get the noble gases, the air is separated into its elements, and the gases are removed one at a time. This is done by chilling air to a very low temperature so that it turns into a liquid. The liquid air is piped into tall towers and heated.

As each gas reaches its boiling point, it boils off from the liquid air as a gas.

Why Does a Diamond Sparkle?

Suppose diamonds were not as rare as they are. Suppose they didn't cost much and almost everyone could have them. Would diamonds still be valuable?

Two things would probably make people still want to have diamonds. One is that a diamond is the hardest substance known to man, so diamonds would still be very useful in industry. The second is that diamonds would still be beautiful, and so people would still enjoy looking at them.

Diamonds are the result of a process that took place in nature. Millions of years ago, the earth was gradually becoming cooler. At that time, there existed beneath the ground a mass of hot liquid rock. This mass was subjected to extreme heat and pressure. As a result of this, molecules of carbon became packed together in dense, clear crystals. A diamond is simply a crystal of pure carbon.

When a diamond is found in "rough" form, its outside appearance is rather dull. Now man takes over to make it into the sparkling gem we all know about. Most diamonds are sawed in two, and each half is shaped and cut into a round diamond called a brilliant.

Then little faces, or facets, are cut into the diamond. The average brilliant is cut into fifty-eight facets, or even more. These facets make a diamond sparkle.

The reason for this is that a diamond has a very high refractive power. This means that when light enters it, the diamond bends the light more than other substances do. The light, instead of passing through the diamond, is bent so that it is reflected back into the stone. So a greater amount of light is returned to our eyes when we look at a diamond and it looks more brilliant. The diamond also breaks up the light into its different colors, which gives a diamond its "fire."

Did you know that diamonds were not worn as personal ornaments until 1430, when a Frenchwoman called Agnes Sorel started the custom? From then on the custom spread.

Where Do Emeralds Come From?

In ancient times, the various gems were distinguished only by their colors. The name ruby was given to all precious stones of a red hue. All green stones were called emeralds. All those of blue were called sapphires.

Later on it was seen that some of the gems were harder than others and endured longer. So it came about that the value of a gem depended not only on its color, brilliancy, and rarity, but also on its hardness.

All the gems are called precious stones. But strictly speaking, "precious" is used only for the four most valuable stones—the diamond, the ruby, the emerald, and the sapphire. The other valuable stones are called semiprecious.

The emerald is one of the softest of the precious gems. It is a variety of beryl. In its perfect state an emerald is a rich, clear green. But flawless stones are seldom found and for that reason are very expensive.

In ancient times, all the emeralds came from the mines of Egypt. These mines are still worked today but yield only a small quantity of the precious stones. The finest emeralds are at present obtained from the mines near Bogota, Colombia. There are also emerald deposits in the Ural Mountains of Russia and in the Salzburg Alps. A few fine emeralds have been found in North Carolina. And more recent discoveries of emeralds have been made in the Transvaal in South Africa.

There are many legends about emeralds. One of them is that the Holy Grail—the cup from which Christ drank at the Last Supper—was carved from a huge emerald. The emerald was believed to have medical power, too. It was supposed to have the power of curing the "falling sickness" (epilepsy). Another old legend about the emerald was that it endowed its owner with the gift of foretelling the future. It was said that by looking into its green depths one could see the things that were to come to pass!

The largest known uncut emerald is two inches long and two inches in diameter.

What Is Jade?

Jade is a gemstone that almost glows. It has been prized by man for thousands of years.

The Chinese language uses the same word to mean both "jade" and "precious stone." The English word "jade" comes from the Spanish *piedra de ijada,* which means "colic stone." The Spanish called it this because they believed jade cured stomach pains!

Jade can be either of two separate minerals, jadeite or nephrite. These look so much alike that only an expert can tell them apart. Jadeite is slightly harder than nephrite. It also has a translucent glow and comes in more colors.

Jade is white in its pure state, but enough mineral impurities are usually present to make jade bright yellow, red, or one of the many shades of green. The most desired shade of jade is an emerald-green, or "Imperial" jade, which may be almost transparent. This type comes from Burma.

Because jade is a tough and hard stone, primitive men used it to make axes, hammers, knives, and other useful tools. Later, men used it for bowls, carvings, jewelry, and charms.

Jade is so tough that it is very difficult to carve. Steel chisels will not work. So instead, gritty materials are rubbed over the surface until it wears away. Making a simple vase may take two or three years of work.

Carved jade pieces have been found in Mexico that are at least three thousand five hundred years old. The early men of Central America used some jade in tools, but used it mostly for religious purposes. The Aztecs considered jade to be worth many times its weight in gold.

China is the country where jade has been of the greatest importance. For three thousand years the Chinese have been making lovely jade carvings. The Chinese admire jade so much that those who can afford it always carry small pieces with them. They believe that when jade is fingered, some of its secret virtues rub off.

GOLD IN QUARTZ

GOLD DUST FROM A MINE BEING CHECKED IN

GOLD NUGGETS

How Is Gold Found?

Probably the first metal known to man was gold. Because of the way it occurs in nature, man knew about it and valued it long before the days of recorded history! Just how is gold found?

Even though it's considered so precious and rare, gold is actually widely distributed in nature. The trouble is that in most cases there isn't enough gold present to make it profitable to extract it. For example, sea water contains a small amount of gold. But it's so tiny in quantity that no one knows how to separate gold from the sea. Yet there's so much water in the oceans that the total amount of gold in them might be as much as ten billion tons!

Gold occurs in two forms: native, which means it's not combined with other minerals, and in combination with the ores of other metals. Native gold occurs mostly in veins of quartz or in masses of iron pyrites.

Sometimes the quartz or pyrites have been exposed to water and wind. The particles of rock surrounding the lumps of gold have been washed away, leaving lumps or nuggets of nearly pure gold.

The nuggets are gradually washed down to the bottom of the valleys and become mixed with the sand and the gravel. In this form it is called "alluvial" or "placer" gold. When man first discovered gold, it was placer gold. These particles of gold vary in size from fine dust to the great nugget found in Australia, the "Welcome Stranger" nugget, weighing nearly 150 pounds!

Gold is often found in the ores of other metals. Silver nearly always contains quantities of gold. Copper ores quite frequently occur in combination with gold.

Today, most of the gold is obtained by mining methods similar to those used for other metals. A deep hole, called a shaft, is dug into the ground toward the gold deposit. This may be more than a mile deep! The ore is then blasted, loaded on carts, brought to the shaft, and hoisted to the surface. It is crushed and ground into a fine sand called pulp, and then by means of chemical action, the gold is extracted from the other material.

The three principal gold-producing countries of the world are South Africa, Russia, and the United States.

Why Is Gold Expensive?

There are three reasons why people have always placed a high value on gold: its beauty, its usefulness, and its scarcity. If iron were as scarce as gold, it would probably be just as treasured.

Gold is a soft, yellow metal. It is one of the heaviest chemical elements. A cubic foot of this metal weighs over 1,200 pounds. Gold is also one of the most easily worked metals. Gold is so easy to hammer and shape that less than 1/25 of an ounce of gold (one gram) can be beaten into a sheet 6 feet square.

Unlike most metals, gold does not tarnish in the air. (You know what happens to silver, for example, when it is left lying about.) Gold remains bright and shiny indefinitely. And this is probably the reason why people first valued it. Gold is also one of the least chemically active metals. It reacts with only a few acids.

The most common use of gold has always been as money. Although coins were also made of metals other than gold, their value was often questioned, but the value of gold coins never was.

By 1914 gold was the measuring stick for almost all the currencies in the world. This means that dollars from the United States, francs from France, marks from Germany, and so on—all had a set value in terms of gold. At any time the currencies could be changed into gold. This system is known as the gold standard and is no longer in use, but gold is still very important in international trade. Gold is used as a "reserve" that backs up a country's international trade.

There are a tremendous number of uses for gold. About 10 percent of the gold produced each year is used by jewelers. Gold is used in dental work. Since gold conducts electricity well, it is used in certain types of electrical contacts.

The scarcity of gold keeps its price high. Today, slightly more than half of all the gold mined comes from South Africa. The world's richest gold deposits were discovered there in 1886.

What Is Uranium?

Uranium is a metal with mysterious properties. It provided man with the key that unlocked the tremendous energy of the atom. The natural radiation of uranium has been put to amazing uses in medicine, agriculture, industry, and biology.

A chunk of pure uranium metal looks about the same as a piece of silver or steel. But it is surprisingly heavy for its size. A one-foot cube of uranium weighs over half a ton! Uranium is the heaviest element found in nature.

Uranium has two very unusual characteristics. It is radioactive, which means its atoms break down slowly, releasing energy in the form of radiation. Some of its atoms are fissionable; that is, they can be made to explode and break in two, releasing vast amounts of energy. Uranium's fissionability is the basis of all nuclear-power plants and nuclear weapons.

Chemically, uranium is very reactive. A piece of uranium exposed to air quickly develops a blackish coating. This coating is a combination of the uranium and the oxygen in the air. Uranium also forms important compounds with many other elements.

Uranium is widely distributed in small amounts, but is never found in nature in a pure state. Extracting uranium from its ores is a long and complicated process. Mills process hundreds of tons of ore a day, but only a few pounds of uranium are collected from each ton.

The ore is first crushed and screened. Then it is treated with various chemicals to remove impurities. The ore is then put through many refining processes until a bright, claylike material called "yellow cake" is obtained. This highly purified form of uranium must be refined still further, for only a small fraction of natural uranium is fissionable.

A single pound of uranium contains as much energy as three million pounds of coal! In nuclear reactors the shattering uranium atoms produce tremendous quantities of heat as the chain reaction builds up. This heat can be used to turn a turbine, which drives an electric generator.

What Is Chromium?

Chromium is a metal. It is hard and brittle, and it is highly resistant to corrosion. It is silvery-white, and when polished, takes on a shiny luster. It is a poor conductor of electricity and heat.

Chromium is never found as a metal in nature. It occurs in a number of minerals, most of which are brightly colored, but chromium is extracted from only one mineral. This is a heavy black mineral called chromite. The largest deposits of this mineral are found in South Africa, the Soviet Union, the Philippines, and Rhodesia.

Most of us know of chromium because it is used as the shiny plating on automobile bumpers and other metal objects. But actually the most important use of chromium is in steel alloys. Adding a small amount of chromium makes steel stronger, harder, and more resistant to corrosion.

Chromium is a vital part of stainless steel, because stainless steel has hundreds of uses where resistance to corrosion is important. For example, stainless steel made with chromium is used for knives, forks, spoons, pots and pans, kitchen sinks and counter tops, tools, dairy equipment, and even surgical instruments.

Chromium metal is used to produce a shiny protective coating on metal objects. This coating is applied by a process called electroplating. Chromium-plating was first used to decorate and protect watches, jewelry, and household appliances. Automobile makers began to use chromium-plating on bumpers and trim about 1925. The automobile industry is now the largest user of chromium-plating.

Machine parts that must withstand a great deal of wear and friction, such as gears and bearing surfaces, are often chromium-plated. Such chromium-plated moving parts can actually be run without oil or grease.

Chromium salts are used to tan leather and in dyes for cloth. Many brightly colored chromium compounds are used in paints. So you see that chromium is one of man's most useful metals.

Of What Is Aluminum Foil Made?

Aluminum is the most abundant metal in the earth's crust. Actually, it makes up between 7 and 8 percent of the crust. But aluminum is never found in a pure state in nature. Rather, it is combined with other chemical elements in compounds that are very hard to break down. The most important ore of aluminum is bauxite, a type of clay. This generally contains from 40 to 60 percent aluminum oxide.

Aluminum has a number of properties that make it useful for many products. Aluminum is light, weighing one-third as much as such metals as iron, copper, nickel, or zinc. Aluminum conducts electricity well and is also a good heat insulator, because its shiny surface reflects away heat rays. And aluminum resists corrosion; when it is exposed to air, aluminum immediately combines with some of the oxygen to form a thin, tough, colorless film that protects the metal against further chemical action, thus preventing rust.

For these and other reasons, aluminum is used in making foil. Foil is any metal sheet that measures 0.005 of an inch or less. To roll a metal this thin, machines of great precision are needed. Even the smallest change in measurement shows up in foil. Different kinds of mills have been developed to roll out aluminum and other metals to the exact thickness desired.

Aluminum is so malleable that it can be rolled into sheets of foil as thin as 0.0002 of an inch. In such cases pure aluminum is used. For most other things, and for greater strength in the foil, aluminum alloys are used. In these instances other metals are combined with aluminum.

The aluminum foil you use at home resists moisture and gas, is greaseproof, odorless, and tasteless, resists corrosion, reflects away heat, and shuts out light.

What Is Pewter?

Pewter is an alloy, which means it is a mixture of metals. The basis of pewter is tin. It is generally mixed with lead in the proportions of six or four parts tin to one part lead.

Pewter has been made for thousands of years, though it is hard to be exact about it. It is said to have been known to the ancient Chinese, the Egyptians, and the Greeks. The ancient Romans made it, too.

Pewter is usually associated with the English, and there is a reason for this. In Cornwall, England, there were mines with deposits of fine tin, and so the English made pewter in very early days, and tin from Cornwall was used for making pewter in other parts of Europe.

Pewter has been used for three basic purposes: for church vessels, for domestic needs, and in civic functions. Chalices of pewter have been used in church services in England since medieval times.

In England, pewter became very popular for use in plates and cups. But in time, the richer people began to prefer silver, and so the middle classes used pewter in place of silver.

In France, pewter was used for drinking vessels, plates, salt-cellars, and cooking pots as far back as the fourteenth century. Germany had a pewter industry established in the fourteenth century, and at about the same time pewter was also being made in Belgium, Holland, Switzerland, Russia, and the Scandinavian countries.

In the United States, pewter was much used in homes in the early Colonial period. There is some that goes back to the seventeenth century, but the great period of production was between 1750 and 1850. Pewter was used for every kind of utensil that was made.

Pewter was also made in China, Korea, and Japan more than one thousand years ago.

What Is a Coral Reef?

Let's start by finding out what coral is. A chunk of coral is made of the skeletons of tiny marine animals called coral polyps.

The polyp's skeleton grows outside its body. It is cup-shaped, and it protects and supports the polyp's body and grows as the animal grows. When the polyp dies, the skeleton is left. Coral reefs and islands are formed of billions upon billions of these tiny skeletons.

A coral colony consists of living corals. Each is attached to a solid base, such as a rock or the skeletons of earlier generations of corals. Coral colonies are found in all the seas, but reef-building coral polyps are found only in warm, shallow waters. A depth of about 150 feet is best for them. Yet in some parts of the world coral reefs rise from great ocean depths.

The mystery of how coral reefs were formed was solved by Charles Darwin, the famous naturalist. Darwin knew that the earth's surface changes. Mountains are forced up in one place; in another, the crust of the earth sinks.

When he was studying coral reefs, he noticed that there were three kinds: fringing reefs, barrier reefs, and atolls (rings of coral). Putting all this information together, he worked out the following theory:

A volcanic island forms where an undersea volcano rises above the surface of the water. In the shallow waters of the island shores,

DETAIL OF CORAL

FRINGING REEF

BARRIER REEF

VOLCANIC ISLAND

corals build a fringing reef. As time passes, the volcano becomes cold and dead; it begins to sink back into the sea. As a result the fringing reef now becomes separated from the island by a wider channel of water, and it goes on growing. It has become a barrier reef.

If the volcano sinks completely and vanishes, only the coral reef is left; it has become an atoll, a ring of coral surrounding a lagoon. In addition, we know today that island shores may rise or sink, and ocean levels may rise or fall. All these changes help explain the building of coral reefs.

How Are Seashells Formed?

If you've ever walked along a beach, you've probably seen a seashell lying on the sand where it has been washed in by the waves. The shell will nearly always be empty, for it is the home of some sea animal that has died.

By the way, shells are also found in woodlands, rivers, and ponds as well as the sea. When people speak of shells, they usually mean those of soft-bodied animals known as mollusks.

Most mollusks have shells outside their soft bodies. The shell is a mollusk's skeleton. It is part of the animal and the mollusk is attached to it by muscles. The soft animal inside can never leave its shell and return to it. As the mollusk grows bigger, its shell increases in size and strength.

The shell is made of a form of limestone and is built by the mollusk itself. Certain glands in the mollusk are able to take limestone from the water and deposit it in tiny particles at the edge of, and along the inside of, the shell. As a mollusk grows in size, its shell increases in thickness and size. You can see the lines of growth that are marked by ridges that run parallel to the outer edge. You've probably noticed these growth lines in the shells of oysters and clams. The other ridges are caused by ridges in the "mantle" of the mollusk, or by muscles in its body.

The shell of a mollusk consists of three layers. The outside is covered with a thin layer of hornlike material that contains no lime. Under this is a layer of carbonate of lime. The inside layer is the "mother-of-pearl," or nacre. It is made up of very thin alternate layers of carbonate of lime and a horny substance.

The coloring of the shell comes from some glands of the mollusk that contain coloring matter. So a shell may be spotted, all one color, or marked with lines. Some shells are so tiny they can only be seen with a magnifying glass, while the giant clam has a shell that can be four feet long.

What Is Plankton?

The word plankton comes from the Greek word for "wandering" or "drifting." And plankton is a drifting mass of life made up of billions of tiny living creatures.

Some of the organisms that make up plankton, such as tiny green plants, always remain plankton. Others, such as fishes and lobsters, are plankton only while they are very young. Sometimes plankton includes large jellyfishes, sometimes creatures so small they cannot even be seen with an ordinary microscope. But all plankton have means of staying afloat and share a drifting way of life.

The smallest plankton organisms are one-celled plants called microscopic algae. One of the most numerous of these is a kind of algae called diatoms. There can be two million diatoms in a single gallon of water.

The animal life included in plankton is quite interesting. One kind is the pear-shaped copepod. Copepod means "oar feet." A copepod swims by jerky, oarlike movements of its tiny legs. The largest copepod is less than one-half inch long.

Young crustaceans of many kinds are plankton. These crustaceans include shrimps, crabs, lobsters, and barnacles in salt water, and crayfish and water fleas in fresh water. The larvae, or developing young, of these crustaceans are tiny or even microscopic, and during this period they cannot move on their own, so they drift with other plankton.

This is also true of the young mollusks, such as snails, clams, and mussels. They are part of the plankton at the first stages of their life. Plankton may also include the eggs and larvae of many fishes.

In fresh water, animal plankton often includes developing insects. Mayflies, dragonflies, mosquitoes, water beetles, and many other insects lay their eggs in water. When the larvae hatch, they live and feed on the plant plankton.

And this is only part of what makes up plankton. So you can see how much this classification includes and how interesting it is to study.

Does Seaweed Have Any Use?

All over the world wherever there is a body of sea water, there seaweed may be found. Seaweed occurs in many varieties. It belongs to a large group of water plants called algae—plants without true leaves, stems, roots, or flowers.

But they do contain a green pigment called chlorophyll. Therefore, they are capable of making their own food. The reason these plants don't look green is that the chlorophyll is often concealed by other pigments. So some seaweed looks brown or red.

In the Temperate Zone, the most common seaweeds belong to the brown algae. This is the seaweed that grows between the high and low-tide lines. It has bubblelike floats that children enjoy crackling open between their fingers. The plants are attached to rocks by means of rootlike holdfasts.

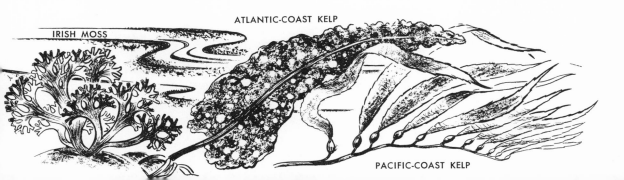

IRISH MOSS

ATLANTIC-COAST KELP

PACIFIC-COAST KELP

Another well-known form of seaweed is the kelp. It has various forms. Most commonly they are long, flat, tough, bladelike forms that fasten to rocks by means of leathery stalks. Some of these seaweeds along the Atlantic Coast grow as long as twenty feet, and the giant kelp of the Pacific Ocean is even longer!

These kelp are among the seaweeds that are useful to man. They are often used as fertilizer because they have a high concentration of potash. They are also a source of iodine.

Another useful kind of seaweed is called Irish moss. It is rather rough and leathery in form. It produces a great deal of agar, which is a colorless substance resembling jelly. In the Orient, tons of seaweed belonging to the red-algae group are dried and used as food! They are not very nourishing, but contain a great deal of agar. They are used in thickening soups and providing bulk in other foods.

Seaweed is also a primary source of food for ocean life. Smaller sea creatures feed on it, and they in turn become food for the larger ones. Seaweed gives off oxygen, and this helps to keep the water pure. So you see why seaweed is considered quite useful to man.

What Causes Ocean Currents?

There are masses of water that are always drifting about in the sea. The circulation is very complicated because many things help to push water about. One of these is the tendency of dense water to sink and lighter water to rise.

The densest water in the ocean is both cold and salty. It is made this way when sea water freezes in the Arctic or Antarctic oceans. There is very little salt in the ice that is formed by this freezing. The cold, salty water left behind when the ice is formed sinks right to the bottom of the sea.

The saltiest water in the ocean is found in the tropics. The water is very warm and therefore not so dense as the cold, less salty water underneath it. It stays at the surface of the ocean. The salty water is pushed about by the winds.

Sometimes the winds and the shape of the coastline push the circulating water together. Then the water has to flow much faster and becomes a current. Currents are like rivers in the sea. The most famous current is the Gulf Stream, which was discovered by Benjamin Franklin.

The Gulf Stream starts in the Atlantic Ocean near the Equator. The steady winds near the Equator are always blowing partly from the east. They push the warm, salty water past the Caribbean islands into the great bay made by Florida and the east coast of the United States. The water piles up and then flows northward past Cape Hatteras.

Here the Gulf Stream is narrow and flows swiftly. Its speed is several miles an hour. The current is less than ten miles wide and is about one thousand eight hundred feet deep. Like a river on land, the Gulf Stream does not flow in a straight path, but it winds its way over the ocean. But, unlike a river, the Gulf Stream is not always found in the same place, for it has no fixed course.

Many surface currents such as the Gulf Stream have currents flowing beneath them. These are called countercurrents. They flow in an opposite direction but in the same path as the surface current.

The rotation of the earth also has a great deal to do with the directions of currents.

What Is the Continental Shelf?

When you think of the Atlantic Ocean, you think of the top surface of the water. But what is under the water, at the bottom of the ocean floor? Let's imagine that we are making a voyage out of New York, due east across the Atlantic Ocean. Here is a picture of the bottom as we move across the ocean.

For about two hundred miles, the bottom gradually slopes down. It is generally flat, but occasionally there is a V-shaped valley or canyon. This is the continental shelf. The continental shelf is part of the North American continent. It just happens to be too low to stand out of the sea.

At the depth of about one thousand two hundred feet, the shelf suddenly comes to an end. It is no longer gently sloping but there is a steep incline. This is the continental edge or slope, and it goes down to the full depth of the ocean.

Moving along past the slope, the ocean depth is about two-and-a-half miles. We are now crossing the deep ocean. Here the ocean bottom is very flat. It is called an abyssal plain. Abyssal plains cover about a third of the sea floor and are among the flattest places found on earth.

As we keep on moving across the ocean, we reach an area where there are humps on the sea floor. Some are the size of hills. This is called the Mid-Atlantic ridge. Near the center of the ridge the hills are higher and steeper, and some rise like mountains to within five thousand feet of the surface.

Between the mountains are deep valleys with flat floors. Right in the middle of the ridge lies the largest valley of all. It is called the mid-ocean rift. The rift is like a crack between the two halves of the ridge.

As we continue eastward, we again cross an abyssal plain. The plain slopes gently upward to the continental shelf off Portugal. And this is a picture of the bottom of the Atlantic Ocean.

SHORELINE

CONTINENTAL SHELF

BERMUDA

What Is a Marine Biologist?

A marine biologist studies the creatures that live in the sea. To do this he has to catch fishes and study them when they are dead. Or else he must go down in the water and watch them while they are alive.

One of the most important tools of the biologist is the pickling bottle, containing alcohol or formalin. Without it he would have very little time to look at a creature he has collected, for the animal would soon decay.

Besides the pickling bottle the marine biologist uses a trawl net to catch fishes and other sea creatures. The trawl net is cone-shaped and looks something like a butterfly net. Its mouth is sewn to a hoop, and the rest trails behind. A towline from a ship is attached to the hoop. A heavy weight pulls down the line as the ship sails along.

Water and fishes flow in through the mouth of the net. The water escapes, but the fishes are caught. To catch bigger and fast-swimming fishes, the net is made with large meshes so that the water can flow through easily and the trawl can be towed very fast. To catch smaller fishes, the meshes are made finer.

When the biologist feels that enough has been caught, the net is hauled in. It is tipped out onto a canvas. The various kinds of creatures are counted, and the ones to be kept are popped into their bottles. What is left is thrown back or sent to the ship's galley.

Sometimes color pictures are taken of the specimens minutes after they die. This is done because many dead fish lose their color very quickly, even when they are preserved.

Back in the laboratory, the specimens are dissected. This means that they are carefully taken apart in order to examine every part of their bodies. The biologist dissects to learn how creatures are built. Then he can determine their differences and similarities.

What Is Anthropology?

Like most sciences, the name of this one tells you what it is about. The name anthropology comes from two Greek words: *anthropos*, meaning "man," and *logos*, meaning "science." So anthropology should mean the study of man.

In a large sense, that is what anthropology is concerned with: man's physical structure, his customs and habits, his languages, arts and religions, and his civilizations. This means that a great many other studies are very closely linked with anthropology—for example, anatomy, physiology, psychology, ethics, sociology, and so on.

But, in actual practice, anthropology limits itself to a much narrower field. You might say that for practical purposes, three studies make up anthropology. The first is the study of man's place in nature. What separates man from other animals? What characteristics of his body set him apart from monkeys and other animals? How does his skull compare with that of a chimpanzee? The purpose of such studies is to trace the connection between man's physical qualities and his development and civilization.

The next study anthropology is concerned with is the various races of man and their classification. This is called ethnology. This science deals with the physical differences between the various human races. It compares the skeletons and skulls of prehistoric man with those of modern man. It also deals with the customs and religions of various tribes and peoples to find out how races differ and how they develop.

There is a third, a special branch of anthropology, called anthropometry. This is the science that deals with the physical measurements of man, the height and weight of various races, the shape of their bones, and so on. It is this science, for example, which tells us that the average height of a man today is 5 feet 5¼ inches.

How Do Archaeologists Know What They Find?

An archaeologist digs up things buried by ancient peoples. The question is, how can he identify cities and people and objects and reconstruct the life of the past from what he has found?

The answer is that he can't always do it—because he doesn't always find the things he needs to build a complete picture of a people or a way of life. After all, what he finds is only what people left behind, usually objects that were used every day. These might be remains of houses, tools, jewelry, dishes, toys, and also bones of animals used for food.

EARTHENWARE WHISTLE

DUG FROM ANCIENT GRAVES IN PANAMA

TERRA COTTA FISH-SHAPED BOWL

PUMA GOLD

But many of the things that were important to the lives of early people cannot be found. Objects made of leather, wood, cloth, wool, or straw usually decay and leave no trace. Another thing that must remain a mystery to the archaeologist is the clothing early people wore. He can probably tell whether they used cloth or animal skins, but unless they left drawings of themselves, he can't tell much more about their clothing.

The archaeologist also may have no clue as to whether the people were artistic, and he may know nothing at all about their thoughts and ideas. So his picture of the life of the early people may be quite incomplete.

But, despite this, the archaeologist can still tell us a great deal. He first finds out the order in which early towns were built, one upon the ruins of another. Then he must know the town in which each object was found. Each object is labeled, photographed, measured, and so on. If the site belongs to historic times, the archaeologist must know the ancient writing used in that place.

There are many experts who help an archaeologist such as geologists, botanists, zoologists, and others, all of whom help him identify and analyze what he has found. Sometimes it takes years of work and study before the archaeologist is ready to publish a work about what he has found. But when he does, it may give us an exciting view into the past—a picture of how ancient peoples lived.

What Is the Sphinx?

Of course, the sphinx most of us think of is the Great Sphinx that stands at Giza, Egypt, near the pyramids. Actually, a sphinx is a monster that was common in the myths of ancient peoples. The Greeks thought of it as having the head of a woman, the body of a lion, and wings. The Egyptians thought of it as a wingless lion with the head and breast of a man.

The Great Sphinx of Egypt was once a hill of rock left over from the building of the Great Pyramid. Later it was carved into a huge lion with the head of a man. It stands 66 feet high with a length of 240 feet. It was probably carved to resemble the face of a king called Chephren, a king of the fourth Egyptian dynasty.

In ancient times, lions lived in the desert just beyond the valley of the Nile. Because they were strong and beautiful, Egyptian sculptors carved statues of them to guard the entrances to temples. Later on, instead of a lion's head, they carved the head of a king.

In ancient Egypt the kings were considered to be descended from the sun god, who was called Ra. When a king died, he himself was supposed to become the sun god. So the Great Sphinx represents the king as the sun god guarding the pyramids.

Although there is no other sphinx as large as the Great Sphinx at Giza, many kings had their likenesses carved as sphinxes. In one case, a sphinx was made with the face of a woman, Queen Hatshepsut, who seized the throne and ruled the country. This sphinx was given a beard to represent Queen Hatshepsut's power.

What Is the Rosetta Stone?

As you know, one of the greatest civilizations of all time was the one of ancient Egypt. A long time ago, man had already begun to unearth monuments and buildings and treasures of all sorts going back to ancient Egypt. There was a strange kind of writing found with many of these objects and buildings, but no one could read it. And there seemed to be no way to figure out what it meant.

The early Greeks believed that Egyptian priests produced these writings for sacred purposes, so they called them *hieroglyphs,* which meant "sacred carvings." And this type of writing came to be known as hieroglyphics.

After the Greeks, no big effort was made to understand these writings until the seventeenth century, when many scholars worked on the problem. But they had no success. Then in 1799, a wonderful discovery was made. A black slab of basalt was found, which had lain for centuries near one of the mouths of the river Nile. It was named the Rosetta stone after the town where it was found.

Now what made the Rosetta stone so valuable was that it had a message written in three different languages. One was Greek; a second, hieroglyphics; and the third, a late form of Egyptian writing called demotic, a sort of abbreviated hieroglyphic.

Many years of study of these writings now began. The Greek text could be read and understood, and by comparing it to the others the long-lost secret of hieroglyphic writing was finally revealed. The man who accomplished this in 1822 was a brilliant young Frenchman called Jean François Champollion.

As a result of his discovery, it has been possible for historians to trace the life, customs, and religion of the Egyptians as far back as 3500 B.C. This was because hieroglyphics were the earliest form of Egyptian writing and one of the oldest-known systems of writing.

Basically it is picture writing. Each picture represents an object. But this writing developed as time went on, and later Egyptians wrote down words and ideas and sounds.

What Is an Obelisk?

An obelisk is a slender stone shaft with a pyramid-shaped top. The first and most famous of these monuments was made in Egypt.

These Egyptian obelisks are considered to be true obelisks, because each one was carved from a single stone. Some famous memorials in the United States, such as the Bunker Hill and Washington monuments, are shaped like obelisks, but they are made of many small pieces of stone.

The Egyptians believed that the obelisk was the home of the spirit of the sun. Obelisks were usually made in pairs and placed on each side of the gates to temples and tombs. The tops were often covered with bright metals, such as gold, to reflect the sun's rays. Inscriptions in hieroglyphics on the four sides praised the pharaohs who had ordered the obelisks.

All Egyptian obelisks came from a granite quarry near Aswan. Some of them were over eighty feet tall. How were the Egyptians able to move these tremendous shafts? No one knows exactly. It has been estimated that more than twenty thousand men would be needed to pull one. From the quarry the obelisks were dragged to the Nile River. They were loaded onto barges and shipped to different cities.

Throughout history, Egyptian obelisks have been sent all over the world. The ancient Romans were very impressed by them. After the Romans conquered Egypt in 30 B.C., they moved about fifteen obelisks to Italy. No one knows how they did this.

The obelisk that stands in front of St. Peter's cathedral in Rome was brought to Rome at about that time. Sixteen centuries later, in 1585, it was moved to the square in front of the cathedral. The operation took nearly a year!

In the nineteenth century three obelisks were moved from Egypt. The first was set up in the Place de la Concorde in Paris in 1836. The second obelisk was set up on the banks of the Thames in London in 1880. The third was placed in Central Park in New York City in 1881. The London and New York obelisks are both called Cleopatra's Needle.

What Are Birthstones?

Many early civilizations believed that precious possessions, including gems, had strange and mysterious powers, and that certain gems could even prevent or cure diseases.

These ideas about gems are still preserved in the custom of wearing a birthstone for the month in which one was born. Even though the idea is a very ancient one, the actual wearing of birthstones started about the sixteenth century.

Here are the traditional birthstones used in America: January, garnet; February, amethyst; March, bloodstone or aquamarine; April, diamond; May, emerald; June, pearl; July, ruby; August, peridot; September, sapphire; October, opal; November, topaz; December, turquoise.

One of the most curious human beliefs is this faith in the power of precious stones. For example, some gems are supposed to have an influence on love and marriage. Turquoise is believed to prevent disagreement between a husband and wife. Aquamarine promotes the love of married couples. Topaz is a symbol of loyalty. Those who wear it are said to be devoted to their husbands or wives for life.

Among the stones believed to have the power to cure or prevent illness, the amethyst is considered especially effective against headache and toothache, and diamonds are believed to cure leprosy, insanity, and nightmares. Agate reduces fever.

Sapphire, it was thought, gave protection from spirits of darkness. The Chinese put jade bracelets or anklets on their children to protect them from harm. The Hindus believe pearls guard them against all evils. The garnet, because it is the color of blood, is worn to make its wearer immune to injury.

A turquoise is said to be a charm against falling from a horse. And there are people who believe an opal necklace guards the life and color of blond hair!

What Is the Zodiac?

In ancient times, when people looked up at the sky at night, they noticed that many of the brightest stars were arranged in a certain pattern, or group. These groups are what we call constellations. The name comes from a Latin word meaning "group of stars."

In every ancient civilization men gave names to these constellations, calling them after gods and heroes, and after animals and familiar objects.

In studying the constellations, early man noticed that they seemed to march in a great procession across the sky. Certain constellations appeared in the spring, traveled across the sky, and then disappeared. They were followed by summer, fall, and winter constellations.

Within the process, twelve constellations were noticed in particular. The sun and the moon always rose and set within the part of the sky that held these twelve. And so the part of the sky through which the sun, moon, and the planets traveled was named the Zodiac, meaning "circle of living things." This was because most of the twelve constellations were named for living things.

The Zodiac was divided by the ancients into twelve sections, each named after one of the twelve constellations. We know these constellations as Taurus, the bull; Aries, the ram; Pisces, the fish; Aquarius, the water carrier; Capricorn, the goat; Sagittarius, the archer; Scorpius, the scorpion; Libra, the scales; Virgo, the virgin; Leo, the lion; Cancer, the crab; and Gemini, the twins.

The twelve constellations were called the signs of the Zodiac. Every month a different sign of the Zodiac appeared on the eastern horizon, and the sun and the moon seemed to rise in this particular sign.

In addition to the twelve constellations of the Zodiac, thirty-six other constellations were familiar to peoples of ancient times. These forty-eight are known as the "ancient" constellations. Later on, forty other constellations were discovered by astronomers, and these became known as the "modern" constellations.

Why Is the Four-Leaf Clover Lucky?

The desire of man to protect himself from unknown forces, or to create good fortune for himself, has led to thousands upon thousands of superstitions the world over. In fact, we can roughly divide superstitions into those that are supposed to bring good luck and those that are supposed to bring bad luck.

The four-leaf clover is believed by people all over the world to be a sign of coming good fortune and happiness. It is such an old superstition that no one can say exactly how or where it began. But there is an old legend about it that some people believe. The legend is that when Eve was sent away from Paradise, she took a four-leaf clover with her. Because the clover was a bit of green from the Garden of Paradise, it came to be considered an omen of good luck if found in one's own garden!

Just as widespread, and just as hard to explain, is the common belief that a horseshoe is lucky. Almost every country has a different legend or tradition concerning the horseshoe. The Irish say that the horse was in the stable where Christ was born, and therefore the horseshoe has magical power. In Russia, the blacksmith used to be considered a kind of magician, and it is claimed he used the horseshoe as a charm in performing his magic. Even the ancient Romans believed that finding a cast-off horseshoe in the road would protect one from illness. This may be because iron at one time was regarded as a good-luck charm.

When it comes to bad-luck omens, the fear of a black cat is one of the oldest. In the Middle Ages, when people believed in witches, it was assumed that witches and evil spirits took the form of the black cat. Today, many people are still uneasy to see a black cat cross their path!

The broken mirror is another bad-luck superstition that goes back to ancient times. In ancient Greece it was believed that one saw the will of the gods in the mirror. Therefore, if a mirror was broken accidentally, it meant that the gods didn't want the person to see the future because it held unpleasant things!

The Romans believed that a person's health changed every seven years. Since the mirror reflected the health of a person, they thought that breaking a mirror meant that the health of a person would be broken for seven years!

What Was the Golden Age?

At certain times, in certain parts of the world, civilization seems to reach unusual heights and men to accomplish great things. One such period was the Golden Age of Greece, which lasted roughly from 500 to 429 B.C.

Early in the fifth century, the Persians invaded Greece, but the Greeks arose and pushed them out. The people of Athens led this fight. Because of this, Athens became the richest and most powerful state in Greece.

Athens built a fleet of ships that was larger than the combined fleets of all the rest of Greece. Wealth began to flow into Athens, some of it as tribute from other states, some from commerce, and some from silver mines.

The population of Athens increased by four times. With all these new people, power, and prosperity, the arts in Athens flourished as never before in history.

It was the Age of Pericles, named after the wise Athenian leader. During this period, construction was begun on the Parthenon, one of the most beautiful and famous buildings in the world. Among the men who lived in Athens at this time were Phidias, the great sculptor; Socrates, the teacher; and Sophocles and Euripides, the playwrights who wrote some of the greatest dramas in history.

PERICLES

Everybody was encouraged to help make Athens more beautiful, and many masterpieces were created. Also, because there was so much wealth and power, men had a great deal of leisure. The citizens of Athens had more intellectual and cultural interests than any other society before or since.

The Golden Age of Greece created treasures and masterpieces and works of art that have had an influence on the whole world, even to this day. Later on in the fifth century B.C., fighting began between Athens and Sparta and their allies. Athenian culture began to decline and the Golden Age ended.

Are Modern Olympic Games the Same as the Ancient Ones?

Even though the modern Olympic Games are patterned after those held in ancient Greece, there are many important differences.

The games are still held every four years, as in ancient times. In those days, wars were stopped so that the games could take place, but in 1916, 1940, and 1944, they were not held, because of World War I and World War II.

The original Olympics were always held in Olympia, Greece. Each modern Olympiad is held in or near a different city of the world.

The earlier games were open only to Greek citizens and athletes from Mediterranean countries. The modern games encourage all nations to compete.

Another big difference is that events for women have become a major part of the modern games. And the female winners receive the same honors as the men who win.

In the ancient games, there were honors for cultural achievements. Modern competition is almost entirely athletic. Many of the contests held in the modern Olympics were unknown in early times. These include bicycle, canoe and yacht racing; soccer; basketball; judo; rifle shooting; and water polo.

One of the most popular events of the modern Olympics is the marathon. This very tiring twenty-six-mile foot race over an open course is the supreme test of the runners' endurance. The marathon was not a part of the ancient Olympics although it originated in Greece.

And finally, a more recent development in the Olympics are the winter games, which were started in 1924. They are held separately from the summer games but in the same year. The winter Olympics provide competition in skiing, speed and figure skating, ice hockey, bobsledding, tobogganing, and rifle shooting. Such cold-weather sports could never have developed in the warm climate of Greece.

Who Were the Knights?

Knights were the highest class of fighting men in Europe during the Middle Ages. The knights, who fought on horseback, were the aristocrats of the battlefield.

Their whole way of life was based on warfare, and they were the great heroes of that time. The high position of the knights was partly due to the fact that during the early Middle Ages kings and governments had very little real authority. Power belonged to the best fighters. The man who had horses and heavy arms and knew how to use them had a great advantage.

From their walled and moated castles the more powerful knights ruled the nearby countryside. They honored no law but their own, and they freely made war against their neighbors. A knight did as he wished, because no one else was powerful enough to stop him. Many knights did keep some sort of order in their land and protected their people from bandits. But many a knight was no better than a bandit himself.

The warfare of the knights was like a game, and their games were like war. The sport that was most like battle was the tournament. In time, tournaments became mock battles in which knights fought with flattened lances and blunted swords. The object of a tournament was about the same as that of a battle—to capture an enemy and collect ransom.

Knights had rules of behavior, called the code of chivalry. A knight was supposed to treat his captive as an honored guest, even if they had been bitter enemies. One knight was not supposed to attack another without warning.

Knights observed this chivalry among themselves because it was a matter of mutual advantage. A knight might be captured by another knight someday.

Knights could be attacked without warning, so no knight left his castle without wearing his heavy, uncomfortable armor for protection.

What Is Falconry?

A falcon is a bird of prey; that is, it catches other animals for food. It has long, pointed wings and a notch or "tooth" in the cutting edge of its beak. The falcon family includes many species, ranging in size from the six-inch falconet to the 24-inch gyrfalcon.

Falconry is the art of training and hunting with birds of prey, usually falcons or hawks. The bird must be strong and fast enough to strike down what it is hunting, and intelligent enough to be trained.

When a falcon is hunting with its master, it begins by rising high in the air. Some falcons go up as high as a thousand feet. When the quarry is sighted, the falcon dives onto it and rakes across its back with its hind talons. The falcon then lands on its prey, bites off the neck, and begins plucking. The falconer must approach the falcon with a piece of meat, and coax it to perch on his fist in order to get the food.

Nobody knows exactly when falconry began, but we do know it was a long, long time ago. According to ancient Japanese writings, the Chinese used trained falcons more than four thousand years ago! Falconry was probably known in Europe by the beginning of the Christian Era.

One of the greatest falconry books of all time was written in the thirteenth century by the Holy Roman Emperor Frederick II. He gained much of his information from the East, where he had been on Crusades. There, falconry was practiced by the khans and their followers.

For four hundred years, from the thirteenth to the seventeenth centuries, falconry was very popular in England. There were many curious customs and laws concerning falconry. For example, the type of bird a falconer could carry depended on his social standing. Kings and emperors could use the eagle and gyrfalcon. Princes, earls, and dukes could carry the peregrine falcon, and so on down the line.

Falconry had nearly died out by the beginning of the eighteenth century, but there are still some fans here and there who carry on this sport.

How Did People Sew in Olden Times?

Sewing is the process of fastening one piece of material to another by stitching with a needle and thread. Now, this seems like such a simple idea that you might imagine it was one of the first ever developed by man. And in fact it was.

Before the needle was developed, however, fabrics were just draped about the body to form garments. But as soon as man became civilized, he felt the need to sew materials together, so needles have existed since the days of the oldest civilizations. Early needles have been found that were made from the bones of birds and fish, as well as from bronze.

In ancient Egypt they not only had needle and thread, but were able to do embroidery! And more than three thousand years ago the Hindus in India had already learned how to cut, fit, and sew what we know as tailored garments.

During the Middle Ages, clothes were very simple. They were made by the mistress of the house and her servants. Later on, as clothing became fancier, it was necessary to make more and stronger seams, because clothes fit the body more closely. Sewing was done entirely by hand, of course. Little girls were taught to sew from early childhood, and every young woman was expected to know how to sew well.

BONE NEEDLE

Who Was Aristotle?

Aristotle was one of the most important men of ancient Greece and one of the greatest philosophers who ever lived.

Aristotle studied under the philosopher Plato for about twenty years. When Plato died, Aristotle began to develop his own method of teaching. He was interested in practically every problem that man faced. How does the mind work? How can we learn what is true and what is false? What is the best form of government?

Aristotle tried to find answers by observing the world around him and gathering facts. He believed that every event had a logical explanation, and he was one of the first men to form conclusions from investigation and observation.

Aristotle opened his own school, called the Lyceum. He urged each man to seek his own place in the world by learning how to live a good and useful life. He believed in the "golden mean," or living the middle way between two extremes.

Aristotle is said to have written about four hundred books on astronomy, physics, poetry, zoology, oratory, biology, logic, politics, government, and ethics.

Aristotle's books have been studied by people all over the world for hundreds of years. No other man has influenced the thinking of so many people for so long.

Modern scientists have found that many of the observations he made more than two thousand years ago are true today. He showed us that every statement should be supported by evidence, and that the basis for knowledge is fact.

Who Was Helen of Troy?

In ancient Greece there were many myths and legends that involved gods and people. The most beautiful woman in Greek mythology was Helen of Troy. Her mother was Leda, who was a mortal. Her father was Zeus, the god.

Helen was supposed to be so beautiful that anyone who saw her was dazzled. As Helen grew into womanhood, the handsomest and most powerful princes of Greece sought her hand. Since there were so many suitors, her stepfather, the king of Sparta, made all of them vow that they would remain loyal to the man who became Helen's husband.

The man who was chosen was Menelaus, the richest and most powerful of all the suitors. He later became king of Sparta, and he and Helen lived happily.

The goddess of love, Aphrodite, wished to reward a man called Paris, who was the son of King Priam of Troy. She promised to give Paris the most beautiful of mortal women. Paris sailed to Sparta. There he saw Helen and fell in love with her. He persuaded her to leave Menelaus and to run away with him to Troy.

Menelaus was furious, and he swore to crush Paris and win Helen back. Remembering the pledge all the former suitors of Helen had made to be loyal to her husband, he asked their help. He decided to wage war against Troy.

In the epic poem called *The Iliad,* the great Greek poet Homer tells of the last battles of the war and of the deaths of many great Greek and Trojan heroes. It is probable that a Trojan war actually took place about 1200 B.C., but no one knows exactly why it started. The story of Helen may only be a legend.

During the course of the war Paris was killed, and Troy was destroyed. Helen begged Menelaus to forgive her, and the king agreed. They returned to Sparta. But there is a legend that after Menelaus died, Helen was driven out of her palace to the island of Rhodes.

How Old Was Joan of Arc?

Saint Joan of Arc is honored by the people of France as one of their greatest heroines. She was born on January 6, 1412, and was burned at the stake on May 30, 1431. So she was only nineteen years old when she died.

When Joan was very young, much of France was ruled by the Burgundians, a powerful group of nobles who had joined with the English to gain control of the country.

When Joan was about thirteen years old, she began to hear "voices," which she said were those of Saints Catherine and Margaret, and of Michael the Archangel. She said the voices told her that she must bring peace to France by having the Dauphin Charles, who was heir to the throne, crowned king.

In time, Joan convinced Charles that she could lead his troops to victory. Joan inspired the French soldiers; they defeated the English, and the Dauphin was crowned Charles VII.

Later on, the king didn't give her full support in her efforts to continue the fight, the French troops began to suffer losses, and Joan was captured by the Burgundians.

She was accused of being a witch. Her judges were French clergymen who supported the Burgundians and English. During her trial, Joan behaved with great bravery. But she was found guilty and sentenced to death.

In 1455 a new court judged that she had been wrongly executed. The Catholic Church declared Joan a saint in 1920, and celebrates her feast on the anniversary of her death, May 30.

The story of Joan of Arc has become one of the most inspiring in history, and many books, plays, and ballads have been written about her.

What Is a Ballad?

The ballad is a form of folk song that tells a story. It developed in Europe during the Middle Ages.

A ballad tells its story simply and directly, often by means of dialogue. Some ballads may be danced to, and ballads may or may not have musical accompaniment. But they are always sung in such a way that the words, rather than the melody, are stressed. While ballads always emphasize the story, the melodies used in ballads are quite beautiful.

The ballad differs from land to land, and goes under a variety of names. In France it is called *ballade;* in Italy, *ballata;* in Spain, *romance;* and in the Soviet Union, *bylina.*

In America, we can divide our ballads into a number of groups. One group consists of the traditional ballads that go back six or seven centuries in British history. They were passed on by word of mouth through many generations, and they developed a large number of variations.

Another group of ballads originated in England during the seventeenth, eighteenth, and nineteenth centuries. They are sometimes called broadside ballads. Many of them were printed on the backs of news sheets, or broadsides, and sold for a penny in the streets.

The British took their ballads to their colonies, where many of them survived. Using these British songs as models, Americans created ballads about bandits like Jesse James and Billy the Kid, strong men like John Henry, and unfortunate girls like "Young Charlotte."

These were often set to old British tunes and even used the same plots, but with an Americanized setting.

BALLAD SINGERS OF THE MIDDLE AGE

What Is an Operetta?

Operetta is a form of light musical theater. It is sentimental drama set to music.

In an operetta the setting is usually some make-believe world or exotic place that lends itself to colorful scenery and costuming. Many of the characters are princes or princesses, with the men wearing officers' uniforms and the ladies in elegant dress.

As for the stories that operettas tell, they are almost always some sort of sentimental romance. The good people triumph, the bad people are punished, and the lovers are united at the end.

The operetta was born in German-speaking countries toward the end of the nineteenth century. Franz von Suppe is the person who really created this form of musical theater. He emphasized romance and sentiment and played down comedy. He was one of the first composers to give the waltz an important part in the musical score, and after that most operettas included a big waltz scene.

Johann Strauss, Jr., wrote some of the greatest operettas and established their main characteristics. His operetta *The Bat* is probably the most famous operetta ever written. It is still being revived in many parts of the world.

The second most popular operetta ever written is probably *The Merry Widow* by Franz Lehar. In the late nineteenth century, operettas became popular in the United States, and soon there were American composers turning out very well-known operettas. Among them were Victor Herbert, who wrote *Babes in Toyland* and *Naughty Marietta,* and Rudolf Friml, who wrote *Rose Marie* and *The Vagabond King.*

Probably the last composer in America to turn out great operettas was Sigmund Romberg, who wrote such famous ones as *The Desert Song* and *The New Moon.*

The operetta was a form of entertainment that gave millions of people a great deal of pleasure.

What Is Jazz?

Jazz is the name of a certain kind of American popular music. It was originally the music of the black people of the United States, but it developed into a coming-together of several different kinds of music from various parts of the world.

One of the basic features of jazz is its rhythm. Jazz melody combines elements from African and European music, but its harmony comes mainly from Europe. One important feature of jazz is improvisation. This means making something up on the spot on the spur of the moment. Much jazz is played that way. The music is made up as the players go along.

Over the years, jazz has changed and developed, but it has retained its basic quality. One of the forms of music that contributed to the development of jazz was the "blues." About a third of jazz music is in the blues form. So are over half of the popular Rock-'n'-Roll pieces. Even some of the Country and Western music of the United States is in the blues form.

A major step in the development of jazz was taken by musicians in New Orleans. New Orleans jazz, sometimes called Dixieland, had the deep emotion of the blues and the black spiritual as well as elements of Ragtime and European folk music.

Later on big-band jazz, or swing music developed. In the 1940's and 1950's came what was called "modern jazz." This modern jazz was more complex in harmony and melody than earlier styles of jazz. But its most outstanding feature was its new approach to rhythm. The players used new rhythms in making their melodies, and the drummers played in a more complex style.

Another major step in the development of jazz was the "new thing" of the 1960's. It is free-form jazz. A whole group of players may change the tempo or speed of a piece several times during a performance without planning to do so beforehand. This doesn't mean that the music is disorganized, but that it is simply freer in spirit and approach. So you see, jazz is a form of music that is always changing, yet one that keeps its basic approach and quality.

Who Was P. T. Barnum?

Phineas T. Barnum was a pioneer showman with a genius for staging unusual entertainment.

Barnum was a master at "humbugging," or fooling the people. He called attention to his shows with loud brass bands, sensational ads in the newspapers, and tricks that he called ballyhoo.

Barnum entered show business in New York City at the age of twenty-five. His career began with Joice Heth, an old Negro woman who Barnum claimed had been George Washington's nurse. Her age was advertised as 161 years old. Hundreds of people flocked to see her.

After her death, the doctor who examined her said she had only been eighty years old. This was the first, but not the last time, that Barnum "humbugged" the people.

In his American Museum, an exhibition hall in New York City, Barnum displayed all kinds of oddities, some real and some fake. One of the most popular was a midget, General Tom Thumb. There were sword swallowers, giants, and bearded ladies. There was also a door marked "Egress." Many people opened this door expecting to find some wonderful oddity. Instead they found themselves outside the museum. "Egress," they learned, was just another word for "Exit."

By the time he was forty, Barnum was rich and famous, but he longed to be known as an important theatrical producer. He persuaded Jenny Lind, one of the greatest singers of the time, to make a concert tour in the United States, which was a great success.

In 1871 Barnum founded a circus that he advertised as "The Greatest Show on Earth." He exhibited it until his death in 1891. The circus continues to this day as the Ringling Brothers Circus.

Who Was Napoleon?

Few men in history have had as great an influence on the world and the times in which they lived as Napoleon Bonaparte.

He was born on August 15, 1769, in Ajaccio on the island of Corsica. When he was a boy, he identified himself with the great heroes of ancient history whom he read about. He was barely sixteen years old when he graduated from the military academy in Paris.

When he was just twenty-four years old, he was promoted to brigadier general for helping recapture the city of Toulon from the British. Later he led armies to victory over Austria, and won a war in Egypt.

Napoleon became the first consul, the ruler of France. He reformed the whole structure of government, enacting the Code Napoleon, which became the basis of modern French law.

In 1804, Napoleon was proclaimed emperor of France. During the ten years of the French Empire under Napoleon, there was almost continuous war. But his victories enabled him to dominate Europe from Spain to the borders of Russia.

In 1812 he decided to invade Russia with an army of more than six hundred thousand men. Even though he captured Moscow, his army didn't have enough supplies, so had to retreat. Only about one hundred thousand men survived the march home.

After several other defeats, Napoleon abdicated and was sent into exile on the island of Elba. He escaped from Elba and gathered a new army, but lost the battle at Waterloo to an allied army.

Napoleon surrendered to the British, who sent him as a prisoner to the barren island of St. Helena. There he remained until his death on May 5, 1821. While he led France to new greatness and power, it can also be said he caused great suffering and ruined the lives of whole nations of people.

Who Was Bolivar?

Napoleon had a tremendous effect on Europe in the early nineteenth century. At almost the same time, a man called Simon Bolivar was influencing nineteenth-century South America.

For nearly three hundred years, most of South America was under Spanish rule. Simon Bolivar vowed to free his native land, Venezuela, from Spain. When he died in 1830, he had freed not only Venezuela, but Ecuador, Bolivia, Peru, and Colombia as well.

Young Bolivar was educated as an aristocrat, but he studied and traveled in Europe, and the examples of the French and American revolutions stirred him deeply. In 1811, he and a group of patriots revolted and declared Venezuela's independence. But they were crushed by Spanish troops, and Bolivar fled the country.

In 1819 he marched with an army over the snow-covered Andes Mountains, surprised the Spanish Army, and was able to bring independence to Colombia. Two years later, Bolivar liberated Venezuela, and the following year Ecuador was freed.

Venezuela, Colombia, and Ecuador were united into the Republic of Gran Colombia, with Bolivar as president. Later he was able to help in the liberation of Peru. Upper Peru was renamed Bolivia in honor of its liberator.

Bolivar had the powers of a dictator, though his ideals were freedom and justice. He encouraged formation of constitutional government, establishment of more schools, and freeing of slaves.

In time, each country wanted its independence, and Gran Colombia fell apart. Bolivar's enemies accused him of being a tyrant. Finally Bolivar resigned as president. He died in 1830 at the age of forty-seven, a disappointed man with many enemies, but to the people of South America he is still El Libertador, the liberator.

Who Was Leonardo da Vinci?

Leonardo da Vinci was one of the most remarkable human beings who ever lived. Probably no one in history achieved so much in so many different fields as this man did.

Leonardo lived from 1452 to 1519. He was an outstanding painter, sculptor, and architect; he also designed bridges, highways, weapons, costumes, and scientific instruments. He invented the diving bell and tank and designed flying machines, though they could not be built with the materials of the time. He made important discoveries about the structure of the human body.

Leonardo approached science and art in the same methodical manner: After studying a problem, he made many sketches to help him find a solution. He saw no difference between planning a machine and a painting, and he became an expert in every field that interested him.

By the time Leonardo was twenty years old, he was listed as a master of the painters' guild. His work had a great influence on other painters, because he was always trying new things, such as the use of chiaroscuro, a technique which creates contrasts of light and dark.

One of Leonardo's greatest works, *The Last Supper,* was painted in Milan. Even though it is one of the world's masterpieces, it was actually an unsuccessful experiment. Because he worked slowly, Leonardo painted in oil on a damp wall. As a result, the painting began to peel, and today it is quite badly damaged.

Leonardo was interested in studying the human body, and he dissected corpses to find out how the body was put together. He also made many discoveries about plant growth.

Probably the single most famous painting in the world, the *Mona Lisa,* was painted by Leonardo in Florence.

Who Was John Calvin?

John Calvin was a leader of the Reformation, the religious movement that swept Europe in the sixteenth century and divided the Christian world into Catholic and Protestant churches.

Calvin was born in France on July 10, 1509. After studying Latin, philosophy, and logic, he turned to the new Protestant faith. He was forced to leave France because of his religious beliefs, and in 1536 he went to Geneva, Switzerland. Except for one short period, he lived there for the rest of his life.

Under his strong leadership, Geneva became the center of Protestantism. The Church wrote the city's laws and governed every part of its daily life. The laws were strict. Genevans were expected to be thrifty, hard working, and serious. Dancing and singing—except hymns—were forbidden. And there was severe punishment for those who disobeyed.

Calvin's religion was stern. Man, he believed, was sinful and could receive salvation only through God's grace. But only the few chosen by God (whom Calvin called the elect) would receive grace. And long ago God had already decided who would be among the elect. This was Calvin's doctrine of predestination.

Calvin died on May 27, 1564. But by then his ideas had spread from Geneva to much of western Europe. The English Puritans who came to America in the seventeenth century were Calvinists. The Presbyterian and other Reformed churches of today base their religious beliefs on John Calvin's teachings.

Who Was Sir Walter Raleigh?

Almost everybody has heard the name of this man, but few people seem to know much about him. In the age of Elizabeth I, there were many great men, but Raleigh was probably the most varied in his genius and talents. He was soldier, sailor, courtier, poet, colonizer, historian, and scientist.

Raleigh was born about 1554 in Devonshire, England. As a youth he fought in the wars in France and later in Ireland. He won the favor of Queen Elizabeth I and was knighted and given various posts in the government.

Then Raleigh decided to do an interesting thing with the money he got from the Queen. He used it to start settlements in America. He sent out the first colony in 1585, a group of about one hundred men who lived on Roanoke Island, off the coast of North Carolina, for a year. This was the first English colony to experience life in the New World. All the later colonies flowed from this first attempt.

Much of our early knowledge of the Indians and of the geography of America and its plant and animal life we owe to Raleigh's efforts. In 1587 he sent out a second colony, but the colonists were all lost in the forests.

Raleigh knew many of the great poets and writers of his time, and he himself was one of the leading poets of his age. In 1595 he made his first voyage to Guiana in South America, where he hoped to find gold.

When King James I came to the throne, he accused Raleigh of being in a conspiracy against him and condemned him to death. Though the sentence was suspended, he spent most of the rest of his life in the Tower of London.

There he wrote a great book, *History of the World,* and made experiments in chemistry. In 1616 he was allowed out of prison and sailed again to Guiana. Instead of finding gold he clashed with the Spaniards and he was executed for this in 1618.

Raleigh was the man who introduced the potato from the New World to Ireland and was also the man who made smoking tobacco popular in Europe.

Who Was Joseph Lister?

There are many things about medicine we take for granted now. If we see a movie or TV show in which a doctor is going to perform an operation, we expect to see him wash his hands and wear a mask.

The idea of germ-free, or antiseptic, surgery was developed by Joseph Lister. He was an English doctor who was born in 1827 and died in 1912. In 1861, Lister became a surgeon in the Glasgow Infirmary, which was the biggest hospital in the city of Glasgow, Scotland.

While at this hospital, Lister had to treat many people who had been hurt in accidents. The wounds of these patients often became infected. The area around the wound would become swollen and inflamed, and pus would begin to form.

Lister became interested in preventing such infections. At first he tried to clean the wounds, but this didn't seem to help. Then, in 1864, he learned of the experiments of the French scientist Louis Pasteur. Pasteur had shown that germs caused the spoiling of milk and rotting of meat. The tiny germs floated in the air and settled in the milk or on the meat. Lister thought that infections in wounds were also caused by such germs in the air.

Lister tried to kill the harmful germs by putting a chemical called carbolic acid on the wounds. He was very successful in reducing the number of infections and was convinced that his germ theory of infection was correct.

In 1867 Lister wrote an article for an important medical journal. In this article he wrote about his theory concerning infections and described his method for preventing them.

At first, Lister's theory was not fully accepted. But within twenty-five years most surgeons were using antiseptics in treating wounds and during surgery. Today there is no doctor or hospital in the world that doesn't follow the ideas first developed by Joseph Lister.

Who Was George Washington Carver?

George Washington Carver was one of America's greatest agricultural scientists. His parents were the black slaves of a man called Moses Carver, who lived in Missouri. Soon after George was born, his father died. A few months later the baby and his mother were kidnapped by bandits. Moses Carver was able to buy George back, but his mother was never found, so the Carvers raised George themselves.

George showed a love for growing things at a very early age. He used to care for and cure sick plants, and the neighbors called him the plant doctor. He wandered about the United States seeking an education, doing all kinds of work to pay for his schooling. Finally he entered Iowa State College. He was the first black person to graduate from the college, and he became their first black teacher.

In 1896, he joined the staff of Tuskegee Institute, a new black college in Alabama. He was appointed to head the school's agriculture department. With the aid of his students, Carver built a homemade laboratory, using for equipment pots, kettles, and whatever else he could find that might be useful.

For nearly fifty years Carver taught at Tuskegee. In his laboratory he worked long hours, seeking ways to help the poor southern farmers. He introduced the peanut, pecan, and sweet potato to the cotton farmers, and showed them how these crops would enrich soil worn out by years of cotton planting.

In his laboratory he discovered new uses for these plants. From peanuts he made butter, coffee, ink, and soap. From sweet potatoes he made flour, cereals, glue, dyes, and rubber. He also made synthetic marble from wood shavings, rope from cornstalk fibers, and paint from Alabama clay.

Carver gave his discoveries to the world, asking no profit for himself. He gave advice freely to all who consulted him. He received offers of many high-paying jobs, but he preferred to remain at Tuskegee and teach. Today his great work is carried on through the George Washington Carver Foundation, which he set up with money from his savings. It provides scholarships for black students in agricultural research.

What Is Psychiatry?

Many people confuse psychiatry and psychology. There is a great deal of difference between them. Let us see what this difference is.

Psychology is the study of how people and animals behave. Psychologists study people to find out how and why people do such things as learn, think, remember, feel, see, hear, and talk.

Psychiatry on the other hand is actually a branch of medical science. It has to do with mental health. Originally, psychiatry was concerned only with insanity. But today this science offers help to people who have all kinds of emotional and mental problems.

Psychiatry moved forward in this way when two important discoveries were made. The first was that there are many kinds of mental disorders and that they have a wide range of seriousness. The other was that even serious mental disorders are more open to cure than was formerly thought possible.

A psychiatrist is always a physician. What he looks for are the motives or causes underlying the illness of one who has a "nervous breakdown" or who is otherwise not in good mental health. He is sure that there are always motives or causes for the illness.

One thing a psychiatrist has learned is that these causes or motives are seldom the ones given by the patient. This is not because the patient deliberately lies about them. It is because the real reasons are often hidden in the unconscious part of his mind.

This means the patient is honestly not aware that there are any reasons other than those on the surface. Once the psychiatrist finds the hidden, unconscious causes that are making the patient sick, he tries to devise a treatment that will do away with these causes and promote the patient's health.

CHARLES DARWIN

GALAPAGOS ANIMALS THAT LED
TO HIS THEORY OF EVOLUTION

IGUANA

SEA IGUANA

What Was Darwin's Theory?

For a long time men believed (and certain religious groups still believe) that each form of life appeared separately on earth and that none had ever changed. They also believed that the earth itself was about four thousand years old. And so there was hardly time for much change to have occurred.

Scientists claim they have shown that these beliefs are wrong. Living forms have undergone many changes in their long history. These changes came about very slowly. All of these changes are summed up in the term, evolution. Evolution describes the many changes that have taken place, and is also a theory developed to explain those changes.

The man who laid the foundations for the modern theory of evolution was Charles Darwin. Darwin said that all life had evolved, and that descendants of a species could become different from the parent forms. These ideas were not new or unusual. But Darwin suggested how evolution might have occurred.

He called the process natural selection. He said that nature "selected" those organisms best suited to survive in the "struggle for existence." Each organism differed slightly from other organisms and had its own individual traits. Some had traits that made them better able to survive than others. Therefore they lived longer and had more offspring. In this way, "beneficial" traits were passed on to a larger number of descendants.

Little by little, living things became so different from their ancestors that biologists classified them as separate and distinct species. Darwin believed that this was how new species originated. His theory still forms the basis of modern thinking on evolution.

Biologists later discovered that certain small chemical units called genes determine the traits that are passed from one generation to another. The genes change, or mutate, from time to time. A changed gene causes a variation in a trait, and if the change is favorable to survival, it may be passed on to the next generation.

Who Was Booker T. Washington?

Booker Taliaferro Washington was one of America's great educators. He was born on a Virginia plantation on April 5, 1856. His mother was a slave who served as cook for the master's family.

After the Emancipation Proclamation was signed by Lincoln in 1863 freeing the slaves, Booker's mother left the plantation and moved with her children to Malden, West Virginia. There Booker entered a school for black children. To help support the family, he worked mornings in salt furnaces and coal mines before going to school.

At the age of seventeen, Booker entered the Hampton Normal and Agricultural Institute for black students in Virginia, and studied there for three years. After graduation he taught school and for awhile served as secretary to General Samuel Armstrong, principal of Hampton.

General Armstrong suggested Washington as organizer of a new industrial and teacher-training school for blacks in Tuskegee, Alabama. The school was very poor; no money was provided for buildings and land, and the first classes met in a run-down old church.

It was at Tuskegee that Washington did his great work as organizer and teacher. For years he traveled widely, sometimes by mule and buggy, to raise funds for the school. He was a stirring orator and made many speeches for the school. Washington was soon recognized as a leader in the field of Negro education.

During Washington's lifetime his school in Tuskegee grew until its campus consisted of over one hundred buildings, and its student body numbered almost one thousand six hundred. When he died in 1915, the school, now called Tuskegee Institute, remained as a monument to his life's work.

He was the author of several books. One of his best known is *Up From Slavery*.

Who Was Helen Keller?

Sometimes a person leads a life that becomes an inspiration to the whole world. And sometimes, what is inspiring about such a life is the way that person overcame tremendous handicaps. Such a person was Helen Keller.

She was deaf, blind, and half mute. She was born on June 27, 1880 in Tuscumbia, Alabama. When she was nineteen months old, an illness made her deaf and blind. She might have led a useless life if it had not been for Anne Sullivan. Miss Sullivan came in 1887 from the Perkins Institution for the Blind in Boston, Massachusetts, to teach Helen.

Helen was a lively child, and she was used to having her own way. Miss Sullivan liked her spirit, but knew she had to teach Helen to love and obey her before she could teach her anything else. She found the way through Helen's wall of darkness and silence. The story is told in Helen Keller's first book, *The Story of My Life*.

Helen was quick and eager to learn. Wealthy people heard about her and gave her money for her schooling. She entered Radcliffe College in 1900. Miss Sullivan sat in the classroom with her, and spelled into her hand in sign language everything that was said.

She read endlessly in this way to Helen, for Helen could read only Braille (the system of raised dots used in books for the blind), and few of the books Helen needed were in Braille. Helen was graduated with honors and decided to spend her life working for the blind.

She wrote articles for magazines and went on lecture tours. She learned to speak, but since she could not be understood easily, Miss Sullivan repeated all that she said. They visited slum areas, factories, and hospitals. Everywhere people became interested in helping, and the blind and deaf took new hope and courage.

Helen Keller visited nearly every country in the world, and kings and emperors welcomed her. She had many famous friends, including Mark Twain.

How Did Lafayette Help the United States?

The Marquis de Lafayette, who was a brilliant leader in the French Revolution, also was a great fighter for the freedom of the American colonies.

He was born on September 6, 1757. At the age of thirteen he inherited a fortune so large that, in terms of today's money, he had an income of two million dollars a year. He was married at the age of sixteen.

In 1776 Lafayette decided to go to America to fight for the freedom of the colonies. Benjamin Franklin and other Americans in France encouraged his sympathy. Lafayette and a few companions reached Georgetown, South Carolina, on June 13, 1777. From Georgetown, Lafayette and his party traveled nine hundred miles overland, by coach and on horseback, to Philadelphia. There the Continental Congress gave him a commission as major general.

He first saw action at the battle of Brandywine, where he was wounded in the leg. He also went through the hardships of Valley Forge and fought at the Battle of Monmouth.

Lafayette then went back to France where he was able to arrange for six thousand French troops to be sent to America. He returned to bring General George Washington the good news.

Washington entrusted him with the defense of Virginia against the British. Lafayette successfully laid seige to the British Army under Lord Cornwallis. The British general had promised that he would capture "the boy." Instead, Lafayette was present at Yorktown on October 19, 1781, when Cornwallis surrendered. Then Lafayette, who knew that American independence was assured, returned to France. He was barely twenty-four years old.

When Lafayette died in Paris on May 20, 1834, flags in the United States were flown at half-mast, and the Army went into mourning for six months, as it had after George Washington's death.

What's the Difference Between a Democracy and a Republic?

We in the United States live in both a democracy and a republic. A republic is a form of government that has no hereditary ruler, such as a king. But a republic need not be a democracy. A republic might have a dictator at the head of the government who holds all power, disregards the will of the people and doesn't allow the people to express their free choice.

On the other hand, a democracy might be a monarchy with a royal family, such as England has. England is one of the world's oldest and greatest democracies, even though it isn't a republic.

The word "democracy" comes from Greek and means the rule of the people. No nation can be considered democratic unless it gives protection to various human liberties. Among the democratic liberties are freedom of speech, movement, and association. The people must be free to express themselves on all issues and questions, and to move about as they please and associate with whom they choose.

Freedom of the press, religious freedom, and equality before the law are other democratic rights. It is very important in a democracy that life, liberty, and property be free from arbitrary and unlawful controls. Men of all races, religions, and degrees of wealth must be treated as equal before the law.

Such liberties are guaranteed by many nations in their constitutions. But such guarantees are not always upheld, and not every nation that claims it is a democracy really is.

Today, all over the world, the idea of democracy is being greatly expanded. It is believed by many that democracy should also include economic democracy, which means more equality in the wealth of men, and social equality, which means equality of opportunity to enjoy all the benefits of society, such as housing, health, and recreation.

What Was the Monroe Doctrine?

Before and during the crisis over Cuba, there was much discussion of the Monroe Doctrine. The American Government said it had a right to keep European powers from trying to run the affairs of countries in the Western Hemisphere.

The Monroe Doctrine is a statement on foreign policy issued by President James Monroe. In December, 1823, he delivered a message to Congress, and part of it was devoted to foreign policy. This part came to be known as the Monroe Doctrine, and the foreign policy of the United States has been guided by it ever since. Here are the four main points included in this famous statement:

1. The American continents are not to be considered open to future colonization by any European powers.

2. The European political system is different from that of America. Any attempt to extend the European system to the Western Hemisphere will be considered dangerous to the peace and safety of the United States.

3. The United States will not interfere with any existing colonies or dependencies of European powers.

4. The United States has never taken any part in the internal affairs of European nations, nor will it do so in the future.

But for a long time the United States was not strong enough to enforce the Monroe Doctrine. For example, Napoleon III of France used French troops to place Archduke Maximilian of Austria upon the Mexican throne. But, in 1904, Theodore Roosevelt said that the United States could interfere in the affairs of Latin America to keep Europeans out, and United States Marines were sent into several countries during the next twenty years to restore order and protect the property of United States citizens.

Today the United States tries to uphold the Monroe Doctrine, but without interfering in the internal affairs of other American nations.

What Is Fascism?

Fascism is the name of a political movement founded by Benito Mussolini in Italy in 1919. Led by Mussolini, the Italian Fascists took over the government in 1922 and set up a one-party and one-man dictatorship that ruled Italy until 1943.

Similar movements in other countries, such as Hitler's Nazis in Germany, copied Mussolini's methods. The word "fascist" is used to describe all of these movements in general.

The fascists hated democracy. They believed ordinary people should not have the right to elect a government. Under fascism the "weak" were forced to obey the "strong." There was no political party but the fascist party.

The fascists had no use for justice or the rights of man. There were police and courts of law, but they were not there to protect the ordinary citizen. They were used to carry out the orders of the men in power.

The fascists had no use for freedom. People were forced to do what the state (which meant the fascists in control of the state) wanted them to do. The schools taught young people to obey and not to ask questions.

The fascist party controlled newspapers, books, and radio. They told editors and writers what to say and write. Nobody was allowed to write or say anything the fascists disliked.

The fascists had no use for peace. They wanted the nation to be strong and united so that it could go to war. They declared that a nation was only great if it made itself feared by others.

When Germany and Italy were defeated in World War II, fascism as a political philosophy and form of government was completely discredited.

What Is Capitalism?

Capitalism is an economic system in which most of the industries and businesses in a country are owned privately. By contrast, under communism, industries and businesses are owned by the state.

A capitalist is a man who uses his own wealth (or other people's money) to make more wealth. The extra money he makes is his profit. Some capitalists manufacture things to sell at a profit. Some are store owners who sell goods at a profit. Others are financiers or investors who lend their money in the hope of getting more back.

No matter what his business, the aim of the capitalist is to make a profit. But, of course, this does not mean that he can get away with any kind of business practice in order to make that profit. For example, he can't charge prices that are too high, or sell bad goods.

If he does, he will probably lose business to others who sell better goods or charge lower prices. So competition forces the capitalist to sell the best possible goods at the lowest possible prices. And that's why competition is an important feature of capitalism.

The profits made by the individual capitalist in free competition can benefit the economy of the whole country. As the capitalist makes profits, he can afford to expand his business and put more people to work.

Today in many capitalist countries, such as the United States, France, and Great Britain, governments own some businesses and regulate many more. For example, the United States Government has always supervised the post office. It regulates public utilities—necessary services like gas, electricity, water, and communications. It also regulates railroads, air travel, television, and other businesses in which the public has a vital interest.

So in a capitalist system, government protects free enterprise and at the same time sees to it that no man is free to run his business in a way that harms other people.

What City Is Really a Country?

By "country" we mean a sovereign state. And the world's smallest sovereign state is Vatican City.

It covers 108.7 acres within the city of Rome. Vatican City is bounded on the southeastern corner by St. Peter's Church and the great square of St. Peter's. The rest of the boundary is formed by the ancient walls of the Vatican Palace and its gardens.

The sovereign of this area is the Pope, who is, of course, the head of the whole Catholic Church. But the Pope is also the civil ruler of about one thousand people in Vatican City. Only persons whose official position, profession, or trade is within the Vatican are citizens.

Vatican City was set up as an independent state in 1929 by the Lateran Treaty. According to this treaty, Italy recognized the independence of the Vatican. And since this treaty, it has been recognized internationally as a sovereign state.

The papal flag (yellow and white with crossed keys and tiara) became one of the world's national flags. The Pope sends ambassadors to many of the world's capitals.

In Vatican City there are Vatican stamps and Vatican money. The Vatican has its own international car-registration plate. The Vatican has a bank and post office, a daily newspaper, and a radio station.

The Vatican even has its own army. This regiment of one hundred men is called the Swiss Guard. The soldiers, who are of Swiss nationality, still wear the colorful uniform designed for them in the sixteenth century. And there are Vatican police who control the traffic and crowds in Vatican City.

VATICAN CITY COAT OF ARMS

What Is a Cathedral?

During the Middle Ages all of Western Europe was Roman Catholic. Each community had its own church. These churches were grouped into districts called dioceses. Each diocese was under the jurisdiction of a bishop.

The principal church of the diocese contained the throne of the bishop. In Latin the name of this church was *ecclesia cathedralis,* or "cathedral church." In English it has been shortened to "cathedral."

Most European cathedrals were constructed with the floor plan in the general shape of a cross. The long part of the cross is the nave and serves as the assembly room for the congregation.

The two arms of the cross are the transepts, and the fourth part, containing the altar and choir, is the apse. The section where the four parts meet is the crossing. Towers or domes were often built over the crossing.

Cathedrals have been built in nearly every style of architecture. But most of the very famous European cathedrals were either Byzantine, Romanesque, Gothic, or Renaissance.

Most of the very famous European cathedrals, such as Notre Dame of Paris, are in the Gothic style of the twelfth and thirteenth centuries. Strangely enough, the world's largest Gothic cathedral, St. John the Divine, was built in the nineteenth and twentieth centuries in New York City, and is not Roman Catholic, but Episcopal.

St. Peter's in Rome is not officially a cathedral, since it is not the seat of a bishop. It is an outstanding example of a Renaissance building. The dome was designed by the great Michelangelo, and is considered to be a masterpiece in itself.

How Many Different Religions Are There?

What is a religion? The word "religion" can mean so many kinds of experiences that it is impossible to describe it in a few words. But there are six things that most religions have in common. Let us consider them briefly:

1. A belief in a power or powers greater than man's. 2. This

power or powers is praised, feared, sacrificed to, and prayed to. 3. Ceremonies are developed for these sacrifices or prayers. 4. Certain places and objects connected with the worship and history of the religion are held sacred. 5. There is hope that through observing the religion, man can have a better life, either on this earth or after death. 6. Proper conduct is one of the best ways for man to please God or the gods, and leads to a better life.

Almost all the religions of the world share these six basic concepts. The religions of primitive peoples, which include the worship of "spirits" in animals, rocks, rivers, and so on, are considered to be on a lower level.

But many of the religions of civilized peoples, who worshipped many gods, died as civilization progressed. For example, among the "dead" religions are the Egyptian, Babylonian, Assyrian, Greek, Roman, Celtic, and Norse.

Today there are many living religions. The chief ones are the Hindu, Buddhist, Confucian, Taoist, Shintoist, Zoroastrian, Mohammedan, Jewish, and Christian. These religions together have a total of about 2,549,161,000 followers, which includes most of the civilized world.

Here is the number of followers in each of the leading religions: Hinduism has about 408,000,000 followers, most of them in India. Buddhism has about 165,000,000 followers in China and Japan. Confucianism has about 358,000,000 followers, and Taoism about 52,-000,000.

Shintoism has about 68,000,000 followers, and the Zoroastrian religion, about 161,000. Mohammedanism's followers total about 465,-000,000 in Asia and Africa. The Jewish religion has about 14,000,000 followers. The Christian religion today has more followers than any other, about 1,019,000,000 people.

What Is Easter?

Easter celebrates the Resurrection of Jesus Christ. It is the most important feast in the Christian calendar.

Easter Sunday does not come on the same date every year, but falls sometime between March 22 and April 25. It falls on the first

Sunday after the first full moon following March 21, the vernal equinox (the time in spring when day and night are of equal length). The date of Easter Sunday was established by the church council of Nicaea in 325 A.D.

Easter Sunday ends a period of preparing for the feast of Easter. This forty-day period of prayer and fasting, called Lent, begins on Ash Wednesday and ends on Holy Saturday, the day before Easter. The Lenten fast commemorates Christ's forty-day fast in the desert.

The week from Palm Sunday to Easter Sunday is known as Holy Week. During Holy Week, church services remind one of the last days of Christ's life on earth. Palm Sunday marks Christ's entry into Jerusalem. Holy Thursday, also called Maundy Thursday, marks the Last Supper. Good Friday marks Christ's crucifixion, and Easter Sunday, his resurrection.

There are many customs that have developed around Easter. The custom of a sunrise service on Easter Sunday can be traced to ancient spring festivals that celebrated the rising sun. The new clothes worn on Easter Sunday are a symbol of new life. The custom comes from the baptism on Easter Sunday of early Christians, who were led into the church wearing new robes of white linen.

The familiar Easter parade goes back to the Middle Ages, when people walked about the countryside on Easter, stopping along the way to pray. Now, of course, it presents an opportunity for people to see and show their new spring clothes.

The egg is an Easter symbol, because it is a symbol of life. The Persians and Egyptians also colored eggs and ate them during their new year's celebration, which came in the spring.

Is New Year's Day the Same Around the World?

Welcoming the new year is one of the oldest and gayest customs celebrated the world over. But no festival has been observed on so many different dates or in so many different ways.

The ancient Greeks began their new year with the new moon after June 21. Before the time of Julius Caesar, the Roman new year started on March 1. In most European countries during the Middle Ages, the new year began on March 25.

What about today? In most Christian countries the new year begins on January 1. But other countries and religions observe New Year's Day on different dates, according to the calendars they use.

The Chinese celebrate two New Year's Days. One is on January 1, and the other takes place on the New Year's Day reckoned according to the Chinese lunar calendar. This may occur any time between January 21 and February 19.

Indonesia also has two New Year celebrations, one on January 1 and another on the Islamic New Year, a date that varies from year to year. The Russian Orthodox Church observes the New Year according to the Julian calendar, which places the day on January 14.

The Jewish New Year, Rosh Hashanah, is celebrated about the time of the autumnal equinox at the end of September or the beginning of October. In Vietnam the New Year usually begins in February.

Iran celebrates New Year's Day on March 21. Each of the religious groups in India has its own date for the beginning of the year. One Hindu New Year comes sometime in April or May.

The people in Morocco observe the beginning of the year on the tenth day of Muharram, the first month of the Islamic year. The Koreans celebrate their New Year during the first three days in January.

By the way, the custom of sending New Year's cards is a very old one. The Chinese have been doing it for more than one thousand years. Their cards carried the name of the visitor who came to call, but no greeting or message.

137

Who Are the Quakers?

In 1650, a man called George Fox was on trial in England because of his religious beliefs. He looked at his judges and commanded them to "tremble at the word of the Lord." One of the judges therefore called him a "quaker." And since Fox and his followers sometimes trembled during religious experiences, the nickname "quakers" became popular for these people. Their official name today is Society of Friends.

George Fox, the founder of the Quakers, taught that men should be guided in their conduct by an inner light, the Holy Spirit that dwells within each person. The Quakers refused to take an oath, even in the courts. They also agreed that they should never use physical force against anyone, or take part in military conflicts.

To set themselves apart from other Christians, they developed different customs, dress, and speech. They wore a plain gray costume, opposed amusements, and used the pronouns "thee" and "thou" in ordinary conversation.

Modern-day Friends have put aside most of the old Quaker customs. But their meetings are still conducted for the most part in the traditional manner. There is no prearranged program. The members gather and sit in silence until the Inner Spirit moves one of them to rise and offer a prayer, or perhaps read from the Scriptures or relate some spiritual experience.

They have no ministers in the usual sense and have no written creed. Men and women, young and old, have equal privileges in all the meetings.

The Quakers maintain many schools and have always been active in charitable and welfare work. They were among the first to establish free schools for the poor. As early as 1688 they took a definite stand against slavery.

GEORGE FOX

What Language Do Gypsies Speak?

Do you know why these people are called Gypsies? Years ago, people in Europe thought that they had originally come from Egypt, and "Gypsy" was derived from the word "Egypt."

But it is believed that about one thousand years ago several tribes from northwest India migrated into other lands, and these were the original Gypsies. Some of these tribes reached Persia; others wandered into what is now Turkey; and still others went into Syria, Egypt, and North Africa. Since they had originally come from India, they spoke an Indian language related to Sanskrit.

Later on, tribes of Gypsies wandered through the Balkans, Russia, Hungary, and then eventually to western Europe, including Germany, France, England, Spain, and even Sweden and Finland.

Through centuries of wandering, the Gypsy language became mixed with words borrowed from the countries in which they lived. An English Gypsy was said to speak *pogado tshib* (broken language), which is a mingling of Gypsy and English words. The English word for the Gypsy language is "Romany." The Romany word for a Gypsy's home on wheels is *vardo*.

Gypsies practiced trades that allowed them to roam the countryside. Some Gypsies were wood carvers, others mended pots and pans, some were minstrels or fortune-tellers.

It is interesting to learn how Gypsies in different countries developed in different ways. English Gypsies became horse traders. In Wales, the Gypsies are singers, violinists, and harpists. Spanish Gypsies are famous for flamenco dancing. In Hungary and Rumania many Gypsies are musicians. In Yugoslavia many Gypsies specialized in making gunpowder.

Did you know that the first groups of Gypsies in the United States came here as long ago as 1715?

דער טאָג מאָרגען זשורנאל

What Is the Yiddish Language?

One of the most curious languages in the world, Yiddish, is the language spoken by the Jewish people practically all over the world. Before World War II eight million Jews spoke or at least understood Yiddish.

But isn't Hebrew, the ancient language of the Old Testament, the language of the Jewish people? The answer is yes. Hebrew is the language of scholars, of religion, of much of the great literature, and in Israel today, of the people, too. There are many Hebrew scholars who consider Yiddish only a dialect spoken by the noneducated classes.

The fact is, Yiddish originally developed in Germany. About a thousand years ago, many Jews from France and northern Italy began to settle in western Germany. As happens whenever languages mix (the German they found and the French and Italian they brought with them), a new dialect or language began to develop, and this became Yiddish. This word, by the way, comes from the German *Judisch*.

After the fourteenth century, many Jews migrated to Poland and nearby countries. In these new places they developed variations on Yiddish to include the local languages. And those who remained in Germany developed Yiddish to its highest form.

Yiddish is written with Hebrew characters, and many of its words are derived from Hebrew, but many are quite different. A curious thing about its development is that for a long time it was chiefly used by women. This was because among the Jews only the men used to be scholars, and they studied Hebrew. So Yiddish came to be called the "mother's tongue."

Probably no other language uses the words of the local country as much as Yiddish does. For example, most people who speak Yiddish in the United States will say the English words for "carpet, floor, dress, hat," and so on. Many learned Jews, however, try to speak a "pure" Yiddish without English words. And by the way, many Yiddish words are used by non-Jews in the United States. For example, you probably know what a *kibitzer* is!

What Is Esperanto?

Man for a long time has been trying to create a universal language that would serve all men all over the world as a common means of communication.

Since the seventeenth century, more than seven hundred such languages have been constructed. There are two kinds of such languages. The "a priori" kind have no connection with any existing language. The "a posteriori" kind use a mixture of existing languages. The most popular of the constructed languages is Esperanto.

It was invented by Ludwik Zamenhof, who lived in the town of Bialystok, Poland. As a young man, he saw that there was a great deal of enmity between the four groups of people who lived there—the Russians, Poles, Germans, and Jews. He felt that a common language would help these people get along better. When he was still in school, he had already worked out the beginnings of his international language.

In 1887, he published a brochure describing his language, and he used the pen name of Dr. Esperanto (one who hopes). Soon people in various parts of the world became interested in this language, which came to be called "Esperanto."

Today, Esperanto is spoken by about eight million people throughout the world. Even governments and international organizations recognize it in many ways. For example, you can send an international telegram in Esperanto. It is often used on radio broadcasts from official government stations.

There are many rules of grammar for this language, and here are a few. The definite article is "la" and does not change. All nouns end in "o," all adjectives in "a," all adverbs in "e," and all infinitives in "i." The plural of nouns and adjectives is formed by adding "j."

Here is the beginning of the Lord's Prayer in Esperanto: "Patro nia, kiu estas en la cielo, snkta estu via nomo; venu regeco via; esto volo via, kiel en la cielo, tiel ankau sur la tero."

What Are the 4-H Clubs?

The four H's in the name of these clubs stand for "Head, Heart, Hands, and Health." There are more than 2,250,000 boys and girls in the United States who are members, and the idea has spread to about seventy countries around the globe.

The slogan of the 4-H club is "Learn by Doing." Many 4-H'ers win prizes at county and state fairs and sometimes become champions in their projects. But the most important 4-H goals are character building and good citizenship.

Nearly five million projects were completed in a single year by 4-H'ers in the United States alone. Some of the most popular projects are foods and nutrition, clothing and home furnishing, home management and landscaping, vegetable and fruit growing, dairy and poultry, dogs and horses, electricity and shop, crops and soil, forestry, and conservation.

In urban communities the projects are naturally a little different. They include such things as automotive care and safety, career exploration, creative crafts, money management, child care, and good grooming.

What is a project? It is a useful piece of work that a boy or girl can enjoy and learn to do well. It is carefully selected to suit the 4-H'er and his parents and is done at home or in club meetings under the guidance of trained leaders or parents.

Most 4-H'ers carry more than one project at a time. The skills they learn may help them in their future careers or may become lifelong hobbies.

What is developing in 4-H clubs are "community clubs"—project groups within the organization. The name of a club is often a clue to the projects of the club—for example, the Dinner Belles, Nimble Thimbles, and Scissors Whizzers. A club that combines sewing and cooking may be called Buttons and Bowls.

In the United States any boy or girl ten to twenty-one years old may join a club by agreeing to follow 4-H ideals and standards. There are no dues to pay.

What's the Difference Between a College and a University?

Someday you may be preparing to enter a college or a university, and then you will become very interested in what each place has to offer and why you should try to go to one rather than another.

The chief difference between a college and a university is that the university usually includes a number of colleges. Many institutions pretend to be universities when they are not. On the other hand, some colleges are more like universities.

Here is one definition of a university given by the National Education Association: "an institution of higher education, having as a nucleus a college in which the so-called liberal arts are taught in a course of three or four years for a degree . . . and in addition one or more departments for the learned professions, medicine, law, or divinity."

The term "college" originally meant any society or union of persons engaged in common activity or granted certain powers and rights to carry on a common work. That's why the cardinals who elect the Pope at Rome are called the "College of Cardinals." And the United States has an "electoral college" that chooses the President and Vice-President. But in the United States, when we say college, we usually mean an institution attended after graduation from high school, and one that gives general, rather than highly specialized or technical training.

There are many "colleges" in the United States, however, that really should not be considered colleges. For example, any institution of higher education that has but one faculty (teachers in only one field of knowledge) and offers a single course of study is likely to be known as a college.

A college and a university differ in that the university includes several special colleges or schools. These special schools give instruction in professions such as law, medicine, forestry, and so on. Sometimes students go to college first, and then take graduate work at a university.

What Is West Point?

West Point is the familiar name for the United States Military Academy, because it is located at West Point, New York. It is the most important school for young men who wish to follow careers as commissioned officers in the Army.

George Washington selected the site for the Academy, which was an important fortress on the Hudson River during the Revolutionary War. On March 16, 1802, the Academy was officially established, and it opened on July 4 of the same year.

Candidates for appointment to the Academy must be male citizens of the United States between the ages of seventeen and twenty-two, who have never been married and are in good health. They must have completed a secondary-school education or the equivalent.

Candidates must be officially appointed by the President, a member of the Congress, or another high member of the United States Government. They may also win an opportunity to be admitted by competing in preparatory programs conducted by the Army.

The candidates next must pass difficult physical and mental examinations. The sons of Medal of Honor winners are admitted without regard to the total number of vacancies, if they are able to pass the minimum requirements.

While in the Academy, cadets follow a four-year course in military and liberal-arts subjects. The purpose of the curriculum is to prepare the cadet for public service in a professional military career.

A cadet who fails in any single subject is usually discharged from the Academy. Cadets who graduate receive commissions as second lieutenants in the regular Army and are awarded Bachelor of Science degrees.

What Is the FBI?

The Federal Bureau of Investigation (FBI) was established in 1908 as a branch of the United States Department of Justice.

It investigates and collects evidence of crimes in which certain federal laws have been broken. These crimes include kidnapping, bank robbery, and transportation of stolen goods from one state to another.

The FBI is mainly a fact-gathering agency. It does not judge the results of its investigation, nor does it recommend prosecution. The information collected by the FBI concerning crimes is presented for action to the United States Attorney General or his representatives.

The FBI helps protect the internal security of the United States. The Bureau investigates cases of espionage (spying), sabotage (destroying property vital to national defense), treason, and subversion (attempts to overthrow the government).

The FBI works closely with other law-enforcement agencies in cities, counties, and states, and helps them by providing various free services. The FBI Identification Division in Washington, D.C. receives an average of twenty-three thousand sets of fingerprints a day! As a result, almost eighteen thousand fugitives a year are identified by their fingerprints.

FBI headquarters are in Washington, D.C. There are fifty-five field offices in large cities of the United States and Puerto Rico. The FBI has nearly fourteen thousand employees. About six thousand are special agents. They are sometimes called G-men, which means "Government men."

What Makes Stamps Valuable?

There are probably several million people in the United States who collect stamps. Some of them are experts, knowing exactly what each stamp in their collection is worth. Others have only the vaguest idea of what makes a stamp valuable.

A stamp catalogue today lists about two hundred thousand different stamps. How is it decided what each one is worth? While we can't possibly begin to tell you all there is to know about stamp collecting, here are a few things that you should know.

A stamp that is damaged is next to valueless. A "damaged" stamp may be torn, stained, discolored, or soiled from bad handling. Unless it is a very rare stamp, such a stamp is practically worthless.

Unused stamps without gum are not in demand and can usually be bought cheaply. Stamps with perforations missing or heavily cancelled stamps are also less valuable.

Now, what makes a stamp valuable? The chief thing is obviously the rarity of the stamp. If only a very few of them were issued or are known to exist, or if some mistake was made and a few of these reached the public, the stamps are likely to be quite valuable.

One famous rarity is a one-penny orange Mauritius stamp of 1847. Instead of having the word "Postpaid," it was inscribed "Post Office." But most collectors can hardly hope to obtain such rare and valuable stamps. Many of them try to collect complete sets of stamps from certain countries. Others try to collect commemorative stamps, which are issued to honor some person, group, or event.

There is a great deal of pleasure in stamp collecting, even if you have no rarities and will never make money from your collection!

What Is Done With Old Money?

Most of us would say: "If they don't know what to do with it, let them send it to me!" But the Government does know what to do with it. In fact, if old money weren't taken out of circulation at a regular rate, we'd find it a big nuisance, for torn and wrinkled paper money is inconvenient to handle.

The average life of a paper bill is only about a year, and for a dollar bill it's even less! So every day, the Treasury receives from banks and other sources worn and dirty bills to replace. How much? From four to five tons of paper money a day!

The old money is cancelled; that is, taken out of circulation. Then the bills are destroyed in a machine called a macerator, which does away with a million dollars a minute.

If you have damaged paper money, this doesn't make it worthless. If three-fifths of the note is preserved, you can send it to the Treasury and redeem it at full value. If more than two-fifths but less than three-fifths is sent in, you will get half of its value.

The paper on which the notes are printed is specially made for the Government. It has in it a mixture of linen and cotton. In the paper are embedded colored fibers of silk, nylon, or other synthetic material. When you hold a bill up to the light, you can see some of these fibers.

United States money used to be of various sizes. From 1861 to 1928 it was 7 and 7/16 inches by 3 and 1/8 inches. But in 1928 it was made smaller, and the new size is what we have today—6 and 5/16 inches by 2 and 11/16 inches.

All United States money is coined or printed by the Treasury Department. Paper money is printed by the Bureau of Engraving and Printing at Washington.

What Country Produces the Most Clocks?

In the early days of mechanical timepieces, there was no particular country that led in clock and watch production. Skilled workers migrated from country to country, and watchmaking and clockmaking became an international trade.

But soon different countries began to specialize in different types of clocks. For example, England has long been famous for its ship chronometers, which are large, accurate watches mounted in a special bracket to keep them level on a rolling sea. England also specializes in chime movements. Many chime-clock movements are shipped from England to case manufacturers all over the world.

The Black Forest of Germany supplies the world with hand-carved cuckoo clocks. The movements are not of the highest quality, but the wood carvings are very attractive. Some jeweled watches are also made there.

Watchmaking in Switzerland is a national industry and is very important to the economy of that country. The Swiss began to lead in the production of watches in the late nineteenth century, when the wrist watch made its appearance.

The Swiss are experts in the production of high-grade, small watch movements. Special-feature watches, such as alarms, calendars, automatics, and chronographs, are made almost exclusively in Switzerland.

What about the United States? Most of the American clock industry is devoted to the manufacture of electric clocks, automobile clocks, and inexpensive alarm clocks. The American watch industry also imports and assembles watches. Individual parts, complete movements, and complete watches are imported by some American companies from Switzerland, Germany, Japan, and France.

It may surprise you to learn that today the largest watch factory in the world is in Japan!

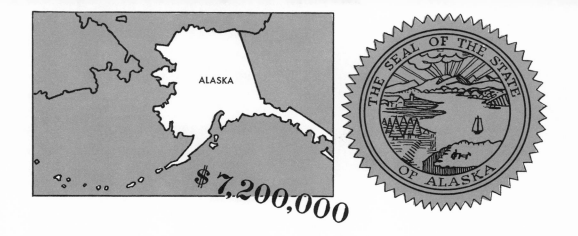

Why Did Russia Sell Alaska?

Today Alaska is our forty-ninth state. But at one time the tremendous potential and importance of this area were recognized by very few people. In fact, when it was bought by the United States in 1867 for $7,200,000 from Russia, it was called Seward's Folly.

William Seward was Secretary of State under Lincoln, and he had urged that we buy it. We obtained an area about twice the size of Texas, 586,400 square miles, at a price a little less than two cents an acre! Most Americans at the time thought it was too much to pay for such a barren, far-off place.

Alaska was one of the last areas of the world to be discovered and explored by white men. In the early eighteenth century, under Peter the Great, Russia extended its empire through Siberia and into the Pacific. In 1741, Vitus Bering, a Dane in the service of the Russian Navy, led an expedition of two small ships (his second expedition) that finally succeeded in reaching Alaska.

Throughout the rest of the eighteenth and much of the nineteenth century, Russia explored its Alaskan territory, then known as Russian America. It governed Alaska through the Russian America Company. But during this time also, sea captains of Spain, France, and Great Britain explored the Alaska coast. The first United States vessels reached Alaska in 1788.

In 1821 Russia declared other nations were not to be allowed to trade or fish or do business north of a certain line. But in 1824 and 1825 Russia signed treaties with England and the United States giving them trading rights.

When the Crimean War broke out in 1854, the Russians felt that they had too much trouble at home to bother with Alaska. They also felt that Alaska was too exposed and too far away for Russia to be able to protect it. Negotiations were started in 1859 to sell Alaska to the United States. The Civil War temporarily halted negotiations, but in 1867 the sale was made.

What Are Public-Opinion Polls?

Occasionally you read in the paper or hear on a news program that a poll has been taken which indicates how most people feel about a certain question.

How did they find this out? It is done through a kind of survey that is called public-opinion research. This kind of research finds out what people think and how they feel about a variety of subjects.

For example, the survey, which is done by asking a representative number of people certain questions, may find out how they feel about labor unions, big companies, the government, the school system, or a certain law that has been passed.

Public-opinion surveys may find out what people's ambitions are, or who makes decisions in a family. They may ask whether people think prices are too high, or whether there should be a change in the draft law.

Probably the best-known kind of public-opinion research is the election poll. In elections for political office, such as for president, governor, or mayor, the polls can find out for whom people are going to vote, as well as the reasons. In some cases, the polls come very close to indicating the actual result of an election. In others, they may be somewhat incorrect, especially when the situation changes quickly or people are still undecided.

Such polls can also be helpful in showing leaders in government what people think about important questions that they may have to deal with when in office.

Another value of public-opinion surveys is that they often show what types of people are ignorant or uninformed about what subjects. With this information, educators can improve their methods of teaching.

Chapter 2

How It Began

30 MILLION YEARS OLD

300 MILLION YEARS OLD

500 MILLION YEARS OLD

330 MILLION YEARS OLD

Where Were the First Fossils Found?

During the past two to three billion years, many forms of life, both plant and animal, have inhabited the earth and then become extinct. We know about them through the study of fossils.

Most fossils are the remains of plants and animals preserved in rock. Fossils take many forms. Sometimes they are shells, bones, scales, or other hard parts of animals; more often, chemicals replace the hard parts. The tracks of animals are also fossils.

Fossils had existed for millions of years before man began to read their story of past life on earth. Yet there is evidence that some early men had seen fossils and recognized them as something special. A necklace of fossil sea shells was found with the skeleton of a woman who died thirty thousand years ago.

The scholars of ancient Greece and Rome found fossil sea shells far up in the mountains. They realized that these shells were the remains of animals that had once lived in the sea. And so they reasoned that in past ages these mountains had been under the sea.

Scientists did not really begin to study fossils until the late 1700's. One of the first men to do so was Baron Georges Cuvier, a great French naturalist. In the rocks along the river banks near Paris, Cuvier found the bones of elephants, hippopotamuses, and many other animals no longer seen in that region. He realized that the climate around Paris must once have been very different, something like the climate of India and Africa today.

Then an Englishman named William Smith began to study fossils all over England. He discovered that each kind of rock had its own group of fossils. Older rocks would generally contain simpler fossils than newer rocks. From this he was able to tell the relative age of the rocks. Charles Darwin later used evidence from fossils to show how living forms developed from past forms, and how higher forms might have developed from simpler ones.

When Did Civilization Begin?

It took man a long, long time to reach what we call a state of civilization. At first he lived in a state of savagery, much like animals. He had no language, and obtained food wherever he could find it.

Later on he had a family organization, learned to make fire, and still later, how to make tools and hunt for food. He invented pottery so that he could cook his food, began to live in tribes, and was able to move to new places.

The next stage of man, which is called barbarism, saw him learn how to raise food from seeds and how to tame animals. Then he began to smelt metals, such as copper and iron, so that he could make better weapons. He also began to build houses. When he invented a system of picture writing, it marked the end of barbarism and the beginning of civilization.

The invention of writing is considered the beginning of civilization, because it enabled man to keep records of past happenings. In this way, people could learn from the experience of others. This happened about five thousand or six thousand years ago.

By the time man reached this stage, he had developed in other ways, too. He had built up agriculture and industry to the point where people could live in villages and even in cities. There was government, there was trade, there were laws, and there were migrations of people.

The earliest civilizations that are known to us in history are those of the Egyptians and the Babylonians. The Egyptians had a form of writing four thousand five hundred years ago. They had a system of government and an understanding of mathematics (used in building the pyramids); they had a calendar, employed architects, and knew how to use various machines.

CAVE PAINTING IN SPAIN

SUMERIAN CLAY TABLET

EGYPTIAN FORM OF WRITING ON STONE

There was also a civilization on the island of Crete about four thousand years ago; and the Sumerian people, who lived along the Tigris and Euphrates rivers, had a civilization as far back as four thousand five hundred years ago.

Did People Always Live in Families?

No one knows how the first family started. Excavations in ancient caves show that men, women, and children lived together in small groups. It is not certain that the groups separated at first into units of father, mother, and children that we think of as a family, although the women probably cared for their own children. The "family" kept warm with fire and protected themselves against wild animals with simple weapons.

A family kind of life is more necessary among human beings than among other creatures. This is because the most helpless creature on earth is the human baby. Most insects and other members of the lower forms of life can move about and get their own food as soon as they are hatched. But the young of the higher forms of life—human infants, baby bears, and other animals—must be fed and protected.

The father (human or animal) usually brings the food for the mother and protects the young against enemies. The mother is most important, for she provides the milk for the baby. Thus the family is formed because it is necessary for the young and adults to stay together.

During the hundreds of thousands of years that family life has existed, different forms of family organization have developed among different peoples. In some tribes, the mother's brother was head of the family. The father had little to do with the children.

The pharaohs in ancient Egypt married their sisters. During Biblical times and earlier, a man might have two or more wives. Among some peoples a woman might have several husbands. The marriage of a man or woman to more than one mate is called polygamy.

There are still families in Africa and the Near East with more than one wife, but the practice seems to be dying out.

Why Do Many Irish Names Start with O'?

How do you feel about your name? Do you think it says anything about the kind of person you are? Would you have chosen it for yourself?

Nowadays, about the only people who have names made up for them to "fit" them are actors and actresses in Hollywood. The rest of us must get along with the names our parents gave us, even though they may say nothing about us.

First names have always been chosen by the parents for the child. At one time, the first name usually had a meaning for the parent. It might describe the appearance of the little baby, or express something the parents felt. For example, the name Samuel means in Hebrew "asked of God." And the name Blanche stands for "white" in French.

As towns grew and many people lived together in the same place, it became hard to tell people apart by their names. There were too many Johns and Williams and Davids. Suppose there were two men called John whom you knew and you had to tell someone which John you meant. You might say: "I'm talking about John who is William's son."

In this way the idea arose of telling people apart by mentioning the father's name. So this particular John came to be called "John Williamson." This might be expressed in many different ways. It might be "John Williams" or "John Wilson" or "John Wills"—all pointing out that John is the son of William!

In Ireland, the prefix O' means "of." So when the Irish wanted to say John, the son of Brian, they used this prefix and made the name "John O'Brian." All the Irish names that start with O' began with this way of identifying the son by the name of the father.

The Scotch did the same thing, only their prefix was Mac, which means "son." This could be shortened to Mc or M with c raised. So John, son of Donald, became known as John MacDonald.

There were many, many other ways in which last names originated. Sometimes the last names were given as the result of the place where a person lived. If Thomas lived near a wood, he might become Thomas Wood or Thomas Atwood. Sometimes the last name came from a nickname, such as Brown, or Longfellow, or Drinkwater.

If you could pick your last name today, what would you choose?

How Did Animals Get Their Names?

Not all the English names of animals came about the same way. Some are just the English word for a name that already existed in another language. Others are combinations of words that describe the animal. Let's consider the names of some animals and see how they originated.

Hippopotamus is the Greek for river horse. *Hippos* meant horse, and *potamos* meant river. Rhinoceros is a Latin term derived from two Greek words. *Rinos* meant the "nose," and *keras* was a "horn." And the rhinoceros has a horn on its nose!

Leopard comes from the Latin *leopardus,* which meant a spotted lion. Lion comes from the Latin *leon.* Camel comes from the Arabic *gamel,* which was *camelos* in Latin.

Wolf is a modern spelling of the Anglo-Saxon *wulf,* which goes back to the Latin *vulpes,* and which meant fox. Our name fox comes from the Icelandic *fax,* which meant a hair-mane. The name opossum comes from *opassum,* which is what the Indians of Virginia called this animal.

Bull comes from the Anglo-Saxon *belkan,* which meant to roar. Deer was originally *deor* in Anglo-Saxon, and meant a wild animal. Porcupine comes from two Latin words: *porcus,* a swine, and *spina,* a thorn. So it's a pig with thorns.

When we call a cat a puss it goes back to the Egyptians. They called a cat *pasht,* which meant the moon, because cats were active at night. This became shortened to *pas,* and that's how we got puss.

The name poodle comes from the German *pudel,* which meant a puddle. This was because it was a water dog. And the word dog itself is a contraction of the Icelandic *doggr.* These are only a few names of animals, but you can see how they originated in many different ways.

160

How Did Fairs Begin?

In ancient times most people lived on farms or on large estates. There were no stores, for the small settlements of people were too far apart. Also, there were not enough goods or people for daily trade.

But people always came together for religious festivals. The merchants waited for the times when people gathered in large groups to sell their goods. This is how the fairs of ancient times began. In fact, the word "fair" comes from a Latin word *feria,* meaning "feast day" or "holiday."

The Egyptians set up markets for buying and selling when they gathered at their tombs and burying grounds for religious ceremonies. The Greeks held their fairs and festivals honoring their gods at Delphi, where there was a famous oracle.

Long before the time of Mohammed, thousands of people used to travel to Mecca, an Arab religious and trading center. After a week of religious ceremonies and feasting, they stayed on to trade precious jewels, oil, and hides. Trade fairs were also important in India, China, and Persia and among the Aztecs of Mexico.

In the Roman Empire, fairs were closely connected with religious harvest festivals. The country people brought their farm products to those festivals. There they exchanged them for cloth and other manufactured articles.

In olden days, only certain towns had the right to hold fairs. This right could be given by a king or an overlord to the lord of the town. The merchants who wanted to sell their goods at the fair had to pay money to the lord who held the license.

Special rules and laws were made for fairs. Honesty was of great importance so that people wouldn't be cheated. In the early civilizations people at war stopped their battles when they met at a fair. They considered the fairgrounds holy.

Fairs played an important part in the development of commerce. They made possible trade between the Orient and eastern and northern Europe.

Who Built the First Castle?

The idea of a castle is connected with defense. In fact, the word "castle" comes from a Latin word meaning *fort*. So a castle was a home of a ruler or lord that could be defended.

Even in ancient Egypt, the royal palaces were fortified with towers and parapets, and so were like castles. In ancient Greece, too, the chieftains fortified their palaces. But the castle as we think of it really came into its own during the Middle Ages in western Europe, from A.D. 1000 to A.D. 1500.

The reason for this was the feudal system. Individual nobles controlled their own sections of the country and their people. They would often attack or take advantage of neighboring areas in order to strengthen their power. And, of course, they would be attacked in return. So they had to make their own homes into strong forts, and thus built what we call castles.

Since the conditions were pretty much alike in most of Europe, the castles that were built were quite similar, whether they were in France, Germany, Spain, or England. One of the first such structures was the Tower of London, begun in 1078 by William the Conqueror.

It was several stories high, had double walls, small windows, and spiral staircases in the corners of the tower. The lord and his garrison of troops lived there.

Another early castle, Hedingham Castle, in Essex, England, was built in 1130. It had double walls of stone twenty feet thick, and its corners were even thicker. There was a great center hall, two stories high. The only light came from a few small windows high up in the wall. It was planned this way for reasons of defense; few and small windows were good protection.

Later on, castles were built around inner courtyards, so that there would be more room for the people living in them, and more comfortable facilities could be set up.

PRIMITIVE STICK PLOWING

MOLDBOARD PLOW
TO ATTACH TO TRACTOR

DISC PLOW TO
ATTACH TO TRACTOR

Who Invented the First Plow?

Before a farmer can plant his seeds, he must prepare the ground by plowing. The plow breaks up the hard ground and turns the soil over.

The plow is a very ancient invention, and no one knows who made the first plow. The earliest plows that have been found are about five thousand years old. The main purpose of all plows is to stir up the soil by dragging or raking something through it. At first the plow was just a forked stick or log, pulled by men or women. Later, men learned to use animals to pull plows.

Gradually the shape of the plowing stick was changed so that it would work better. The bottom of the stick was shaped into a pointed blade called the plowshare. This helped the plow cut through the ground more easily.

Then curved sides were added to the plow. These sides turn the soil over as it is plowed up and break it up more thoroughly. The sides are called moldboards. Together the plowshare and moldboards are called the plow bottom. The type of plow that is most commonly used today is called a moldboard plow.

The plowshare was made much stronger and sharper by cutting it out of metal. In the eighteenth century the British began making cast-iron plowshares. In 1797 Charles Newbold, an American inventor, patented the first American cast-iron plow. Modern plows are made of cast iron or steel, depending on what kind of soil the plow is to be used in.

Did you know that Thomas Jefferson used mathematics to find the best shape for a plow bottom (the plowshare plus the moldboards) and helped make the cast-iron plow popular?

In dry, hard soils, disk plows are used instead of moldboard plows. Instead of pointed blades on the bottom, disk plows have sharp-edged steel disks. Disk plows are good for rocky soil because they can roll over rocks that might stop or damage a moldboard plow. Disk plows are also very good for plowing old plants into the soil to enrich it.

How Long Has Man Been Growing Vegetables?

Vegetables are herbaceous plants, the kind of plant that has a soft stem and little or no woody tissues. The part of the plant that we eat may be a root (beets), a stem (asparagus), leaves (spinach), flower buds (broccoli), a fruit (tomatoes), or seeds (peas).

Early man probably gathered wild pod-bearing plants, such as beans and peas, and root plants, such as carrots. Vegetables such as these and leafy plants such as cabbage and lettuce are believed to have been in the first primitive gardens, though we don't know when such gardens were started.

The ancient Egyptians cultivated lettuce, cabbage, cress, melons, broad beans, radishes, onions, garlic, artichokes, and possibly peas. So thousands of years ago people were already eating quite a variety of vegetables.

The Greeks and Romans later were familiar with all the vegetables the Egyptians used. In addition, they raised cucumbers, asparagus, and celery.

When the explorers came to America, they found vegetables that were completely unknown in Europe. Even the familiar bean was not the same plant in the New World. Here they found string beans, lima beans, potatoes, sweet potatoes, corn, and tomatoes. These were all native to the New World and were not grown in Europe until the explorers brought back seeds and tubers. Many of these new vegetables didn't become popular until the nineteenth cntury.

In the nineteenth century a revolution took place in farming of all kinds. Farmers improved crops by using better farming methods and by selecting only seeds from the best plants for the next year's crop. In this way, vegetables became larger, better tasting, and more nutritious than they had ever been before.

When Was Fertilizer First Used?

Any material that is added to the soil to give it the elements that will help plants grow is a fertilizer. Why are fertilizers needed? Basically they keep up the fertility of good soils, and correct or cure the lack of fertility of poor soils.

When crops are harvested, all the food elements that have gone into them are taken away from the land. In this way, crops use up the supply of food elements in soil. The farmer uses fertilizers to put them back, or to build up the supply of elements that are naturally low in soil.

There are natural fertilizers that come from things that were once alive, such as humus, which is made from decaying plants; meal, made from animal bones or seeds; and animal manures. And there are chemical fertilizers that come from many sources.

Man has used fertilizers for a long time. We do not know just how long, but we do know the Chinese used animal and plant wastes as fertilizers thousands of years ago.

The Romans as early as the second century B.C. rotated their crops, put lime in the soil, and added nitrogen by planting peas and beans. During the seventeenth century, in parts of Europe, manure was used as fertilizer, town wastes were taken to farms, and clover was used in crop rotation.

In 1748, Benjamin Franklin demonstrated in America the value of a lime fertilizer. He laid out lime plaster in the form of huge letters in a field along a highway near Philadelphia. The letters spelled out the message: THIS FIELD HAS BEEN PLASTERED. The white letters soon disappeared, but when the crop came up, the message reappeared, because the fertilized area was much greener than the rest of the field.

Where Did Corn Originate?

Corn, or maize, is one of the most useful plants known to man. Today it is an important crop in southern Europe, Africa, parts of Asia, and, of course, the United States.

Scientists believe that it originated somewhere in Central or South America. Prehistoric Indians probably selected seeds year after year from wild grasses. After several centuries they had developed a plant very much like the corn we know today. Corn is a plant that cannot survive unless man cares for it. No wild plants closely resembling corn are now known.

Indians had their own stories about the origin of corn. In one tale a young girl turned herself into a corn plant to give mankind a new grain. She left her hair on the plant as corn silks to remind people to take good care of her gift.

The Indians liked corn with blue, red, and black kernels. They gave their colorful corn to the Pilgrims to feed them during the first cold winter in America. The next year the Pilgrims shared their own harvest with the Indians. This was the first Thanksgiving.

Corn was first introduced to the Old World as maize by Christopher Columbus. Maize was the Indian name for the grain. It has kept this name, spelled in a variety of ways, in most countries. Since the word "corn" in England meant any kind of grain, the Pilgrims called this new grain "Indian corn."

Today there are six chief types of corn. Dent corn is the most widely grown. It has a notch at the top of the kernel. Flint corn has hard kernels and withstands cold and disease.

The corn we eat is usually sweet corn, flour corn, or popcorn. Sweet corn is high in sugar. Flour corn is used to make flour. Popcorn is corn that bursts from its small, hard-shelled kernels when heated.

ANCIENT CORN

MODERN CORN

Where Did Oranges Originate?

There are records that show that in China the orange was known at least four thousand years ago!

There are two kinds of orange tree, the sweet and the sour. The sour orange was the first orange grown in Europe. It was introduced by the Moors who invaded southern Spain and Sicily around the ninth century.

By the eleventh century the Moors were quite strongly in control of the conquered countries, and they planted sour orange and other trees. Sour oranges were widely grown in southern Europe until the fifteenth century, when increased trade with the Orient brought sweet oranges to Europe. Although some sour oranges are still grown and eaten, they are now used mainly as rootstocks for sweet oranges.

Sweet oranges were at first a luxury that only very rich people could afford. Kings and nobles paid great prices to obtain orange trees, which they planted in their gardens.

In the colder countries the delicate trees would be killed during a cold winter, so special greenhouses, called orangeries, were built. The orange trees were planted in tubs. During the summer they were moved outside, but in winter they were kept safe behind glass in the orangeries, where they could bloom despite the cold outside.

Did you know that when Christopher Columbus sailed for the New World he carried seeds of oranges and many other citrus fruits with him? The seeds were planted on the island of Hispaniola. Citrus trees flourished in the tropical climate of the West Indies and what is now Florida.

The Indians ate the oranges and, as they traveled about, they dropped the seeds. Planted in this way, groves of citrus trees were soon growing wild.

Today the United States leads the world in the production of oranges. The state of Florida has the greatest number of orange trees and produces more sweet oranges than any other state—or country!

WATERMELON   MUSKMELON   HONEYDEW MELON

Where Did Watermelons Originate?

On a hot summer day is there anything that tastes as good as a cold, juicy watermelon? It's no wonder then that this fruit has been enjoyed by man for thousands of years.

The watermelon originated in tropical Africa and spread from there to every possible place where the soil and climate were right. In ancient Sanskrit there is a word for watermelon, and there are early Egyptian drawings that show watermelons. So we know that it has been cultivated for more than four thousand years!

The watermelon is one of several types of melons, all of which belong to the gourd family. Like cucumbers, they are trailing annual vines with flat, lobed leaves and bell-shaped flowers.

Muskmelons are another ancient type of melon, which grew originally in southern Asia. All muskmelons have a faint, musky perfume, which gives them their name. Muskmelons are often called cantaloupes.

The Casaba and the honeydew melons ripen late in the season and keep better than other melons. Casaba melons are large, with smooth, yellowish-green rinds. Their flavor is delicate and their flesh is pale green. Honeydew melons have an even smoother rind, and their flesh is deeper green than that of Casaba melons.

Watermelons are considerably larger than muskmelons, and much juicier. Some watermelons weigh more than fifty pounds, but most of them are smaller. The rind is hard and green, often mottled or striped with lighter green. The flesh is pinkish, yellowish, or red.

Watermelons need a long growing season and a hot climate. They are planted after the ground is warm and there is no danger of frost. Watermelons are usually eaten fresh, but they can be pickled and the rind made into a preserve. In Oriental countries their seeds are considered a delicacy.

Where Did Olives Come From?

The original home of the olive is southwest Asia. For many centuries olives have provided food for people and have been carried by caravan to distant markets.

An unusual thing about the olive is that it cannot be eaten fresh from the tree. The bitter taste of the fruit must be removed by pickling, before the olive can be eaten.

Oil from olive trees was very important in trade between ancient peoples. Kings used to judge how wealthy they were by the number of jars filled with olive oil in their storerooms. On the tiny island of Crete the remains of storerooms for olive oil have been found that date back as far as 2000 B.C.

171

Olive trees were planted in all the countries that border the Mediterranean Sea. At one time even the bare desert regions of North Africa were covered with olive groves. It is said that once upon a time a person could travel from Mecca to Morocco in the shade of olive, date, and fig trees.

The Spaniards brought olive seeds and cuttings to the New World. They planted them around their missions in California, where the trees thrived in the warm, dry climate.

Today olives are a major crop in California, which produces almost all the olives grown in the United States. But Spain and Italy are still the leading olive-producing countries in the world, and California's production is only 0.9 percent of the world's total.

Olive trees are raised either from seeds or from cuttings. A cutting is a stem or other part of the plant that will grow into a new tree if properly planted. An olive tree lives a long time. In the Garden of Gethsemane on the Mount of Olives, there are olive trees that have been alive for two thousand years, though they may not have the same trunks as originally. They were probably renewed by new shoots growing from their bases.

When Was Wine First Made?

Wine is the fermented juice of grapes. It has been enjoyed by man for thousands of years.

Probably the first people to make wine were Persian farmers living near the Caspian Sea. The Egyptians learned how to make wine from them as long ago as 3000 B.C. Pictures on the walls of tombs in the pyramids show the ancient Egyptians making wine.

Wine was common in the everyday life of the early Greeks and Romans. It was important to their religious ceremonies. The god of wine was called Bacchus by the Romans and Dionysus by the Greeks.

In the fourth century B.C., the Greek conqueror Alexander the Great carried grapevines and the knowledge of wine-making to Central Asia. The Greeks also took vines to southern France. Roman invaders probably took vines to northern France and Germany in later centuries.

When Leif Ericson landed on the eastern coast of North America in about 1000 A.D. he found so many wild grapevines growing there that he called the place Vinland. Later, Spanish explorers and missionaries brought grapevines from Europe to California.

Wine was used ceremonially in many ancient religions. And it is used today in many Christian and Jewish religious ceremonies. In times when pure water was scarce, wine was considered safe and healthful to drink.

Wine can be made from many fruits and plants that contain natural sugar. But most wine is made from grapes. When we say "wine," without using a descriptive name, such as "peach wine" or "blackberry wine," we always mean grape wine.

There are more than eight thousand varieties of grapes that can be used to make wine.

When Were Pretzels First Made?

Pretzels may not taste or look like cookies, crackers, and biscuits —but all of these are actually alike in many ways.

They are all small and crisp, and keep well. They are even made on the same kinds of machines and packaged in the same way. Special baking plants turn out all four with only slight changes in equipment and recipes.

They are made with the same ingredients—flour, leavening, shortening, sweetening, and liquid. Usually the leavening in these products is baking powder instead of yeast. In the oven the baking powder creates carbon-dioxide gas, which makes the baked goods light without making them rise too high.

Pretzels have a long history. They date back to the early Christians in the Roman Empire. They were used at that time solely for religious purposes. Fat, milk, and eggs were forbidden during the Lenten season, and people ate dry pretzels instead of bread. They were especially popular on Ash Wednesday. It was only in modern times that they became popular as snacks to nibble on.

In northern Europe and the Scandinavian countries, the pretzel has become the sign of the baker. A large golden pretzel is usually seen hanging outside each bakery.

The original pretzel was a large twist with a soft inside and a crusty outside. By baking out almost all of the moisture, manufacturers produce the crisp, hard pretzel we eat today. Made from very stiff dough, the pretzels are actually salty baked biscuits. They are twisted or shaped into sticks.

By the way, the name "biscuit" comes from the early French word for "twice cooked." During the Middle Ages, French travelers, soldiers, and sailors carried a strange, hard bread. The bread had been cooked twice to keep it from spoiling. This hard bread was what we call the biscuit.

When we buy biscuits today, they come wrapped to keep the moisture out so that they will be as crisp as when they left the oven.

EARLY IRON STOVE

When Were Stoves First Used?

Stoves were used as early as the fifteenth century, even though the fireplace was still the main source of heat in the house. Stoves were more efficient than fireplaces, because a stove sits inside a room and heats by convection as well as by radiation. Convection means air flowing around a room in a circular fashion, due to the fact that air rises as it warms and drops when it cools off.

The earliest stoves were made of clay or brick with wrought-iron or bronze doors. As wrought iron became less expensive, the stoves themselves were made of wrought iron. Metal conducts heat much better than clay or brick, so these iron stoves were a big improvement. They conducted more of the heat from the fire to the air in the room.

The first metal stoves were called five-plate stoves. They were just boxes made of five wrought-iron plates: one for the top, one for the bottom, and one for each of three sides. The fourth side was left open and was put into a fireplace so that the smoke could go up the chimney.

The first metal stoves that did not need to be set in a fireplace were made in Holland and Scandinavia. They were called six-plate stoves because they were made of six cast-iron plates, which formed the six sides of the box.

The stoves had a door for putting in fuel and removing ashes. They also had a hole that allowed air to enter for proper draft, and they had a hole at the top to which a chimney pipe could be attached. The Pilgrims lived in Holland for several years before they sailed to America, and were familiar with these stoves. When American colonists in Massachusetts began making iron and iron products, this was the type of stove they made before 1650.

Early stoves burned wood, coal, or the cheapest local fuel. In the 1820's a coal-burning stove, called the baseburner, came into use. The baseburner was designed to burn small pieces of coal, which were cheap. The coal burned on a grate near the bottom of the stove. Such a stove could stay lit for twenty-four hours a day.

When Were Bathtubs First Used?

In ancient times there were two reasons why people bathed in water: for cleanliness and for religious observance.

The ancient Greeks and Romans liked to take warm baths for relaxation and pleasure. Bathing places became social centers. And bathing was also considered a way of treating diseases.

Among the ancient Egyptians, bathing was chiefly a religious rite. The Hebrews also believed in bathing for religious reasons, as did the Hindus.

The earliest baths known to man are the palace baths at Knossos, on Crete. They are about four thousand years old. The palace had bathrooms with foot baths and tubs. In this palace, in the

WATER AND BATHING OIL BEARERS OF KNOSSIS

QUEEN'S BATHTUB FROM KNOSSIS—1400 B.C.

queen's apartments, a bathtub has been found that goes back to between 1700 and 1400 B.C. It is a very modern-looking tub. In fact, since a tub has to be shaped a certain way to be used by human beings, the design of bathtubs has remained much the same throughout history.

In ancient times, Greeks were already bathing in tubs. They were usually made of polished stone, marble, or wood. Homer, the great Greek poet, describes an especially beautiful silver tub that was brought from Egypt.

The early Christian church did not preach that cleanliness had anything to do with religion. There were even some Christians in early times who regarded being dirty as a way of atoning for sin. This attitude began to change about the time of the Middle Ages.

After the Middle Ages, most Europeans used perfumes and cosmetics as a substitute for bathing. There were very few private baths in homes. Even the colonists who came to America frowned on bathing. Benjamin Franklin, who took a bath regularly, was one of the pioneers of American bathing.

It was not until Victorian times that the bathroom developed as a separate unit in a house. The tub, made of wood, copper, or iron, often had a cover over it to make it look like a sofa.

How Did Clothes Develop?

Man has always wanted to improve his appearance. Early man put on animal skins and hung strings of beads and stones around his neck. Bark, leaves, straw, feathers, or whatever material was closest at hand were turned into clothing.

For early man, clothing may also have had magical qualities. By wrapping himself in a certain skin, he may have been trying to keep away evil spirits. During the ice ages, people had to wear animal furs to keep warm.

The hides were first scraped. Then holes were pierced in the skins. Strips of leather or animal tendons were drawn through the holes to tie the pieces of fur together and to help keep the garment on the body.

Gradually, man learned to make the skins softer and more supple. About forty thousand to fifty thousand years ago the needle was invented; it became a key tool for making clothes.

Later, man learned how to twist wool and animal hair into long strands. The Egyptians wove light fabrics out of the flax and cotton that grew in the Valley of the Nile. Wool was spun into yarn for robes and tunics by other ancient peoples.

In colder climates, clothes covered all of the body as a protection against the elements. Because of cold weather, the clothes that were developed here were closer-fitting. So trousers, tunics, and warm, protective cloaks came from these areas.

As communication improved between the sections of the globe, clothing styles from different regions began to influence each other. But different social groups wore different types of clothing. The clothes of the lower classes were looser and easier to work in. Wealthier people liked to wear clothing that showed everyone that they didn't have to do manual work.

When Did Women Begin to Style Their Hair?

Considering what we know about women, it probably won't surprise you to learn that women have dressed and decorated their hair from as far back as we have any records in history!

Combs of some sort or other, for example, have been used by women since the very earliest times. Primitive peoples have made combs of bone, wood, or even bronze.

Savage races have always paid a great deal of attention to their hair. Some of them have dyed their hair black, white, or red. In the Belgian Congo in Africa, natives used the oil from the castor bean for dressing their hair, and many tribes would plaster their hair with mud.

In ancient Greek times, women used long hairpins that were quite elaborate and sometimes had sculpture on them. On special occasions they would adorn their hair with garlands and wreaths of flowers, and they also used ribbons for their hair.

As for what women did about arranging their hair in ancient times, it varied from place to place and customs were constantly changing. But even in ancient times, it seems that curled hair was considered more attractive than straight hair. There are pictures and statues that show women with rows of small curls arranged over the brows and temples, and these curls must have been made and kept in place by some artificial means. And not only did men also curl their hair, they even used to curl their beards!

EGYPTIAN

GREEK

EARLY COMBS

As civilization advanced, hair styles and methods of arranging and dressing the hair became more varied. In some places the style was straight; in others the fashion was curled hair.

The custom of short hair for men and long hair for women is quite recent in the history of mankind and goes back only to the end of the Middle Ages.

Why Do Men Raise Their Hats to Ladies?

This custom, like so many others that we practice today, passed through many stages of development before it came down to us.

Long, long ago, uncovering one's body in the presence of another person was considered a sign of respect and deference. Usually, it was the upper part of the body that was uncovered. In time, instead of uncovering the body, it was considered enough to uncover one's head. And gradually, the mere raising of the hat was all that was necessary to show respect.

During the age of knights, it was the custom for a knight to wear his full armor in public. But when a knight came among friends, he would remove his helmet. This was a symbol of the fact that he felt safe among friends and didn't need the protection of his helmet.

This custom, combined with the already existing custom of uncovering one's head as a sign of respect, created the tradition of raising the hat as a mark of courtesy. In our civilization, of course, it is men who are expected to show signs of courtesy to women, so the custom of raising the hat is still practiced by men today!

When Did Man Begin to Use
Knives, Forks, and Spoons?

Let's see if you can figure this out by using logic. Imagine the time when knives, forks, and spoons didn't even exist. Which one of them do you think man would "invent" first?

Not the knife—because man can tear his food apart with his hands. Not the fork—because he can pick it up with his fingers. But for picking up liquids, especially hot liquids, he needs a spoon! Hence man invented the spoon first. In fact, spoonlike implements have been found going back to the Stone Age! The Egyptians had spoons made of wood, stone, and ivory. And the Greeks used spoons of bronze and silver.

When man began to use the knife and fork, however, he really made a great advance in dining. And this advance came about quite recently in his history. Even only three hundred years ago, knives and forks were great curiosities. As a matter of fact, in France everyone ate with his fingers until the seventeenth century.

This doesn't mean that knives and forks didn't exist before that time. The primitive savage actually used a kind of fork, but it was nothing like ours. It may have been made of a small pronged twig.

As far as is known, the first real forks were long, two-pronged utensils made of iron, bone, and hard wood. They were used only in cooking and for holding the meat while it was being carved.

Forks were used for dining in the eleventh century, but only a very few people were so dainty that they had to have one. The knife, of course, was one of man's first inventions, in the sense that he made a cutting tool of flint or other stones. But there was no such thing as a table knife in early times. Even three hundred years ago, it was so rare, most people didn't know about it. After the seventeenth century, table knives were introduced in England, and soon they became popular. But the poor people couldn't afford them, and so most people still ate with their hands.

ROMAN TABLE

Who Made the First Table?

Can you imagine a house without a table in it? A table fills so many needs—eating, writing, playing games, holding lamps, and so on—that tables seem to have existed since the beginning of civilization.

A small table, made of metal or wood, was known to the Sumerians, and theirs is the first civilization of which we have any records. The Babylonians and Assyrians got the idea from them, as did the Egyptians. The Egyptians produced small, low tables that were beautifully designed and had fine workmanship.

The Greeks, who adapted many things from the Egyptian civilization, developed all kinds of furniture, including tables. Their tables were made of marble, metals, and inlaid woods.

Then the Romans carried the development of furniture to an even higher level. They not only had tables made entirely of metal or wood, but they also made costly ornamental tables that were delicately carved and inlaid with ivory and precious metals. The legs were carved into sphinxes, fluted columns, or to resemble the legs of rams or lions.

It was the custom among them to recline rather than sit at the dining table, so the tables were low in height. By the way, in ancient times, tables of any kind were owned only by the rich.

During the Middle Ages, tables appeared in all kinds of shapes: circular, oval, and oblong. But they were made quite simply—just boards supported by a fixed or folding trestle. They were covered with tablecloths that reached to the floor in order to hide the supports. After a meal, they were cleared out of the way.

During the sixteenth century, in the castles of the rich, there would be a fixed table in the great hall. This was reserved for the nobility, and ordinary people sat at smaller, separate tables or boards.

When Did People First Freeze Food?

We think of frozen food as a new invention, but it is actually one of the oldest methods known for preserving food. From the days when man first inhabited cold regions, he froze fish, game, and other meats for future use.

The first known patent for freezing food was granted as early as 1852 in England. The method used was to immerse the food in an ice-and-salt brine. Many other patents were granted for freezing food at that time, all using ice-and-salt mixtures.

But frozen foods could not be used extensively until the development of mechanical refrigeration. This made it possible to freeze and transport meats over long distances.

Early in the twentieth century, attempts were made to preserve foods other than meats and fish by freezing. A man called H. S. Baker froze fruits in Colorado as early as 1908. The purpose of this was to freeze the part of the fruit crop that couldn't be marketed and sell it for use later.

Only certain fruits were frozen at first, chiefly strawberries and cherries. They were frozen by what is known as the cold-pack method. This means placing barrels or containers of the fruit in large storage rooms where the temperature is maintained at 10 and 15 degrees below zero fahrenheit.

In 1916, experiments in Germany showed that foods could be frozen by the quick-freeze method, which meant freezing the food in a few hours instead of in several days. In 1917 a man called Clarence Birdseye began to work on methods for freezing food in small containers for sale in stores. It wasn't until 1919 that the first commercial pack of this type was put on the market.

As the result of his experiments and the work of others, it was found that many vegetables could also be preserved in this manner, and the frozen-food industry was on its way.

When Was Coal First Used?

Coal has been used by man since very ancient times. Probably the first people to use it were the Chinese. There are records to show the Chinese used coal to smelt copper and iron perhaps as far back in time as three thousand years ago.

Coal is mentioned in the Bible. In the Book of Proverbs we read: "As coals are to burning coals, and wood to fire, so is a contentious man to kindle strife." The Greek philosopher Aristotle, who lived from 384 to 322 B.C., mentions coal in his writings.

During the period when the Romans occupied Britain, which began about 50 B.C., coal was used. We know this because in the ruins of Roman villas in Britain both coal and cinders have been found.

Here is an interesting fact about a certain coal mine. There are records that show that coal was mined in the Dutch province of Limburg in the year 1113. This mine, now known as the Domaniale Mine, is still being used and produces the most coal in the Netherlands!

During the mid-thirteenth century, women and children gathered what was known as sea coal along the English coast, and there were already several mines in England. Blacksmiths needed the coal for heating the iron for their smithies. Owners of small shops kept their

EARLY COAL MINE

places warm with coal. And poor people preferred coal to wood for heating purposes because it was cheaper.

By the way, the nobility at that time refused to have anything to do with coal. They wouldn't enter a house in which coal was burned or eat food that had been cooked over coal fires. They believed the smoke poisoned the food. And, of course, since houses at that time didn't have chimneys, smoke used to fill the rooms, which is what made people suspicious of coal.

After the invention of the steam engine, which made it possible to transport coal from the mines, the use of coal finally became common.

BRONZE AGE ARTIFACTS

When Was Metal First Used?

About six thousand years ago man lived in what we call the Stone Age. This is because he made most of his tools and weapons out of stone. He had not yet learned how to use metals.

Probably the first metals man learned how to use were copper and gold. The reason is that these metals occur in nature in a free state as well as in ores. Man found nuggets of copper and gold and was able to hammer them into various shapes without having to melt them. We don't know the date when man discovered how to use these metals, but we do know that copper was used as long ago as 5000 B.C. Gold was first used some time before 4000 B.C.

By about 3000 B.C., man had learned some of the most important things about using metals. By this time the metals silver and lead had been discovered, too, but copper was the one used most since it was the strongest and most plentiful.

Man first learned to beat metal into useful shapes, such as bowls, tools, and weapons. Once he began using metals, he discovered the processes of annealing (making a metal soft and tough by heating and then slowly cooling it), melting, casting, and smelting. Also, he could get copper from its ore, which was more plentiful than the nuggets.

Later man discovered tin and learned to mix copper and tin, which made bronze. From about 3500 B.C. to about 1200 B.C., bronze was the most important material for making tools and weapons. This period is called the Bronze Age.

Man knew about iron from meteorites he found, long before he discovered how to smelt it from its ore. By about 1200 B.C., man had learned how to work iron, and this knowledge spread all over the world. Iron replaced bronze for most uses. This was the beginning of the Iron Age.

By the time of the Romans, seven metals were known: gold, copper, silver, lead, tin, iron, and mercury.

When Were Eyeglasses Invented?

If you look around you, you'll notice that an amazing number of people wear eyeglasses. We are so used to seeing people wear glasses that it's hard for us to imagine a time when there was no such thing. People with poor eyesight simply had to get along as best they could.

Nobody is really sure when eyeglasses were invented. In the year 1266, Roger Bacon, an English monk who made many interesting experiments, found a way to make the letters in a book larger and easier to read. He simply put a piece from a ball of glass on the book! Of course, this wasn't the same as having eyeglasses to help him.

The first evidence we have of someone actually wearing spectacles is a portrait of a cardinal painted in 1352 in Italy. He wears two framed lenses with their handles riveted together and attached over the eyes.

When printed books began to appear, eyeglasses became a real necessity for many people and the use of them began to spread. During the sixteenth century, eyeglasses were being made in large quantities in northern Italy and southern Germany. In 1784, Benjamin Franklin invented bifocals, which are two different kinds of lenses in the same pair of eyeglasses.

To understand how eyeglasses can help a person see better, you must know something about the eye. The eye is shaped like a ball, with a slight bulge at the front. At the center of this bulge is the pupil, which lets the light into the dark inside of the eye. Light passes through the pupil to the lens. The lens focuses the light, forming a picture at the back of the eyeball. Here there is a screen of light-sensitive cells called the retina.

Some people have eyeballs that are a little longer than normal, front to back; with others the eyeball may be too short, and the lens may not be able to focus a sharp picture on the retina. Eyeglasses provide the eye with an extra lens. The extra lens corrects what your own lens does, so that there is a sharp picture focused on the retina and you can see better.

Who Made the First Timepiece?

When we talk of a timepiece, we mean an instrument to measure time. But man found ways of measuring time long before he invented any instruments to do so.

The rising and setting of the sun were man's first units of time. The lengthening and shortening of shadows made by sticks, stones, and trees also gave him an idea of the general time of the day. And the movements of the stars furnished him with a kind of gigantic clock. Man noticed that as the night passed, different stars became visible.

The ancient Egyptians divided the night into twelve time periods, corresponding to the rising of twelve stars. They divided the day into twelve periods also, and our twenty-four-hour day is based on the Egyptian division of day and night. The Egyptians also made shadow clocks—blocks of wood with pointers. Eventually these shadow clocks,

SUNDIAL

CANDLE

HOURGLASS

or sundials, had twelve periods of time to divide the day—so they were the first timepieces.

The next kind of timepiece developed by man used fire and water. A candle with notches cut in the side will measure time as it burns from notch to notch. A dish with a small hole in the bottom can be set on water. After a certain period of time the floating dish will fill with water and sink.

About two thousand years ago, man developed still another kind of timepiece—the hourglass. This consisted of two hollow glass containers connected so that sand could flow from one to the other. The top container was filled with enough sand to flow through the hole for one hour.

About 140 B.C. the Greeks and Romans used the toothed wheel to improve the water clock. A float placed in a container rose as water trickled into the container. The float was connected to a toothed wheel. The wheel turned a pointer that gradually moved from one hour-mark to another.

The first true mechanical clock was invented about fourteen hundred years later. A weight was attached to a cord wound on a spool. As the cord unwound, it turned the spool, which moved a series of toothed wheels, or gears. The wheels turned a hand on a dial.

AGITATOR POST

When Was the Washing Machine Invented?

Everybody knows about washing machines, but in many homes they are still a luxury. Before any kind of mechanical washers were invented, home washing was done in a wooden or galvanized tub. The wash was rubbed on a corrugated washboard to force the water through and the dirt out. Then the wash was put through a wringer to squeeze out the excess water, and finally it was hung out on a line to dry.

One of the first home washing machines was made in 1858 by Hamilton Smith of Pittsburgh, Pennsylvania. This home washer was operated by turning a crank at the side that rotated paddles that were inside the tub. There was another early washing machine that imitated the scrubbing action of a washboard.

But these first machines were not successful. The clothes often became tangled, knotted, or torn. It wasn't until 1907 that a practical washing machine was developed that operated by motor. By 1912 nearly all makers of home washing machines were making them to be driven by electric power.

The tubs of the first washing machines were made of wood. Gradually, the manufacturers turned to metal: copper, galvanized steel, aluminum, and zinc. By 1961 practically all tubs were made of porcelain enamel, because such machines could resist the strong washing powders and all temperatures of water.

The agitator was developed in 1922. Most agitators consist of a cone with several fins at its lower end. The agitator moves the wash up and down and side to side. The fully automatic washing machine first appeared in 1937.

Most washing machines hold between eight and ten pounds of wash. They generally use between thirty-five and forty-five gallons of water per wash, and the water temperature is usually kept between 135 and 165 degrees fahrenheit.

The first successful home dryer was built in 1930. A combination washer-dryer was first put on the market in 1953.

When Were Wheels Invented?

The wheel was one of man's greatest inventions. Before men had wheels, they moved heavy loads on sleds pulled by men or oxen.

The earliest known wheels were made in ancient Mesopotamia (modern Iraq) between 3500 and 3000 B.C. They were of two kinds: the cart wheel and the potter's wheel. The potter's wheel was the ancestor of our pulleys, water wheels, gear wheels, clockwork, and other wheeled machinery.

The first carts were simply sleds mounted on wheels. The idea of mounting a sled on wheels probably came from the practice of putting logs under a sled to act as rollers. As the sled rolled forward, the rollers were picked up behind it and laid down again in front of the sled.

The earliest wheels were probably fastened solidly to their axles. Wheel and axle turned together. When a cart with wheels of this kind rounded a corner, the outer wheel traveled farther than the inner wheel. So one wheel or the other had to skid or drag.

A later invention—fastening the axle to the vehicle and letting the wheels spin freely—made turning much easier.

The first wheeled vehicles were farm carts, war chariots, royal hearses, and the sacred wagons of the gods.

Early carts and chariots were made with two wheels or with four. But the early four-wheeled vehicles were not practical. Both the front and rear axles were fastened to the body. Since neither axle could swing, the vehicle could not make sharp turns. About two thousand years ago someone developed a front axle that was pivotal so it could turn right and left.

The spoked wheel was invented in southwestern Asia about 2000 B.C.

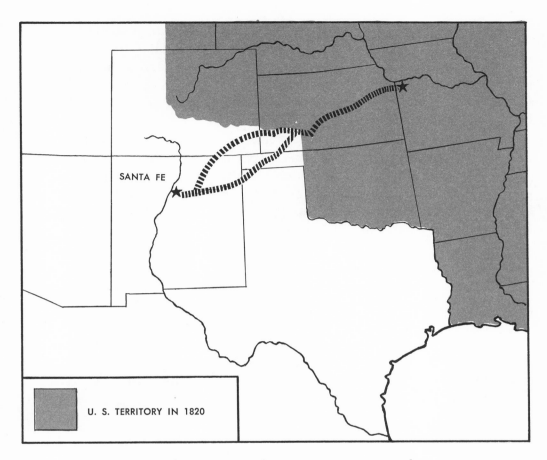

SANTA FE

U. S. TERRITORY IN 1820

What Was the Santa Fe Trail?

The Santa Fe Trail was a traders' path. It was never an actual road, but rather a broad route that followed rivers and wagon ruts. It led from the Missouri River to Santa Fe, New Mexico.

The people of Santa Fe, which was a Mexican mission town, wanted to trade with Americans, but Mexico's rulers forbade this. When Mexico rebelled against Spain in 1820, Santa Fe was opened to American trade.

The first man to reach Mexico after trade was opened was William Becknell, who is called the "Father of the Sante Fe Trail." On his return trip, snow clogged the northern trail he had planned to follow, so he took a shortcut across the Cimarron Desert. This Cimarron Cutoff became part of the Santa Fe Trail.

When Becknell returned to his home in Franklin, Missouri in January, 1822, he poured out the Mexican silver dollars he had received for his goods onto the sidewalk, to the amazement of his neighbors. People became interested in carrying on such profitable trade, so Becknell organized a trading party. They planned to take wagons where wagons had never gone before.

Becknell and his party crossed the Missouri, struck out across the Great Plains to the Arkansas River, and followed its course. Often they had to float or drag wagons across the river to avoid steep cliffs. Going through the Cimarron Cutoff meant crossing fifty miles of dry, hot wasteland without a landmark to help them find their way.

Finally they reached the Cimarron River and crossed it. They were safely past the desert. Over three hundred miles of rough travel through foothills brought them to Sante Fe. They had proved men could take wagons over the Trail.

When they returned and showed their rich profits, others flocked to the trade. From 1822 to 1843, caravans headed west each spring over the Sante Fe Trail. Trouble with Mexico stopped the trade in 1843, but after the Mexican War ended, Sante Fe was in American territory. The Trail became one of the roads serving California gold hunters.

Why Were Covered Bridges Built?

There are not many covered bridges left in America today, and those that still stand have become tourist attractions. This is not only because they are rare, but many are quite beautiful and quaint.

At one time, covered bridges dotted the American countryside from the Atlantic coast to the Ohio River. The bridges looked like square tunnels with peaked roofs. Why were these bridges built with covers?

Some people claim that the bridges were covered so that horses would not be frightened by the water underneath. Others say that they were built as a shelter for travelers in bad weather.

Actually the coverings were designed to protect the wooden framework and flooring of the bridges and keep them from rotting. Some of these covered bridges still standing today are more than one hundred years old!

Many of these bridges have been destroyed to make room for modern highways. To protect the bridges that are left, the National Society for the Preservation of Covered Bridges has been established. Many states also try to protect the bridges by making them historical landmarks.

When it comes to unusual bridges, two of the most interesting are London Bridge and the Ponte Vecchio in Florence, Italy. London Bridge was the first one over the Thames River to be built entirely of masonry. Houses were gradually erected on the bridge until it was covered with buildings. The old London Bridge was replaced by the new London Bridge about 1830.

The Ponte Vecchio was another bridge on which people lived. It was built in 1345, and is still lined with houses. Most of these houses are now used for shops.

Who Made the First Boat?

If you lived near a body of water and had never seen or heard of a boat before, what would you do? You'd probably want to get across the water or move down it in some way, and you'd look for something that would hold you up on the water.

In very much this way, primitive man probably discovered that if he tied some brush or tree trunks together, and if he used a stick or a branch as a pole or paddle, he could get across a river or lake. And thus the idea of a boat was born.

This kind of boat, consisting of objects that float being tied together, was really a raft. But the problem with a raft is that it doesn't move very fast, and water washes over it and through it.

So in looking for some kind of faster and drier boat, primitive man thought of hollowing out a tree trunk. It was faster and fairly watertight. But you couldn't carry as much in this kind of boat as on a raft, and it could easily tip over.

So primitive man tried to improve the "dug-out" kind of boat. He shaped the bow and stern for greater speed; he bulged out the sides for more stability; he flattened out the bottom. Then he invented the keel, and he tried to raise the sides by building them up with planks.

Meanwhile, those who were still using the raft began to make improvements on it, too. They put a floor on the raft composed of timbers that were squared and shaped. They built a platform on it for greater comfort and protection (which was the beginning of the deck). They built up the sides and turned up the ends. And they had a kind of boat that later on was to become an ark, or punt, or junk—all types of flat-bottomed boats.

In time, the raft and the dug-out boats began to have many features in common. From then on it was a question of combining the best features of each, depending on what kind of boat was needed. So we can say that boats as we know them today began with both these ideas first thought of by primitive man.

Who Were the First People to Use Sails?

A long, long time ago man made an important discovery, though nobody knows exactly when it happened. The discovery was that it was easy to move a boat along in the same direction as the wind.

All that was needed was to hoist up a section of skins, cloth, or something like it on a stick. With such a crude sail the boat would move along easily and it wouldn't be necessary to row it.

Of course, a real sailing vessel has another advantage: it can also sail against the wind. For this, it is necessary to know how to tack, or to approach by zigzags. It was a long time before ships and sails and this kind of know-how were developed.

On the way to this kind of use of sails, there were many steps. The ancient Egyptians had ships that used both oars and huge sails. At first, their ships were used only on the Nile River, but later they went out to sea. But the sails were only used with a following wind.

The Greeks and Romans developed a kind of ship called a galley. It used slaves to do the rowing, and it also had a sail that was used only with a following wind.

Another kind of ship they developed, called "round" ships, were used to carry cargoes. At first, these ships had only one mast with one great sail. But around the time of Christ these ships already had an additional small mast and sail in the bow, and sometimes also a small topsail.

These ships were still not able to head into the wind, but some of them could operate with the wind coming in on the side.

The Vikings also developed ships with sails, and by 800 A.D. had ships with large square sails.

EGYPTIAN

What Were the First Ocean Liners?

Today most travel across oceans is done by air, though ocean liners are still in use. Ocean-liner service across the Atlantic started in 1816. The first line to run ships on a regular schedule was the Black Ball Line of New York. Its ships sailed between New York and Liverpool, England. Soon afterward other ship lines began operating.

The early liners were sailing ships. They were called packet ships because they carried packets of mail as well as passengers. The ships were not very comfortable. First-class passengers had only small cabins. Travelers in the cheapest class, called the steerage, had no cabins at all. They slept on bunks of rough boards, stacked three deep in low, narrow spaces below decks.

On some ship lines the steerage passengers had to bring their own food. Each passenger had to show his supply of food before he was allowed aboard. The required supply included quantities of biscuits, flour, potatoes, tea, sugar, molasses, two hams, a tin pot, frying pan, mug, teapot, knife, fork and spoon. To help provide milk and food for other passengers, most packet ships had a cow and a flock of chickens on board!

The first steam-powered ship to cross the Atlantic was the American vessel *Savannah*. In 1819 she made the trip from Savannah, Georgia, to Liverpool in twenty-nine days. The *Savannah* used her sails most of the way, running on steam power only when the winds died down.

THE SAVANNAH, 1819

Sails were carried on the early steamships because seamen didn't trust the new steam power. They were afraid that the steam engine might break down in mid-ocean or that the fuel might run out.

One of the famous early steamships had paddle wheels and screw propellers. This was the *Great Eastern*. She was 692 feet long and 83 feet wide, and remained the world's largest ship for forty years.

GREEK LONG SHIP

How Did Navies Originate?

Did you know that originally the navy of a country meant all of its ships, whether used for war, the carrying of merchandise, or fishing? Today, of course, the word "navy" has come to mean a country's fighting ships and those that help in warfare.

The first navies were created when the armed men of a tribe or town went to sea in the largest ships they had in order to give battle to their enemies or raid territory from the sea. The ships used were ordinary fishing or commercial ships. Only later on were ships especially designed for purposes of war.

At the time of the ancient Greeks and Romans, the very first long ships were built for speed in war, instead of round ones to carry merchandise. When the Persians threatened to attack Athens in 483 B.C., the Greeks increased their navy from fifty to one hundred long ships. By the end of the fifth century B.C. this fleet of long ships had increased to 300 and later even to 360, which makes it quite a navy! In times of peace these warships were kept on slips and under cover in sheds.

The most ancient warships were many-oared galleys, each requiring a great number of rowers. These great rowing galleys were used to ram other ships or as a means of boarding the enemy ships.

In both the ancient Greek and Roman navies there were many similarities to the organization of a modern navy. The Greeks had a captain, a sailing master, a number of petty officers, seamen and oarsmen, and soldiers or marines who did the fighting. The Romans always had a body of soldiers, called the *classici,* who were especially assigned to service in the navy.

Today, of course, a navy is a very complicated organization with dozens of types of ships and units organized to maintain them.

When Did Men Begin Underwater Exploration?

The first underwater explorer was probably looking for something to eat.

Hundreds of thousands of years ago, people knew how to get fish from the water. These early fishermen lived on the shores of lakes in Africa, and they probably waded in to make the catch with their hands.

Wading led to swimming. Then swimmers learned how to hold their breath and became divers. The first dives were along lakeshores and seacoasts where the water was deep and clear. Gradually divers learned to explore at greater and greater depths.

They found all sorts of interesting and useful things to bring back. There were shellfish to eat, and there were beautiful colored corals and shells that people used for beads or for money. As far back as four thousand years ago, Indians did deep diving off the coast of Peru to obtain mussels, a kind of shellfish, which was one of their favorite foods.

At the same time—thousands of years ago —on the other side of the world, men were bringing up oysters from the Arabian Gulf, but not to eat. These divers wanted the pearls that sometimes grew inside the shell in the soft part of the oyster's body. The pearls were made into jewelry, just as they are now.

The men of ancient Greece and Turkey are sometimes called the fathers of modern diving. They began exploring for sponges in the Aegean Sea more than two thousand years ago, and what they learned is still useful today.

They discovered that the more air they could take down with them, the longer they could stay underwater. One of them finally thought of carrying extra air down in a device called a water bladder.

This was made from the skin of a goat, sheep, or pig. It was oiled and made waterproof. All but one opening was sewn up tightly. The diver would blow the skin full of air, and with a heavy stone to keep himself underwater, would go down into the water. He could work for some time, getting air from the inflated skin as he needed it.

DIVING WITH A WATER BLADDER

How Did Swimming Start?

Man does not swim naturally, as certain animals do. He has had to learn how to swim.

Originally, man must have learned to swim by watching animals that swim by instinct. Early man probably had to learn how to swim in order to survive under certain conditions.

The first effort man made to swim imitated a dog. Such a stroke has always been known as the "dog paddle." But then man wanted to find a way of swimming that gave him more buoyancy and an opportunity to coordinate the motions of the arms and legs. So more than two thousand years ago he developed the method of swimming known as the breast stroke. This stroke is still used by many people for restful distance swimming in rough open water.

The next stroke that man developed in swimming was the side stroke. In this stroke the "scissors kick" was used. After that came the "over-arm" side stroke. In this, the upper arm was extended out of water. It allowed a longer arm pull and produced greater speed.

The next stroke to be developed is called the Trudgen, after John Trudgen, an Englishman who introduced it in 1783. This consists of an alternate over-arm stroke and a scissors kick. He broke so many records with this stroke that many people adopted it.

Next we come to the crawl stroke. It is called that because in its original form it resembled a man crawling. It was brought to England in 1902 by Richard Cavill, who had learned it in Australia, where the natives used it. It was first called the Australian crawl. People using the crawl stroke broke so many swimming records that it was adopted as the speediest of all strokes.

By the way, swimming was rated highly in the ancient days of Greece and Rome and was used as part of the training of warriors.

How Old is the Sport of Diving?

Man probably learned to dive shortly after he learned to swim. He started jumping into the water after he found that he was able to walk into the water from land.

After he had learned to jump, he probably began to enter the water by diving head first. But it wasn't until the late nineteenth century that acrobatic or fancy diving was developed.

Gymnasts from such countries as Sweden, Germany, and Finland, who wanted to improve their acrobatic techniques, found during their practice sessions that water was softer to land on than the ground or tumbling pads. As a result of these practice sessions, the sport of fancy diving, now usually called competitive diving, was developed in Europe.

By 1904 there was great international interest in the sport. There were enough assorted dives to hold an Olympic diving championship during the Olympic Games of that year. The event was called high diving in the program of the Olympic Games.

Each dive that is permitted in competition has a value based on how difficult it is to perform. Since the first Olympic diving event, held in 1904, the list of competitive dives has been continually changing. Old-fashioned dives are discontinued, and new ones are added.

Platform diving is diving without a springboard. It is usually performed from a high platform. In springboard diving a long, flexible board that bends very easily is used. Springboard diving was developed after platform diving. It is performed closer to the water than platform diving.

Today competitive diving is one of the top sports in high schools and colleges. Many divers who enter competition during their high-school and college days continue to compete for many years.

Who Was the First to Go Up in a Balloon?

Why does a balloon go up? Air itself is made up of gases, the chief ones being oxygen and nitrogen. Certain other gases are lighter than air. One of these is helium, and that is why a balloon filled with helium rises. Hot air will also make a balloon rise, because it is lighter than cold air.

Man sent balloons up into the air before he went up with them. The first big balloon was built by two French brothers called Montgolfier. On June 5, 1783, they launched their balloon by building a fire under it. When hot air from the fire filled the balloon, the brothers released it and it floated hundreds of feet into the air.

The first live passengers in a balloon were a rooster, a duck, and a young sheep. The Montgolfier brothers put them in a basket carrier and filled a huge balloon with hot air from a fire.

This inspired two brave men to risk their lives by being the first humans to leave the ground and fly in the air. One man was the Marquis d'Arlandes; the other was Jean de Rozier, a French doctor.

In a Paris park they tied a basket to the bottom of their beautifully decorated balloon. A roaring fire filled the balloon with hot air. The two men jumped into the basket and released the ropes. They rose above the heads of the people on the ground for the first human flight. The year was still 1783.

That same year, a French scientist, Jacques Charles, filled a balloon with hydrogen and sent it up into the air. This was to avoid the danger of fire when hot air was used to fill balloons.

Later that year, Charles and a friend, Jean Robert, went up in a balloon that was filled with hydrogen. They also invented a valve that enabled them to come down by letting hydrogen escape from inside the balloon.

DURYEA

When Did Automobile Racing Begin?

Did you know that the best-attended sporting event in the whole world is the Indianapolis 500 (500-mile race) held each Memorial Day at Speedway, Indiana? Millions of people all over the world watch automobile races every year.

Quite soon after the automobile was developed, different manufacturers became involved in arguments as to who was making the fastest and most durable automobile. This led to the first international auto race in history. It was run in France in 1895, and was a 732-mile race from Paris to Bordeaux and back. The race was won by a French Panhard, traveling at an average speed of 15 miles per hour!

In 1900, James Gordon Bennett put up a trophy for a series of races. The cars that competed had to be entirely the products of the country they represented. This really started international automobile racing.

In 1906, the Automobile Club of France decided to run its own race, the Grand Prix. The cars in this contest took two days to complete 12 laps on a 64-mile course near Le Mans. Grand Prix racing developed from this and there are now such international races in Monaco, Belgium, Holland, France, England, Germany, Italy, Mexico, South Africa, and the United States.

The first important automobile race in the United States was spurred by the success of the race in France from Paris to Bordeaux. It was held in Chicago on November 28, 1895. The object was to test the speed and the stamina of American-made cars. J. Frank Duryea, one of America's leading auto manufacturing pioneers, won in a Duryea car at a speed of 7½ miles per hour.

Today, automobile racing is divided into many groups. There is stock car racing, in which a car must not be over three years old, must resemble a showroom automobile, and must use a stock production engine. There are also sports-car racing and drag racing. In drag racing, the object is to cover a prescribed straightaway distance, usually ¼ of a mile, as quickly as possible. Even drag racing has over 75 classes of cars.

Where Was Polo First Played?

Did you know that polo is the oldest game in the world played with a stick and ball? The name comes from the Tibetan word *pulu,* which means "ball."

The game of hockey, and possibly even golf and cricket, is derived from polo. The first written records of the game of polo are Persian. A book published in the year 1613 describes the game of polo already being played in Persia.

From Persia, the game spread to Constantinople, then Turkestan, Tibet, China, and Japan. From China it was imported into India. Europeans who were in India saw the game and decided to play it, too. In 1859, the first European polo club was formed, and the first rules of the European version of the game were drawn up.

In 1869 a group of officers in the British Army read about this game being played in India and decided to play it in England. The first match in England was played in 1871.

You've probably heard the expression "polo pony" in connection with this game. This comes from the early days of the game when there was a limit set to the height of the horse that could be used in a game. But there are no such limits today, and no particular breed of horse is used. But because top speed is so important, the horses are usually thoroughbreds. They are trained for the game for at least a year before they are used.

Outdoors, polo is played by two teams made up of four players each. The field is bounded on each side by sideboards eleven inches wide, and by white lines that extend across both ends. Goal posts are placed on these lines twenty-four feet apart and equidistant from the sideboards.

There are six periods of seven and one half minutes each. Horses used in the game can play only two periods each, so each player requires three horses for a game. Team play is very important in the game of polo, since changes in the position of the ball happen very suddenly, and the object is to set up a situation that will result in a score.

VEGETABLE GUM

LEATHER AND FEATHERS

GREEK BOY BLOWING
UP AIR BALL

Who Invented the Ball?

No one knows who first played with a ball. Men have been playing ball since prehistoric times. Every civilization, from primitive times to the present, has played a game using some kind of a ball.

Some early people wove reeds into rounded shapes. Others used leather stuffed with feathers for playing ball. Later, generations of Greeks and Romans added a new idea—air. A blown-up leather ball called a *follis* was used in games of catch. They also inflated balls of larger sizes with which they played a kind of football and other kicking games.

Balls have been made from many materials, depending on what was available in the particular country. North American Indians, for example, were hunters, so they used balls made of deer hide. Japanese children, on the other hand, played with balls of tightly-wadded tissue wrapped with string.

It is said that Columbus found the Indians of Central America playing with solid, black balls of vegetable gum. He took some of these balls to Europe with him and thus introduced the idea of a bouncy rubber ball.

Many of our modern ball games started as religious and magical ceremonies. Ball games were once carried on seriously by older people. Often the games retold the old beliefs about war, gods and devils, life and death.

The Egyptians were among the first people to have ceremonial ball games. Each spring two large groups of people acted out a contest between two of their gods. A round, wooden ball and crooked sticks were used. The object was to drive the ball through the opposing goal. The side that was able to knock the ball past the defenders won a victory for the god their team represented.

How Did Kindergartens Start?

Most children start first grade when they are five, six, or seven years old. But many children start going to school before first grade. They attend kindergarten or nursery school.

In the public school system of the United States, kindergarten is the class in elementary school that comes before the first grade. Children in kindergarten are at play most of their day, but they are constantly learning through their play. They learn to plan activities, to follow simple directions, and to adjust to school life.

The idea of schools for the very young began in Europe in the late 1700's and early 1800's. Industry was growing, and many mothers who went to work had to take their youngest children into the factories with them.

One answer to this problem was the development of the infant school. The first infant school was started in Scotland in 1816 by a man called Robert Owen. He set up a system of schools for all the children in a mill town who were under twelve. The very youngest children were placed in an infant school as soon as they had learned to walk.

But even before this, educators had been concerned with the training of young children, and had many theories about this. A German teacher called Friedrich Froebel developed his own theory and method of teaching young children. He opened a school in Blankenburg, Germany, in 1837, and named his school *Kindergarten,* or "children's garden." This was the first kindergarten.

FRIEDRICH FROEBEL

Froebel believed that children expressed their interests through their play. He developed a set of play materials, which he called gifts, for use in the kindergarten. The gifts included six soft, colored balls, and several wooden spheres, cubes, and cylinders. In addition to using the gifts, children in Froebel's kindergarten sang songs, played games, and listened to stories.

Other educators later developed other ways of helping very young children start learning in kindergarten.

When Did Free Education Start in America?

It is hard for today's student to realize how difficult it was to get free schooling for everyone, and to make sure that all children went to school.

Many people thought that poor children did not need to be educated. They insisted that the government had no right to take tax money from one man to educate another man's children. And poor families wanted their children to work, because they needed the money.

In 1647, the colony of Massachusetts passed a school law that required every town with at least fifty families to have an elementary school, and every town with one hundred families to have a Latin grammar school (these were schools that taught reading, writing and Latin, but no science, history, mathematics, or English).

This law marked the beginning of American public education. Other New England colonies passed similar laws. The New Englanders who settled the West took this idea with them.

The New England elementary schools were public schools open to all children. They were built by the town, and some tax money was used to run them. But parents who could afford it had to pay a fee for each child.

Sometimes there was not enough money to keep these schools going. Then parents had to pay if they wanted their children in school. In 1827 Massachusetts passed a law saying that the schools would have to be paid for entirely out of tax money. Most of the other New England states soon followed.

The struggle for tax money to pay for schools went on, state by state. It was not completely won in New York until 1867, and in

Pennsylvania until 1868. Public schools in New Jersey were not free until 1871. Delaware, Maryland, and the southern states did not have free education until after the Civil War.

The midwestern states did better, because the Federal Government helped start their school systems. It gave the states free, unsettled land that could be sold for money to start school funds. Before the end of the nineteenth century, there was free education in all the states.

EAGLE ON AMERICAN COINS

Why Is the Eagle Our National Symbol?

In 1782 Congress decided that the American bald eagle would be the emblem of the United States. The eagle is shown on our national seal with wings outstretched, holding a spray of olives in one claw and arrows in the other. But when shown on such things as coins or military emblems, the eagle can be pictured in a variety of other postures.

211

Why did we choose the eagle to be our national symbol? Eagles, which are the most kingly of birds, have always been considered symbols of power. In ancient times, the Roman legions had images of the imperial eagle on their standards. Many European empires since that time have had eagles as their symbols. So it was natural to turn to this majestic bird when our country was deciding on a national symbol.

The bald eagle, which is the American symbol, is found only in the United States and Canada. In fact, when the colonists came here from Europe, they saw this bird for the first time and called it "bald headed." By this they meant that it had a white head, since "bald" originally meant "white." The bald eagle is dark brown, except for white tail feathers and white plumes on the head and neck.

It is not among the largest eagles. Its wingspread, from tip to tip, is six to eight feet, and the length of its body is about thirty-five inches. It has fierce yellow eyes and big "brows" that give it an imposing look.

The bald eagle is very majestic in its flight, especially when it soars or swoops. It has such good eyesight that it can see a small object on the water from a distance of three miles!

During the summer, the bald eagle eats dead fish or goes after its favorite prey, the fish hawk. In winter, it stuffs itself on the flesh of a dead calf if it can find one in the fields, and it will try to kill wild ducks or geese.

It likes to live near a river, lake, or seacoast. It builds its nest in a tall tree or sometimes on a rock ledge. The nest is a great heap of sticks, to which the pair of eagles return every year. Their big white eggs are usually two in number. It is believed that some bald eagles live as long as one hundred years!

Where Did Hummingbirds Originate?

Sometimes we hear about strange and interesting creatures that are found far off in exotic lands. Well, one of the most remarkable creatures of all is found right here—a native of North and South America. This is the hummingbird, the smallest and most brilliant of birds.

There are about five hundred different kinds of hummingbirds in South America and sixteen species in western North America. The only hummingbird found east of the Mississippi River is the ruby-throated hummingbird.

The hummingbird gets its name from the humming sound made by its vibrating wings. A hummingbird doesn't fly the way other birds do. Its wings move so rapidly that they cannot be seen clearly by the eye, so that when you look at a hummingbird hovering over a flower, it seems to be suspended in mid-air as if by magic!

A hummingbird has a long tongue that can be folded lengthwise to form a sucking tube. It sticks this tongue into flowers and sucks up the nectar, somewhat the way butterflies do. It eats spiders and insects it finds on plants, and sometimes it captures them on the wing!

The bill of the hummingbird varies with the species. In some cases, the slender bill is shorter than the rest of the head, as with most birds. But some hummingbirds have a bill that is actually longer than the rest of the body. One kind, the sicklebill hummingbird, has a bill that curves downward like a hook.

The ruby-throated hummingbird, which is found in the eastern part of the United States, is only about three-and-a-half inches long, including the bill. It builds a nest shaped like a cup that is only an inch and a half wide! This delicate little nest is made of fine fibers, plant down, and bits of lichens, and is fastened in place with spider webs.

The way the hummingbird feeds its young is interesting, too. After swallowing soft insects and partly digesting them, the mother bird puts her bill into the open beak of the nestling and squirts the food into the young bird's mouth!

How Did National Anthems Originate?

A national anthem is a patriotic song that is sung or played on official occasions as a special sign of respect for a country. National anthems and patriotic songs serve to unite a people in their common hopes and ideals.

The origin of many national anthems is unknown. Often a melody was already popular as a folk song when someone set a patriotic text to it. Only a few melodies were actually written to be national anthems. The most famous of these is the anthem of West Germany, which was originally composed for Austria by the great composer Franz Joseph Haydn.

Several older national anthems and patriotic songs have the same melodies but different words. Some of them have even been sung as war songs by opposing armies in the same battle. The British anthem, "God Save the Queen," has provided the melody for patriotic songs in Denmark, Germany, Russia, Switzerland, and all English-speaking areas of the world. In the United States the words of "America" are sung to this same melody.

"God Save the Queen" first appeared as a tune in 1619. It was written by the English composer John Bull. The first public performance of the anthem took place on September 28, 1745.

The national anthem of the United States was written during the War of 1812. Francis Scott Key, a Baltimore lawyer, was aboard one of the British ships that attacked Fort McHenry. All night long, Key watched the attack. When he saw the American flag at dawn, still flying over the fort, he was so moved that he wrote the words of "The Star-Spangled Banner" on the back of an envelope. For the tune, he had in mind an old English song called "To Anacreon in Heaven."

The "Marseillaise," the French national anthem, was the battle song of the French revolutionary period (1789–1815). The words and music were written by Claude Joseph Rouget de Lisle, a captain in the French Army. It was declared the official national anthem of France in July, 1795.

FRANCIS SCOTT KEY

JOHN BULL

FRANZ JOSEPH HAYDN

ROUGET DE LISLE

215

U. S. FLAG OF 1777

UNION FLAG OF HOLLAND

Why Does the American Flag
Have Stars and Stripes?

It may surprise a great many people, but the exact reason why the American flag has stars and stripes is not really known. Scholars have studied the question and there are many explanations, but no one is really sure.

The Continental Congress, on June 14, 1777, "Resolved that the Flag of the United States be 13 stripes alternate red and white, that the Union be 13 stars white in a blue field representing a new constellation." But nobody knows why Congress adopted that design.

Some scholars believe that perhaps Congress had taken the idea of using stars and stripes from George Washington's coat of arms. But others believe that Washington would not have allowed his coat of arms to be used for the Republic's first flag.

There is also the story that relates how Betsy Ross made the first flag for George Washington. He is supposed to have come to her sewing shop with a rough drawing. Betsy Ross probably did make the first official flag with stars and stripes, because there is a record that Congress paid her for the job. Yet scholars believe that the American flag did not originate with Betsy Ross, George Washington, or the Continental Congress. They now trace the idea for it back to the Dutch flag as well as the English flag.

The Dutch flag goes back to the sixteenth century and was a striped red-and-white flag. The striped flag was also the flag of the Dutch, who settled in 1639 in New York. So it was a common sight in the northern colonies and became a symbol of religious and political freedom. Striped flags were used by various groups right up to the time of the Revolution.

The stars are believed to have come from the Dutch flag, from Rhode Island's flag, or from the stars on Washington's coat of arms. They were probably chosen to represent a new country being born, the way a new constellation suddenly appears in the sky.

How Did National Parks Start?

One of the greatest pleasures in traveling through the United States is to visit a national park or national monument. Just think what a loss it would be to us if these lovely or historic places weren't preserved and guarded and kept up in good condition.

National parks and monuments are areas of great scenic, historic, and scientific importance that have been set aside by the United States Government for the use and enjoyment of the people. Every year millions of people visit the parks, monuments, and other areas that make up the National Park System. The national parks in Canada are also popular with tourists.

The National Park System had its beginning in 1870. A small group of men had just completed a month-long exploration of the Yellowstone region. They were gathered around a campfire, and after hours of discussion the men decided that they should not claim this wonderland for themselves. They felt that it should be set aside for the use and enjoyment of all the people.

So they started a campaign, and two years later, in 1872, an Act of Congress, signed by President Ulysses S. Grant, made the Yellowstone region a "public park or pleasuring ground." This was the first national park in the whole world!

In the years that followed, other beautiful regions of the country were set aside for the people. To manage these parks, the National Park Service was set up by Act of Congress on August 25, 1916.

In a national park, park rangers are on duty at all times to answer questions and to help visitors in any difficulty. Nature walks, guided tours, and campfire talks are offered by specially-trained staff members. The park service also protects the animals and plants within the parks.

When Was the Capitol in Washington Built?

In the Capitol Building in Washington, D.C., the Congress of the United States meets to debate bills and make laws. The Capitol is also the site of the Presidential Inauguration.

This huge, impressive building dominates the skyline of Washington. Wide avenues radiate from the Capitol like spokes of a great wheel.

The cornerstone of the Capitol was laid in 1793 by George Washington. The main portion of the building, made of Virginia sandstone, was constructed between 1793 and 1827. The House and Senate wings, built of Massachusetts white marble, were added between 1851 and 1865.

The Capitol's iron dome, which rises to a height of 288 feet, is capped by the Statue of Freedom. This statue, made by the American sculptor Thomas Crawford, was set onto the dome during the Civil War in 1862. Abraham Lincoln watched as it was placed in position and 35 cannons roared in salute. Encircling the base of the dome are 36 columns, representing the states in the Union when the dome was completed.

The Capitol has had several renovations. It was burned by the British in the War of 1812. The fire destroyed the original wooden roofing, much of the Capitol's interior, and many marble columns. Then in 1961 the East Front of the Capitol was remodeled. It is on the steps of the East Front that the President takes his oath on Inauguration Day.

Near the Capitol are the Supreme Court and the Library of Congress. The Court, of white marble, symbolizes the prestige and solemnity of the law. Here, in the highest court of the land, the nine justices of the Supreme Court meet.

THE U. S. CAPITOL IN 1800

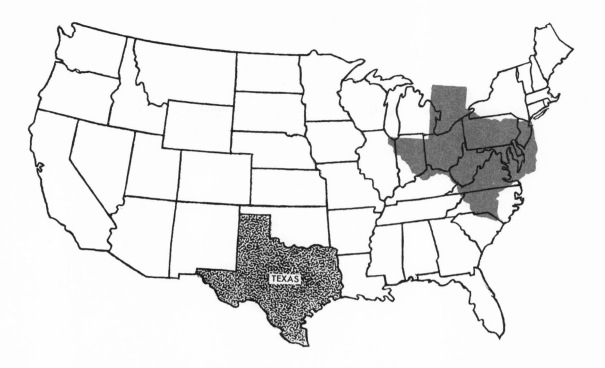

Why Is Texas Called the "Lone Star State"?

For a long time it has been very popular to make jokes about Texas. Usually these jokes refer to its tremendous size and the size of everything in it.

There's a good reason for this. It's as far across Texas as it is from New York City to Chicago. The area of Texas is 267,339 square miles, which makes it 25 percent larger than France and five times as large as England. It is as large as the whole of New England plus New York, New Jersey, Pennsylvania, Delaware, Maryland, Virginia, and West Virginia!

The first white men in the land now called Texas were survivors from a party of shipwrecked Spaniards. They were cast on the Gulf shore in 1528, and some of them later wandered across to the Gulf of California. As a result of their wandering, Spain claimed not only Texas, but all the region that is now southwestern United States.

But Spain made no effort to take possession of Texas for more than 150 years. In the meantime, France also established a claim to Texas. Then the Spaniards began to settle the country. By 1750 they had established several missions.

In 1821 Mexico, of which Texas was then a part, broke away from Spain and became an independent nation. That same year Stephen F. Austin came to Texas with a colony of immigrants from the United States. Quarrels arose between the colonists and the Mexican Government. The Texans revolted against Mexico in 1835.

The Mexicans tried to put down the revolt but were defeated by Sam Houston in 1836. This made Texas independent, and for ten years Texas was a republic, with a congress and government like that of the United States. The congress adopted a red, white, and blue flag bearing a single star. This gave Texas its popular name, the "Lone Star State." In 1845 Texas was admitted as a state into the United States.

When Was the First Oil Well Drilled in the United States?

Long before man thought of drilling for oil, or petroleum, he was using it. Ancient peoples, including the Egyptians and Chinese, used it as a medicine. In India it was used for lighting. And more recently, the American Indians were using petroleum before the white man came. To hold it, they dug pits in the ground. The white men imitated the practice of the Indians and used to sell the mineral oil as a cure for many ailments!

Until the middle of the nineteenth century, men collected crude oil where it seeped naturally from the earth. At that time, people lighted their homes with lamps in which they burned whale oil. Then they began to distil oil from coal, which produced a product called kerosene. At the same time, work was being done on petroleum to make it a source of lamp oil. So the time was ripe for someone to find a way of obtaining more of this petroleum, which was becoming more and more useful.

Two New York lawyers named George Bissel and Jonathan Eveleth, formed a company to prospect for oil in Pennsylvania. They secured the services of Colonel E. L. Drake, a retired railroad conductor, and set him to drilling near the little town of Titusville, Pennsylvania.

On August 27, 1859, after he had drilled down only 69½ feet, Drake struck oil. Soon he was pumping eight barrels a day, then twenty. The petroleum was a cheaper and surer source of lamp oil than the dangerous business of hunting whales. So it quickly found a market.

Excitement ran high. Thousands of people came to see the Drake well. Soon the first oil rush in history was on! Farms were leased. More wells were sunk. Many people became suddenly rich. Oil towns sprang up overnight. The flood of oil mounted, and now the refining and transportation of the oil became the big problems. But the age of petroleum had come!

Today there are four great oil regions on earth, but the United States still supplies about 60 percent of the world's petroleum.

Who Discovered Greenland?

If there is any part of the world that you would not expect to be called a green land, it is Greenland!

Most of Greenland is covered by an icecap more than ten thousand feet thick in some places. Only the hardiest plants and animals can survive the climate at the edges of this icecap. Winters are bitter cold, and summers are short and cool.

There are thin patches of soil with grasses, heather, and low, flowering plants. But much of the ice-free surface is barren rock, thinly covered by mosses and lichens.

Why then is this place called Greenland?—for the same reason a real-estate development is called "Pleasant Hills," or some such name, when actually the place may be quite unattractive: the real-estate developer wants to attract customers.

In A.D. 982 an Icelander named Eric Thorvaldsson came to southwestern Greenland. This rugged man, better known as Eric the Red, had been exiled from Iceland for three years for killing a man. Eric spent his three-year exile exploring the western land described by Icelandic sailors.

Three years later he returned to Iceland and told the people about his explorations. He wanted settlers to be eager to go to this land, so he made it sound attractive by naming it Greenland!

Today there are fewer than thirty-five thousand people living in Greenland, which is a very small number for such a large place. Most of them live in the ice-free areas of the island's southwest coast. Only two thousand five hundred persons live in eastern Greenland, and fewer than six hundred live in the north.

Who Discovered Medicine?

A doctor practices medicine—and so the first man who could help someone feel better was really, in a way, the first doctor. For example, a caveman who pulled a thorn out of somebody's finger was doing what a doctor does.

Primitive people practiced a kind of medicine that we would call magic. They used chants or songs, or a stew of herbs and leaves. Or, by accident, they may have discovered that the warmth of a fire eased a sprained shoulder, or an herb drink helped a stomach-ache. Many primitive peoples of today can set and splint a broken bone, or use plants that are laxatives or that will put people to sleep.

But doctors as such seem to have existed from the earliest civilizations. The Babylonians left medical writings describing various diseases so clearly that doctors today can recognize them. The ancient Egyptians had medical treatments, and these included pills and ointments containing drugs. They even performed surgical operations on the outer surfaces of the body.

A man called Aesculapius was the earliest physician in Greek history. He practiced a kind of magic medicine. But gradually true medicine began to develop. A man called Hippocrates, who lived about 400 B.C., did so much to rescue medicine from such magic and superstition that he is called the "Father of Medicine."

WITCH DOCTOR USING MAGIC

In his writings he taught that the physician should observe the patient closely and accurately. He should use gentle treatment and try to encourage the natural healing process. The physician should never risk harming the patient. He should keep the patient's secrets.

Hippocrates also recognized and described many diseases. Some of the medical facts he observed are as true today as they were over two thousand years ago. So perhaps we can call him the world's first doctor in terms of what we mean by that today.

Who Discovered Insulin?

Insulin is used for the treatment of a disease called diabetes. When a person has this disease, some fault in his body chemistry keeps it from using starches and sugar to make energy.

A large gland called the pancreas makes a substance called insulin that the body needs to use starches and sugar. The body of a person with diabetes either does not make enough insulin or does not use its insulin. If this disease goes untreated, he suffers from extreme thirst, loses weight, feels weak, and may eventually become unconscious and die.

However, these things need not happen to a person with diabetes now that insulin is manufactured. The diabetic patient can take it by daily injection. With this manufactured insulin and a regular diet, he can lead a normal life.

Doctors had known for some time that a person suffering from diabetes could not make use of the sugar in his body. The problem was how to provide diabetics with insulin. Scientists thought they knew the answer: give a diabetic insulin taken from the pancreas of a healthy animal. But no one had been able to extract insulin.

This was the achievement of Frederick Grant Banting, a Canadian doctor and scientist who was born in 1891 near Alliston, Ontario. He was teaching in London, Ontario, and one evening, while preparing a lecture on the pancreas, he suddenly realized how he might extract insulin. He went to the University of Toronto and asked Professor John Macleod, director of a large laboratory, for help. Macleod agreed to let him use the laboratory for a few weeks.

In May, 1921, with the help of Charles Best, a young graduate student, he set to work. They worked day and night, and within several weeks obtained the first insulin from the pancreas of a dog. By January, 1922, after many tests, they were able to give insulin to a diabetic, a young boy near death. He showed immediate improvement. Other patients given insulin improved, too. An important step forward in medical history had been made.

X-RAY TUBE   ROENTGEN

Who Discovered the X-Ray?

Did you know that the story of X-rays started more than a hundred years ago?

In the middle of the nineteenth century, a man named Heinrich Geissler discovered that when electricity was discharged under high voltage through tubes in a partial vacuum, beautiful light effects were produced. Later on, Sir William Crookes proved that the luminosity was caused by electrified particles.

Next, Heinrich Hertz showed that these rays would pass through thin sheets of gold or platinum. His pupil, Lenard, made "windows" of such substances, so that the rays could pass out of the tube to the outer air.

Now we come to the actual discovery of the X-ray. In 1895, Wilhelm Roentgen was experimenting with one of these tubes, but one without "windows." He noticed that certain nearby crystals were glowing brilliantly. Since he knew that the rays that had been discovered before (called cathode rays) could not pass through the glass to produce this effect, he suspected that there must be some other kind of rays present, too.

These invisible rays, which were so different from the other rays and from light, could not be explained so he called them X-rays. By this he meant "rays of unknown nature." Later on, scientists called them Roentgen Rays, and this name is still used by many scientists.

X-rays are produced in an X-ray tube. Most of the air is pumped out. There are two electrodes, and the electrons travel from one (the cathode) to the other (the anode). The target is made of tungsten, and it stops the electrons suddenly. Most of the energy of these electrons is changed to heat, but some of it becomes X-radiation. X-rays can penetrate objects, because they have a very short wavelength. The shorter the wavelength, the more penetrating the rays become.

When Was the Computer Developed?

What is a computer? An automatic computer may run by itself for hours or days, performing millions and millions of steps in solving a problem. A computer is able to handle whole problems, which may include thousands of pieces of information. This information may be numbers made up of digits; words made up of letters; or sets of digits, letters, and other signs. Such information is called a machine word.

The computer then adds, multiplies, sorts, compares, or does any one of hundreds of other kinds of figuring or reasoning. The computer carries out all its work on the machine words by following a long list of instructions called a program. The instructions on a program are fed into the computer by a person. But the computer analyzes for itself all of these detailed instructions. And finally, the computer solves the problem and prints out the answers on special, coded computer forms.

Computers usually do not have any moving parts, but do their work by means of small flows of electrons or particles of electricity.

The first automatic computer that really worked came into being in 1944 at Harvard University. The men who made the computer were Professor Howard Aiken of Harvard and a group of engineers from International Business Machines Corporation.

They called the machine the Harvard IBM Mark I. This was the first machine that could carry out long lists of figuring operations of a great many kinds, all in the proper order.

This machine worked with twenty-three decimal digits; it could add two such numbers in 3/10 of a second, and it could multiply them in four seconds. The machine used electrical and mechanical parts, but not electronic ones. As soon as good electronic parts were put into use, the speed of computers rose rapidly.

Now the most powerful automatic computers can add more than one hundred thousand numbers a second, and they can multiply more than ten thousand numbers a second.

How Long Have Secret Codes Been Used?

Codes are a way of writing something in secret; that is, no one will be able to read it who doesn't know the code. Ciphers are another way of doing this. In a code, each word is written as a secret code word or code number. In a cipher each letter is changed. Secret writing that uses codes and ciphers is called cryptography.

Codes and ciphers have played an important part in the history of the world. Julius Caesar, the Roman ruler who conquered almost all of Europe about two thousand years ago, used a cipher when he sent secret messages to his generals. During the American Revolution, George Washington's spies used a code to send him information about the enemy. His spies had a code book that listed numbers for all the words they might need. The messages were written and decoded according to the numbers given in the book.

Do you know that today you see codes being used all around you? When you go into a store, you may find numbers or letters on certain goods. These are codes used by storekeepers. The codes show how much was paid for the goods, or when they were added to the stock.

Businessmen use codes to hide plans from competitors. Sometimes personal letters or diaries are written in code. Many people enjoy working out codes and ciphers simply as a hobby.

In the sixteenth century, codes and ciphers were very popular among scientists. They wrote messages to each other in code so that no one would learn their secrets.

An Italian scientist of that time, Giambattista della Porta, wrote a book about codes. He is sometimes called "The Father of Modern Cryptography." When Galileo, the famous Italian astronomer and physicist, discovered the phases of Venus, he recorded his discovery in a kind of cipher.

Who Started the Boy Scouts of America?

Many years ago, an American businessman called W. D. Boyce was in London. In the fog, he couldn't find the house of a friend he was looking for, so he stopped a boy who was passing and asked for directions.

The boy not only gave him directions, but guided Mr. Boyce to the house. When the American offered the boy a coin, it was refused. "I am a Boy Scout," the boy said. "Helping you was my daily good turn—Boy Scouts do not accept tips."

Mr. Boyce was so interested by this explanation that he wanted to learn more about Boy Scouts. He went to the London Scout headquarters, where he was told the history of the movement and provided with pamphlets and other printed matter.

He learned that the Boy Scout movement had been founded in England by Lord Baden-Powell when he returned to England after the Boer War. Baden-Powell had become interested in various boys' organizations and had combined their best features with ideas of his own, finally developing the Boy Scout program.

Mr. Boyce was so impressed with what he learned that on February 8, 1910, he incorporated the Boy Scouts of America. Scouts observe this anniversary with much ceremony every year. In 1916 the Boy Scouts of America were granted a federal charter, because Boy Scouts had been so helpful in many ways in their various communities. The charter gives protection to the name and insignia of scouting and authorizes the members to wear an official uniform.

From the time the Boy Scout movement started in the United States, more than seventeen million boys and leaders have been registered members. There are three age groups in scouting, with programs and activities adapted to the interests of boys at each level. The Cub Scouts are boys eight through ten years of age; the Boy Scouts, eleven through thirteen; and the Explorers, fourteen and up.

WILLIAM BOOTH

How Did the Salvation Army Start?

Today there are very few countries in the world where the Salvation Army and its work are not known. Yet this great organization began in the mind of a single man. This man was William Booth.

In 1865 Booth was a young Methodist revivalist who walked the dreariest streets in London's East End. There he prayed for the men and women who gathered around him, though they usually jeered at him and even threw stones.

But Booth refused to be discouraged. Day after day, he went into the streets with his wife and a few followers. Day after day, this small group invited people to come to meetings held in a tent, a dance hall or an old warehouse. During these meetings they tried to bring religion to the poor and to do whatever they could to relieve their misery.

At first the group called themselves the Christian Mission, but in 1878 they organized themselves as the Salvation Army. The organization adopted a kind of "military" system. Its founder, William Booth, was called General, and its workers wore uniforms. It grew with amazing speed.

The Army as a whole is divided into territories, which are made up of divisions, which in turn consist of corps and outposts (mission stations). The General and other international officers operate from the international headquarters in London.

The Salvation Army has set up about eighteen thousand posts throughout the world. At these posts it carries on its social work. Its services include hotels with inexpensive food and lodging, factories, farm colonies, orphanages, rescue homes, day nurseries, insurance societies, and so on.

The Salvation Army was organized in the United States by George Scott Railton in 1880. Evangeline Booth, daughter of William Booth, became the Commander in the United States in 1904, and in 1934 she became the first woman General of the Salvation Army.

FIRE ENGINE ABOUT 1825
HAND-PULLED
HAND-PUMPED

When Were the First Fire Fighters Organized?

Man has always known that fire can be his friend and servant, and can also be a great destroyer. Primitive man, however, didn't have the problem of fighting fires as we have, simply because he didn't live in houses that were grouped together—in other words, in villages, towns, and cities.

But when men began to live together in large groups, they had to concern themselves with the problem of fighting fires. And so, long before Christ (in fact, many centuries before), fire brigades were organized. They existed in many cities throughout the world. The ancient Romans had fire brigades to protect the city, and used slaves for this work.

By the way, the Romans also developed the first means of throwing a continuous stream of water. Roman firemen used axes, blankets, buckets, ladders, and poles! In the Middle Ages there was some organized fire fighting here and there, but it was not very efficient.

Fire fighting as we know it was started in England. It came about because fire-insurance companies were organized, and they, of course, were interested in cutting down the loss from fires and preventing their spread. The officials of London hadn't done much about this problem, so the insurance companies organized fire brigades of their own.

Probably the first such brigade was organized in 1722, and then others followed. These insurance companies would place fire marks on the buildings they insured, and probably didn't bother too much with other buildings. In 1833 the first organized fire fighting system for the city of London was set up.

In the United States, as in most parts of the world, before the local authorities (of the city or town) set up fire brigades, the citizens themselves would organize volunteer fire fighters. In fact, the job of fighting fires is still done mostly by volunteers. There are about one million fire fighters in the United States—and only one out of ten is a paid fireman working full time!

When Did Labor Unions Begin?

In ancient Greece and Rome slaves did much of the labor. Food and shelter were provided by their masters in return. During the Middle Ages, serfs were required to work for the lord of the manor in return for protection. Laborers were tillers of the soil, not wage earners.

As trade increased, the town replaced the feudal manor as the principal place where people worked. Merchants and artisans organized into associations, or guilds, for each craft. These artisans and craftsmen worked at home or in small shops, and there were a few factories with many workers laboring together.

This was all changed toward the end of the eighteenth century with the coming of the Industrial Revolution. As machines were developed that could produce more goods faster than the individual worker, factories were built to house the machines. Handwork and small shops all but disappeared. The worker had to seek a job from an employer, and he was paid in wages for his services. And when workers had problems, they had no one who would listen to them.

Conditions in the early English cotton mills were particularly bad. So the workers began to organize into unions. They felt that if they stood together, their grievances and complaints had a better chance of a fair hearing.

These trade unions were founded in the towns as small clubs of skilled craftsmen. In 1868 the Trades Union Congress, the first big and successful union organization, was formed in Manchester, England.

There was a great need for unions in the early days of the American Republic, but they were hard to organize and public opinion was against them. The first union in the United States was formed in 1792 by eight shoemakers in Philadelphia. It did not last a year.

During the early years of the nineteenth century, unions began to form city-wide trade associations. The first was the Mechanics' Union of Trade Associations. It was founded in Philadelphia in 1828. The first important national labor federation was formed in 1866.

How Old Is Weaving?

Weaving is the method by which threads are interlaced to make cloth. The principles of weaving have not changed through the ages. Modern textile mills do quickly on machines what ancient peoples did slowly by hand.

Cavemen, who lived about thirty thousand years ago, learned how to weave. They used straw, stalks of reed, or other materials to weave baskets. Nets for fishing and the capture of game were also woven by man in prehistoric times.

What these ancient peoples didn't realize was that cords, which are really yarns, could be interlaced to make soft fabrics or cloths. The idea of weaving cloth seems to have developed in certain particular places and then spread all over the world.

The most ancient woven cloths that we have records of are these: the Near East, about 5000 B.C.; Egypt, about 4000 B.C.; central Europe, about 2500 B.C.; China, about 1200 B.C.; and the Peruvian coast of South America, about 1500 B.C.

The use of different fibers for weaving developed in various places according to what was available. Wool was first used when the sheep was domesticated, about 1600 B.C. Cotton was first used in India and spread from there through Asia and finally to Europe.

Silk fibers were first used in China. On the other side of the world, in ancient Peru, the cotton plant and llamas and alpacas were providing material for making cloth. And since man has always liked to have colorful clothing, it is interesting to know that the ancient Peruvians had already found ways to have more than 150 tints and shades in their cloth.

Today, of course, most weaving is done in mills. But in many cases the weaving of rugs and tapestries is still done by hand by skillful artists.

EARLY GREEK POTTER

When Was the First Pottery Made?

Wet clay can be modeled into almost any shape. After a few days the clay becomes dry and hard. If the clay is baked, or fired, the nature of the clay changes. It can no longer be made soft and workable. Objects made of baked clay are called ceramics. Ceramic vessels (containers) are called pottery.

The first pottery was made about ten thousand years ago. To keep grain from spilling through the holes in baskets, the insides were smeared with wet clay. Perhaps one day a basket of this kind fell unnoticed on a campfire. The reeds burned away, and the first piece of pottery had been made.

There are three kinds of pottery—earthenware, stoneware, and porcelain. The simplest kind of pottery is made from clay and then fired. It is called earthenware. It is porous, and water will slowly leak out of it.

As time passed, people learned that certain rocks could be melted into a kind of glass. The rocks were crushed to a fine powder and mixed with clay. The pottery made from this clay is called stoneware. Stoneware, which does not leak, can be used over a fire for cooking.

During the Tang dynasty (618–906 A.D.) the Chinese began to make another kind of pottery. It was made from a special white clay mixed with powdered rock. This pottery, called porcelain, was fired in a kiln almost hot enough to melt iron. Porcelain is translucent (light can be seen through it) and hard.

About 3300 B.C., the potter's wheel came into use. The potter puts a ball of wet clay onto the center of the wheel. As the wheel spins, the potter shapes the clay by pressing it with his fingers. Pots made on wheels are always round.

All the ancient civilizations—Egyptians, Persians, Mesopotamians—made beautiful pottery. The Egyptians used glazes of many colors. The Persians painted on their pottery as far back as 4000 B.C. The ancient Greeks and Romans also made large pottery vases. But it was the Chinese who made the most beautiful pottery in ancient times.

Who Painted the First Pictures?

The first artists on earth were the cavemen. On the walls of caves in southern France and Spain there are colored drawings of animals that were made from 30,000 to 10,000 B.C.

Many of these drawings are amazingly well-preserved, because the caves were sealed up for many centuries. Early man drew the wild animals that he saw all around him. Very crude human figures, drawn in lifelike positions, have been found in Africa and eastern Spain.

The cave artists filled the cave walls with drawings in rich, bright colors. The pigments used were earth ochers (iron oxides varying in color from light yellow to deep orange) and manganese (a metallic element). These were crushed into a fine powder, mixed with grease, like animal fat, and put on with some sort of brush.

Sometimes the pigments were used in sticks, like crayons. The grease mixed with the powdered pigments made the paint fluid and the pigment particles stuck together. The cavemen must have made brushes out of animal hairs or plants, and sharp tools out of flint for drawing and scratching lines.

One of the first civilizations was developed in Egypt, and they had artists who painted pictures. Much Egyptian art was created for the pyramids and tombs of kings and other important people. Artists recorded scenes from the life of the person in wall paintings in the burial chamber. They used watercolor paints and washes.

Another early civilization, the Aegean, also developed the art of painting to a surprising degree. Their artists had a free and graceful style, and they painted sea life, animals, flowers, athletic games, and processionals. Their paintings were made on wet plaster walls, a kind of painting we now call fresco.

So you see that painting goes back to the very earliest times of man and civilization.

When Was Sculpture First Created?

It may be that sculpture is the oldest of the arts. People carved before they painted or even designed homes.

Only a few objects survive to show what sculpture was like thousands of years ago. But people living today in primitive societies often carve things that may be similar to prehistoric sculpture.

Prehistoric sculpture was never made to be beautiful. It was always made to be used in rituals. Figures of men, women, and animals were made to honor the forces of nature, which were worshipped as evil or good spirits.

The earliest civilizations of man also used sculpture to express their beliefs. The ancient Egyptians believed in life after death, and they carved life-size and even larger statues of their rulers, nobles, and gods. They were placed in tombs, and the Egyptians believed the spirit of the dead person would return to these images.

One of the greatest periods in the history of sculpture came with the Greek civilization that started about 600 B.C. For the Greeks, sculpture became one of their most important forms of expression.

The Greeks made the human figure the principal object of their art. Sculptors in Greece were always looking for better ways to represent the human figure.

During the first one thousand years of Christianity, very little sculpture was produced. But after the year 1000, and for the next three centuries, some of the most impressive Christian churches were built and much great sculpture was created for these churches.

Later on, during the Renaissance, the human figure was again glorified and great sculptors produced masterpieces that are among the world's greatest treasures.

How Did Poetry Originate?

First of all, what is poetry? Poetry is language that is deeply felt and deeply moving, written or spoken in a special form. The rhythm of a poem is what makes it different from prose.

From this we can get an idea of how poetry began. Of course, we can never know who first created it or where. But because we know something of the way primitive people acted, we can guess at the beginnings of poetry.

Man had some sort of rhythmic dance even before he had a language. He made sounds and gestures and uttered grunts and cries at special times, such as before a battle or a hunt. Also, he created a drum on which he could beat in many ways. And soon he was using sounds and the drums to send magic words to his gods.

Primitive man then began to develop the dance, and it became more and more complicated as it advanced. Soon the words of the chant to the gods became more important than just sounds from the drum. The words could be understood. In time, the leading performer of such a ceremony was actually a kind of poet, or bard.

At the same time, over thousands of years, man was influenced by rhythms he saw everywhere about him—in the sound of water, winds, in the flight of birds, in the rhythmic movements of animals. In trying to imitate some of the rhythms, he was using a kind of poetic imagination.

Then, but still centuries ago, these dances, chants, and incantations reached a point where men kept a record of them. They were handed down from generation to generation, and they were a form of poetry.

By the time of the Greeks, during the fifth century B.C., poetry was being written especially for certain occasions, but it was still performed with music and dance. Later on, a type of poetry was developed by the Greeks that told stories of heroic events or described the lives of various types of people.

Where Was the First Theater?

The theater as we know it took a long time to develop. The idea of drama itself had its beginnings in religion.

The Chinese first performed dramalike dances in their temples. Later a playhouse was used. It was just a platform without curtains or changes of lights that had a roof decorated like the roof of a temple.

The Japanese also developed a form of theater in ancient times. One type of drama was called *No,* and a popular form of drama was called *Kabuki*. They were performed on a platform with a temple roof.

In ancient India, dramatic performances were given on specially-built raised platforms, with draperies as background.

The ancient Greeks developed a very great form of drama. The audience was seated on a hillside. The action of the play took place in a grassy circle. There was a building called the *skene,* which was used for the entrances of the actors, for dressing, and for scenic background.

During the Middle Ages, the Christian church condemned all forms of drama, but later religious drama became an important part of church life. Priests in the Middle Ages acted out bible stories as part of the church services.

NO SPIRITUAL MASK

NO PERFORMER

KABUKI PERFORMER

During the reign of Elizabeth I, the theater in England took a great step forward. In 1576 an actor, James Burbage, built the first playhouse. It was known simply as "the Theatre" and was patterned after the stages that used to be set up in inn courtyards.

Soon other theaters were built, and these included the Globe, where many of Shakespeare's plays were performed; the Red Bull; and the Blackfriars. The audience stood in the pit, in front or around the sides of the stage, or were seated in boxes around and above the stage. Our modern theater had its beginnings with these early English theaters.

CLAUDIO MONTEVERDI

How Did the Orchestra Develop?

An orchestra is a large group of musicians playing many kinds of instruments. The standard orchestra has at least seventy-five to one hundred players. Of these, more than half play stringed instruments, which form the foundation of an orchestra. The rest play woodwind, brass, and percussion instruments.

An orchestra such as this is called a symphony orchestra. An orchestra that has fifteen to thirty players is called a chamber orchestra. It is small enough to play in a small hall or "chamber." A string orchestra is made up of only the stringed instruments of the symphony orchestra.

The modern symphony orchestra developed over hundreds of years. There were many experiments and changes, and it was actually the composers of music who had a great deal to do with shaping the orchestra.

The first great pioneer in writing for the orchestra was the Italian, Claudio Monteverdi (1567–1643). He was also the first great composer of opera. In one of his works he used an orchestra of thirty-five musicians playing violas, guitars, harpsichords, organs, trumpets, trombones, and flutes.

When the violin was perfected in the seventeenth century, the strings became the leading instruments of the orchestra. The great French opera composer Rameau (1683–1764) was one of the first composers to use clarinets in the orchestra. He also used bassoons and horns regularly.

Turkish bands traveling in Europe introduced several new percussion instruments. These included the bass drum, triangle, cymbals, and others in this family. So we see how the orchestra grew in terms of the kinds and the number of instruments composers could use. And composers wrote music designed to get new sounds and tone color from the orchestra.

The first orchestra in the United States, still in existence, was the New York Philharmonic, founded in 1842. The Boston Symphony was founded in 1881.

PAGANINI

A STRADIVARIUS

Who Made the First Violin?

Did you know that of the one hundred or more musicians in a symphony orchestra, over thirty are violinists? The beauty of tone and wide range of expression of a violin are considered greater than those of any other instrument.

The violin took many centuries to develop. Its history begins in India. It was here that the use of a bow to play stringed instruments was probably invented. During the Middle Ages in Europe, various stringed instruments were played with a bow.

One of these was the vielle, which was probably introduced to Europe in the tenth century. Like the violin, the vielle was held against the player's shoulder. Later the vielle was changed through the influence of the rebec. This was an Arabic instrument that spread from Spain to the rest of Europe. By combining the sturdy body of the vielle with the clever arrangement of the pegs in the rebec, a new group of instruments was born.

The violin received its basic shape between 1550 and 1600, and it is impossible to say which one individual first made this instrument as we know it today. The most successful violins were made in the seventeenth and eighteenth centuries.

Italy produced outstanding families of violin makers. Each had its own secrets that the father handed down to his sons. The Amati family of the city of Cremona produced violins that had a tone of rare sweetness and softness. For a long time it was believed that no one would ever be able to make better violins.

But Niccolo Amati had a star pupil called Antonio Stradivari. He has been called the master of all masters, and he developed a larger, flatter type of violin with more tone and power. Stradivari is reported to have built 1,116 instruments, and of these 540 are still known to exist. Each one is worth a great deal of money and is considered to be a great work of art.

The greatest violinist of all time is said to be Niccolo Paganini, who lived from 1784 to 1840.

Who Made the First Phonograph Record?

Thomas A. Edison invented recording in 1877, when he noticed two things about sound.

He noticed that a small disk inside a telephone receiver vibrated as the person at the other end of the line spoke. So he had the idea of attaching a tiny needle to the center of the disk; the force of the needle could tell him the amount of sound that was being sent out.

He also noticed that when he ran a paper tape covered with Morse code dots and dashes through an instrument at high speed, it produced little noises that were much like the sound of people talking. If the human voice could make a needle move, why couldn't the same needle prick the pattern of the sound waves on paper tape?

After a few experiments, he replaced the paraffin paper with a metal cylinder. He wrapped a piece of tin foil around the cylinder and attached two disk-and-needle units. One was to speak into; the other was for sound to come out of. When the "in" disk vibrated, the needle should make little indentations in the tin foil as the cylinder turned. When the "out" needle traveled over these same indentations, its disk should vibrate, too, recreating the sounds.

Edison put on the first cylinder, leaned close to the "in" disk, and shouted, "Mary had a little lamb." He then set the needle in the same groove and turned the crank of the cylinder. Back came the voice! He had made the first recording of sound! This was in 1877.

In 1895, a man called Emile Berliner put the first phonograph record on the market. This was a record instead of a cylinder. It was made of zinc and coated with wax. When the "in" needle vibrated to the sound of a voice, it scratched a wiggly pattern in the wax. Then the record was put into acid, which ate into the zinc where the needle cut its path. This was a way of "etching" the human voice, and became the way to make records.

When Did Ballet Dancing Begin?

What is a ballet? It is a kind of theatrical entertainment that combines several things: dancing, stage design, and music. Some ballets tell a story, but others just depict an idea or mood.

When you see a ballet, you see the human body performing in the most elegant and harmonious way possible. And it takes strict and strenuous training to enable the dancers to look natural and beautiful as they perform.

Ballet is nearly five hundred years old. It began in Italy about the time Columbus discovered America. It was quite different then from what it is today. At that time ballet was a form of court entertainment. Italian noblemen amused themselves and their guests by combining dancing, music, pantomime, poetry and drama.

So the first ballet dancers were the royalty and nobles of the court, since there were no professional dancers. The steps were modeled on the elegant and rather simple court dances of the day, and the dancers didn't wear toe slippers. However, dancing of this kind was not called ballet until almost one hundred years later at the court of King Henry III of France.

In 1581 Queen Catherine de Médicis ordered a grand entertainment to celebrate a royal wedding. The result was a spectacular ballet. There were hundreds of dancers, singers, and actors. The Italian musician de Beaujoyeulx organized it. He was probably the first choreographer, or maker of dances, as we know the word today. He called his work *The Queen's Comic Ballet,* and ever since performances of this kind have been called ballets.

The leading lady in a ballet company is called a prima ballerina. The first of these was a woman called Lafontaine, who danced in 1681. Later on, various individuals introduced changes and improvements in ballet.

Chapter 3

The Human Body

What Is Life?

This is probably one of the deepest questions man can ask and one of the greatest mysteries facing him.

Scientists have discovered that all living things are made of a material called protoplasm. They can make a chemical formula for protoplasm, and they can take molecules of various elements and compounds and put them together and make materials like protoplasm. But the materials they make are not alive!

All man can do is examine the living creatures on earth, in all sizes and shapes and wherever they live, and find what it is they have in common. Then we can say that these common qualities make up life.

Let's see what these qualities are. All living things must be able to grow. They grow to a fairly definite size and shape. A kitten becomes a cat; an acorn becomes an oak tree. For some living things it takes a short time to grow to full size; a redwood tree may take thousands of years. But all living things grow.

All living things can replace and repair parts of themselves. A lobster can grow a new claw, human beings can grow new skin or bones, trees grow new leaves.

Another characteristic shared by living things, and living things only, is the ability to reproduce. If this ability didn't exist, living things would disappear from the earth as they grew old and died. Animals, fish, birds, insects, plants—all produce offspring.

Living things are able to adapt to their environment. Man can do this better than any other creatures because of his brain. But plants can do this only to a limited extent.

Living things can also respond to stimuli. This means if something outside of themselves affects them they can react. When you smell food, you respond, and flowers grow toward the light.

This doesn't tell you what life is, but it does describe the qualities that things must have to be considered "alive."

2 TO REPRODUCE

4 TO RESPOND TO STIMULI

1 TO REPAIR

3 TO ADAPT TO ENVIRONMENT

Why Must We Breathe?

We all know instinctively that we must breathe. But why is it necessary for all living plants and animals to breathe? The reason is a very simple one. By breathing we take in air that provides oxygen. Without this gas, no life can exist.

When we exhale the air, it has changed. As it made its way through our system, some of the oxygen was used up, while the amounts of carbon dioxide and water were increased.

Nature keeps up a constant supply of oxygen for our breathing. In fact, from year to year, there is little change in the amounts of oxygen and carbon dioxide found in the air. This is because the carbon dioxide we breathe out into the air is taken in by plants. They breathe out oxygen, which we need.

Breathing, or respiration, is made up of two parts: external and internal breathing. External breathing is what most of us think of when we refer to breathing. It consists of inhaling and exhaling, or inspiration and expiration. Inspiration means taking in air through the mouth, the nose, or both. Expiration means sending out air through those same channels, but air that has had about one-fifth of its oxygen exchanged for an equal amount of carbon dioxide. This happens in the lungs.

Internal breathing is the opposite of external. The oxygen taken from the air in the lungs is carried to the tissues of the body by the red cells in the blood. In the tissues this oxygen burns certain food products, making them available for use by the body. The blood takes away the waste products, including water and carbon dioxide. These are returned in the blood to the lungs for exhaling.

Since an exchange of gases (oxygen and carbon dioxide) takes place both in the lungs and in the tissues, a large surface is needed to make this possible. The linings of the lungs of an adult, for example, are equal to a space about 36 feet square. This is larger than the ceiling space of one floor of an average house! Much of this area is kept in reserve, since we might need 8 or 10 times as much oxygen during work as we need at rest. If we need more oxygen, we breathe more deeply or more quickly.

Different creatures breathe at different rates, depending on the oxygen they need.

A newborn baby breathes about once a second, but at the age of 15, breathing is about 20 times a minute. An elephant breathes 10 times a minute; a dog, 25 times a minute.

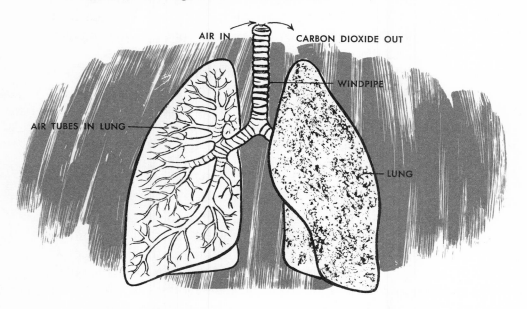

What Keeps the Heart Beating?

As most of us know, the heart is a pump. It drives the blood through the body, thus making life possible.

But what an amazing pump it is! With each beat of the heart, it sends out about one hundred cubic centimeters of blood. In the course of a day this amounts to about 10,567 quarts of blood that are pumped through the blood vessels. In an average lifetime, a heart pumps about 264,175,000 quarts of blood!

Each beat of the human heart lasts about eight-tenths of a second. The heart beats about one hundred thousand times a day, and rests an equal number of times between beats. So it rests about six hours total per day.

Now, what we call the "beat" of the heart is a contracting and a relaxing. During the contracting the blood is pumped out; during the relaxing new blood enters. But this doesn't take place in a simple

10,567 QTS. PER DAY

WHY

way as, for example, you might open and close your fist. The contraction takes place in a kind of wave that starts at the bottom of the heart and moves up toward the top.

What keeps the heart beating? Does this impulse to contract and relax come from somewhere else? Is it self-starting? It is one of the most fascinating questions in biology, and much about it still remains a mystery. Let me tell you about an interesting experiment that has been known about for hundreds of years.

Suppose you take a chicken egg and incubate it about twenty-six hours. Now you open it and with a magnifying glass study those cells in the egg from which the chick's heart will later develop. You will see those cells beating! Even before those cells have become a heart, they are already beating!

Now suppose you remove this mass of cells and allow them to grow in a medium. If you cut the growing heart into six pieces, each piece continues to contract for some time! What is the explanation? We don't know. All we can say, it seems, is that the heart has a certain characteristic of automatically contracting. And one of the secrets of life—why it keeps beating—remains a riddle!

253

What Is Heredity?

Every new organism, whether it is a plant, fish, animal, or human, resembles its parents—and yet it differs from them. For example, children may look like one parent or the other, but usually they have some features of each parent. What has happened is that the parents have passed down to the children certain characteristics. The children have "inherited" them. So heredity is the study of how offspring resemble their parents.

The unit of heredity is called the "gene." Genes are large molecules found in the nuclei of both sperm cells and egg cells. Within the nucleus of each cell are long, thin strands, or threads. They are called "chromosomes," and they carry the genes.

Since chromosomes occur in pairs, their genes are also paired. The chromosomes of a cell may contain hundreds of thousands of pairs of genes. Each gene pair controls one or more features of the organism, such as color of hair, shape of nose, size of body, and so on.

There are many "laws" of heredity, which means that the process takes place in certain ways. For example, every trait that is inherited depends on a single "factor," and each factor behaves independently. Because a certain trait is inherited from the parents, it doesn't mean that any other trait will also necessarily be inherited. In other words, the factors, or genes, have nothing to do with each other.

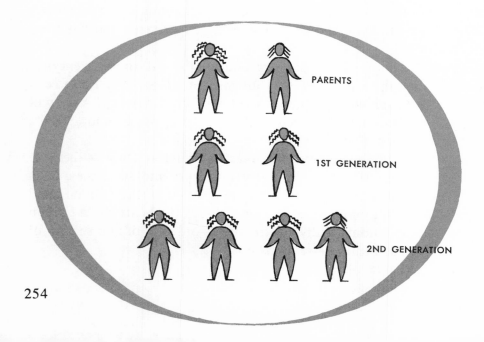

PARENTS

1ST GENERATION

2ND GENERATION

Some genes carry traits that are "dominant," and others carry traits that are "recessive." For example, the gene for curly hair seems to be dominant to the gene for straight hair. When both parents are curly-haired, they usually have curly-haired children. But if each parent carries a recessive gene for straight hair, some children may be straight-haired.

Scientists have studied such human traits as color of eyes, hair, and skin, so that they usually can tell how they will be inherited by people whose family history is known for several generations.

Is Cancer Hereditary?

We are concerned today with the terrible toll of lives that cancer is taking in the world. Naturally, when such a dread disease exists, there is also a great deal of misunderstanding about it, including such matters as heredity. Anyone with any question at all concerning cancer should talk to his doctor about it.

Cancer is a disease in which there is an abnormal growth of tissue. A tumor is considered malignant, and therefore a cancer, if it can spread to remote areas of the body. Cells from the original tumor break off and set up a "colony" elsewhere. Cancers grow locally by extending into the normal surrounding tissue. A cancer can arise in any of the body's tissues, wherever those tissues begin to grow wildly and uncontrollably.

Cancer is chiefly a disease of middle and old age, but may occur at any time of life. Certain peoples of the world seem, for some reason, to get one type of cancer more commonly than another type. For example, cancer of the stomach is twice as frequent among the Japanese as it is among Caucasians.

The question of whether cancer is hereditary is not an easy one to answer. What may happen sometimes is that the child may inherit the type of skin, for example, in which cancer is more prone to occur, rather than inherit the disease itself. As a rule, two factors are necessary: the susceptibility, which may be inherited; and some factor that incites the cancer in this tissue. It has been found that sometimes marriage between certain people magnifies the hereditary factor. For example, in some families cancer of the stomach is a common ailment, while in others it may be a cancer of the breast.

But to any one human being, the inheritance of a tendency to cancer need not be a source of fear. It is a good policy for people with a history of cancer in parents or close relatives to be alert and have regular physical examinations to detect any signs or symptoms.

Why Are Some People Smarter Than Others?

One thing everybody seems to realize is that some people seem to be bright and intelligent, and others seem to be backward and learn slowly. But not everybody agrees as to why this is so.

We do know that many cases of low mental ability are the result of injuries at birth, glandular disorders occurring before or after birth, or diseases that have caused damage to the brain. In many cases the causes of retarded mental development cannot be determined.

There is a great deal of disagreement among experts as to the influence of heredity on intelligence. Some believe that in most cases a child inherits his intelligence. Others think that a child's intelligence is a result of the experiences he has had and the kind of environment in which he has lived.

Probably both of these opinions are partially true. The most common belief is that a child inherits a capacity for mental growth. But the degree to which he develops within that capacity depends upon a great many factors in his environment. There are perhaps many people who could have developed higher mental abilities if during childhood they had had better opportunities.

How is intelligence measured? What is really measured is "mental age." This is done through a series of mental tests. For example, most children of six years can do the problems and perform the tasks required in a certain test. A few four and five-year-olds can also do them. On the other hand, there may be children of ten or twelve years of age, or even adults, for whom they are too difficult.

The first group are "average," the second group are "superior," and the third, "retarded." If a child passes enough tests so that his average is that of a six-year-old, his mental age is said to be six years.

If a six-year-old has a mental age of six years, his intelligence quotient (IQ) is 100. If a five-year-old has a mental age of six, his IQ is 120. IQ's above 110 are generally considered superior.

How Does the Brain Store Information?

Storing information is remembering, and remembering is closely linked to learning.

Psychologists have tried to explain how people remember and why they forget many of the things they learn. No one has yet found all the answers. It is believed, according to one theory, that when a person learns something, a physical change of some kind takes place. A trace, or pattern, is left in the brain. And it is believed that memories, or the traces memory may leave in the brain, simply fade away in the course of time.

The way you feel about a particular experience may also determine whether you remember or forget it. In general, people are apt to forget things that are unpleasant or upsetting and remember things that are pleasant.

NERVE CELLS

Brains can learn different kinds of tasks. Better-developed brains can learn more complicated tasks. In the simplest brains, learning is very crude. Humans show the greatest learning abilities.

But how and where does the brain store the information that we call memory? As we said, scientists are not yet able to fully explain it. In the human brain, areas of the cortex appear to be involved. The cortex is the twisted, wrinkled, and knotted surface of the largest part of the brain (the cerebrum).

When these areas are excited by weak electrical currents, a person "relives" past experiences. These stimuli force the brain to reproduce experiences that are stored within it from the past. And it is known that injury to certain areas of the brain will result in loss of memory.

But are these the places in the brain where the information is stored? We don't know. Nor do we know how the information is stored. Some scientists think that storing information is a chemical process—the individual nerve cells have chemically-coded information within them. Other scientists believe that memory is the result of some permanent change in the structure of the nerve. So memory is still a mystery!

What Is Multiple Sclerosis?

It is always unpleasant to read about diseases that afflict people, but they are part of our knowledge of man and how he lives.

Multiple sclerosis is a disorder of the brain and nervous system. It usually develops early in adult life, and it seems to attack people who are otherwise healthy. The disease often stops and then reappears again, and it may last over a period of years.

What happens in this disease is that certain matter in the nervous system, in the spinal cord, and in the brain is destroyed. This happens in tiny spots scattered through the nervous system.

Because this disease shows up in many different symptoms and fluctuates so much, it is hard to diagnose. Often, at the beginning of multiple sclerosis there is a temporary mistiness of vision. There may be no pain, and the person doesn't become blind. In fact, this symptom may be so mild that the person may let it pass without going to a doctor.

Then later the person begins to have double vision and a tingling or burning sensation in the skin. The patient may also not be able to coordinate his movements, and he may feel weak and may shake or even begin to stammer. In some cases, the person starts to talk in a strange way, slurring his speech, or talking monotonously.

Eventually, the muscles of the legs become stiff or have spasms. In some patients there are also mental symptoms. The mind doesn't seem able to work well. And a person may be very depressed or very elated.

When a case is far advanced, the patient may become very aggressive. A curious thing is that the most common symptom is that the person feels everything is fine; he is very optimistic even though he has severe symptoms. He might smile or giggle frequently.

At present there is no known cure for multiple sclerosis.

What Is a Phobia?

Did you ever know anybody who was afraid of high places, or someone who was afraid of closed places? There are people who are afraid of crowds, or of being touched by others. There is a name for behaving this way: it is called a "phobic reaction," and we say the person has a "phobia."

Is something "wrong" with such people? Are they "sick" in some way? No—but we might say they are suffering from some emotional disturbance. Something upsets them—or has upset them in the past—

very strongly. And such a person is trying to deal with this emotional disturbance—it can be called "emotional pain"—just as you would try to deal with physical pain.

We all react to emotional upsets. We cry, we blush, we might break out in a sweat. But some people, who feel this emotional stress more strongly, or whose power of resistance is weaker, try to deal with this emotional pain in an unnatural, unusual way. This kind of reaction is sometimes called "neurotic."

One such way of reacting is to develop a phobia, which is un-reasonable fear of a specific thing, such as fear of high places, or closed-in places. An interesting thing about a phobia is that the thing the person is afraid of is usually a thing or situation he can avoid. After all, nobody forces people to climb to high places or get into closed places. And as long as a person can avoid these things, he feels· fine. He doesn't have what is called "anxiety."

But why should a particular person have a fear of high places, to take an example? The truth is, he is really afraid of something else, or perhaps felt afraid of something else when he was a child. It might have been his father whom he loved and feared at the same time. He didn't want to admit he was afraid of his father, so he substituted a fear of high places, which is a symbol of his father. And since he can avoid high places, he can avoid facing the fact that he is afraid of his father. All of this seems very complicated, doesn't it? But then the human being and how he behaves is a very complicated matter!

What Makes People Laugh?

If this question had a simple answer, such as a formula that could be learned, every comedian would know it! But laughter is a complicated thing, and the best explanations of it are still only theories.

We know, of course, that laughter is an expression of many feelings and that laughter is found only among human beings. But psychologists are still studying two basic questions about laughter: What makes people laugh, and what is the function or purpose of laughter?

When you try to think of what makes people laugh, or what people consider funny, you find yourself thinking like a psychologist or philosopher. You become concerned with people's reactions to other people in all kinds of situations—for example, why people laugh when they see awkwardness or some kind of weakness or imperfection in another person.

Another explanation of laughter is that it depends on our suddenly seeing some incongruity; that is, things that don't normally or naturally go together. A big fat man wearing a tiny hat, or a very short man dancing with a big, tall woman are examples of this. But this theory doesn't explain many of our other reasons for laughter that have to do with the comic, the humorous, and so on.

From the physical point of view, laughter is good for us. It's good for our lungs, and it's an outlet for some extra energy. Laughter also has a great social value. We usually laugh as members of a group. According to this theory, laughter is used by social groups as a way of commenting on the behavior of people and making them conform to our standards.

How Does a Baby Learn to Talk?

What is the first word a baby says? We all know the answer—"Mama!" Now, that seems like a very simple thing to do, doesn't it? But it's a very complicated process indeed. Not only does it require many steps of development, but do you realize that no other creature on earth is capable of accomplishing this?

Let's go through the process step by step. When a baby is born, his brain is like an unwritten page. There is nothing there. The areas in the brain that receive sense impressions haven't yet received any. The baby's eyes are open, but the nerves between the eyes and the brain are not yet developed, so the brain doesn't register anything.

After one or two months, these nerves are developed and now the baby "sees" its mother. As a result of seeing the same object again and again, the visual memory center in the brain develops. The infant's impressions of the mother register in this center as memories. So now the child "recognizes" the mother.

As soon as the mother realizes this has happened, she keeps pointing to herself and saying "Mama" at the same time. At first the child can't hear, but gradually the nerves develop and the baby "hears" the sound "Mama." Through repetition, the child forms a memory image of the sound. The baby now remembers and "understands" the word "Mama."

Now the mother has to teach the child to speak. By repeating the word "Mama" over and over, she makes this happen: A connection is made in the brain between the image of the mother in the visual center and the sound of "Mama" in the hearing center. This is called an association. Now the child not only recognizes Mama's face, but also thinks of the sound "Mama" when he sees the mother. He "identifies" her. The child now begins to imitate the mother. He forms the word without saying it at first. After trying to say the word many times, the baby can make the vocal muscles move when it sees the mother. Finally he is able to say "Mama." And, of course, the proud mother says, "My baby is talking already!"

What Makes Your Voice Change?

The kind of voice you have depends chiefly on your vocal cords. These vocal cords are made of elastic fibers. You might compare them to the very best violin strings.

The vocal cords can be made tense or slack. In fact, your vocal cords can be in any of about 170 different positions. When a column of air (which you push upward) strikes the vocal cords, they begin to vibrate. This vibration produces sound waves.

If the vocal cords are slack, they may vibrate about eighty times per second and the result is deep tones. If they are tensed, they vibrate

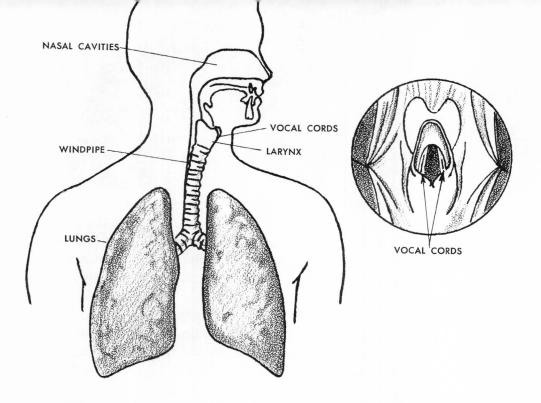

NASAL CAVITIES

VOCAL CORDS

WINDPIPE

LARYNX

LUNGS

VOCAL CORDS

rapidly, perhaps one thousand times a second, and produce short sound waves or high tones.

A child has short vocal cords. So they produce short air waves and a child has a high-pitched voice. As a child grows, the vocal cords become longer. As they become longer, the voice becomes deeper. The average length of a man's vocal cords is greater than that of a woman's, which is why men's voices are deeper.

In boys, growth often takes place so quickly, and the whole larynx changes so quickly, that they can't get used to it and can't control it perfectly. That's why we often have "the breaking of the voice" with young boys.

While the general pitch of an adult's voice depends on the length of the vocal cords, each voice has a certain range. It is this range that determines what kind of voice the person has. Voices can be divided into six groups: bass, baritone, and tenor for men, and alto, mezzo-soprano, and soprano for women.

The quality of a human voice, however, depends on many other things as well, especially the resonating spaces such as windpipe, lungs, nasal cavities, and so on. People with beautiful voices have resonating spaces shaped a certain way and know how to control them.

Why Do People Stutter?

All of us have met people who stutter or stammer. Such people should be treated with understanding and sympathy, but unfortunately there are many, including "entertainers," who think this is a subject for humor.

Stuttering or stammering occurs when the organs of speech have certain spasms, so that words suddenly can't be articulated and there is a pause in the speech. This is often followed by a repetition in rapid sequence of the particular sound at which the stoppage occurred.

There are many degrees of stuttering. In some cases it's only a slight inability to pronounce certain letters or syllables with ease. In extreme cases, the muscles of the tongue, throat, face—and even those connected with breathing—are involved in a spasm.

Normal speech, which most of us carry on without even thinking about it, is quite a complicated procedure. The most amazing kind of coordination is necessary in the larynx, cheeks, tongue, and lips. When this coordination is not done with enough precision, the result is stammering.

Stammering rarely shows itself before the age of four or five. When it develops, it may be due to some physical disorder or emotional disturbance.

In some cases, it seems, stuttering may be overcome by instruction in reading and speaking slowly and deliberately, carefully pronouncing each syllable. When feeling a tendency to stammer, the person should also be taught how to regulate respiration during speech. Sounds or combinations of sounds that present special problems should be carefully studied, and the defect may be largely overcome by a series of graduated exercises in reading.

In any case, the treatment should be done by experts in the field, and the emotional basis of stammering requires serious attention, too.

How Are Deaf-Mutes Taught to Speak?

Until the sixteenth century, deaf-mutes were treated very cruelly. They were regarded as idiots, incapable of intelligence, and were locked up in asylums or even killed. But in the sixteenth century, an Italian doctor named Jerome Cardan got the idea of teaching deaf-mutes through written characters.

As the result of his work, about a hundred years later a finger alphabet was developed, similar to the finger alphabet used today. With the finger alphabet, a deaf-mute makes the letters with his fingers and spells out words. He also depends on sign language. For example, sweeping the forefinger across the lips means "You are not telling me the truth." A tap on the chin with three fingers means "My uncle." With this alphabet some deaf-mutes can spell out as many as 130 words a minute!

But many teachers of deaf-mutes believe that the use of sign language and the finger alphabet is not the best method. It forces the deaf-mute to communicate only with other people in the same condition. So these teachers use a method known as "oral instruction." In this method the deaf are taught to understand what is spoken to them, and even to speak themselves.

Nowadays many of the deaf and hard-of-hearing learn to interpret what is said by watching the lips of the speaker. They learn to speak themselves by observing and feeling the lips and vocal organs of the teacher and then imitating the motions.

Hearing aids are being used more and more. In schools and classes for deaf and hard-of-hearing children, group hearing aids are used. The group hearing aids have individual earphones for each child so that the volume and tone can be adjusted. The teacher speaks through a microphone, and the children hear her in the same manner as if they were listening to a radio with earphones.

APPLE

Should Left-Handedness Be Corrected?

If you're left-handed, or know anyone who is, then you've noticed that a left-handed person has to make certain adjustments to get along in this world. For we live in a right-handed world.

With 96 percent of the people right-handed, it's natural that everything from doorknobs, locks, screwdrivers, automobiles, musical instruments, and machines to such things as the buttons on our clothing are designed for right-handed people. But somehow most left-handed people seem to get along quite well. And, of course, there are cases of left-handed people who got along very well indeed! For example, Leonardo da Vinci and Michelangelo, two of the world's greatest geniuses, were left-handed.

While some parents worry if their child is left-handed, most medical authorities believe it is wiser not to do anything about it. Being left-handed is not a defect in a person, so a child should not be scolded or punished, and no effort should be made to try to change him to a right-handed person, these authorities believe.

Now, what is it that makes most people right-handed? For a long time it was believed that we are right-handed because of such things as training, custom, and the fact that most people are right-handed. So a left-handed person had something wrong with him because he couldn't do things the way other people did.

Today it is believed that most people are right-handed because the brains of most people function in a certain way. One-half of the brain "dominates" over the other half. The left half of the brain controls the functions on the right side of the body, and the right half of the brain controls the functions on the left side of the body. And in most people the left half of the brain is dominant, so the right half of their body is more skilled and better able to develop. Our right hand works better than our left hand.

In left-handed people, the brain develops in a reverse way. The right half of the brain is dominant, so the left half of the body works better. It works just as well, just as skillfully—it just happens to make them left-handed! And it's no more serious than that!

Do Human Beings Alone Have Fingerprints?

If there's one thing in the world you have that nobody else has, it's your own particular set of fingerprints! What are fingerprints, and what makes them so different for each person?

To begin with, our skin consists of two layers of tissue. One is a thick, deep layer, the "corium," and over it is a delicate membrane called the "epidermis." In cold-blooded animals, the epidermis fits smoothly on the corium. There are no "ridges" to make "prints."

But in mammals, these two layers of the skin are joined very closely. The under layer, the corium, buckles where it meets the upper layer, the epidermis. Some of the tissue of the lower layer projects up into the upper layer molded over these projections, so that they are firmly and closely attached.

Now, among the lower animals, these "pegs" that stick up are scattered at random. There is no pattern of any kind. Among the apes, these pegs are arranged in rows. So the ridges in the upper layer of skin form parallel rows. But since all apes have these parallel rows of ridges, their "fingerprints" are pretty much alike.

But in human beings, the rows of ridges form definite patterns. In fact, the system of classifying human fingerprints was developed by studying these patterns. An Englishman named Sir Edward Henry developed the system of classifying fingerprints that is the basis for the system used today by authorities all over the world.

According to this system, all ridges on human fingers can be divided into the following patterns: loops, central pocket loops, double loops, arches, tented arches, whorls, and accidentals. (If you press your finger on an ink pad and then onto a piece of paper, you should be able to see some of these patterns.)

By counting the ridges between fixed points in the pattern, it is possible to classify each of the ten fingers into a definite fixed group. The ten fingers are then considered as a unit to classify a person's fingerprints. By the way, the chances that two people will have the same ridge pattern on just one finger are one in twenty-four million!

Why Do Humans Have Hair on Their Bodies?

Birds have feathers, and mammals, such as man, have hair. It is believed that feathers and hair enabled birds and mammals to develop far beyond their common ancestors, the reptiles.

In human beings, there are only two parts of the body where there is no hair: the palms of the hand and the soles of the feet. The hair on the rest of the body is believed to be a leftover from the coat of heavy hair that our prehistoric ancestors had.

When a human baby is about a hundred days old in the mother's body, a thick coat of hair sprouts from the skin. After another hundred days, these hairs are shed. This is called the embryonal hair.

This hair is replaced by the delicate hair of a newborn baby. Then this hair is transformed at the time of puberty (about fourteen years in boys and twelve years in girls) into the final coat of hair that the person will have.

The development of the adult coat of hair is regulated by the sex glands. In males, certain hormones promote the development of hair on the face and body, and keep down the growth of hair on the head. The female hormones act in just the opposite way.

Why we need this hair is not quite understood by science. We can say that the hair of the eyebrows, lashes, ears, and nose, are probably there to protect us against dust and insects. A man's beard, in prehistoric times, probably helped set men apart from women—even at a distance—and helped give the man an appearance of power. According to Charles Darwin, the fine hairs of the body help us to shed perspiration and water.

An adult male has from three hundred thousand to five hundred thousand hairs in his skin. Blond persons with finer hair have the most hair; red-haired people, who have the coarsest hair, have the fewest hairs on their bodies.

Why Is Some Hair Curly?

We all have a great deal of curiosity about our hair. What gives hair its color? Why does hair turn gray? Why is some hair curly? Science still doesn't have all the answers to all the questions about our hair, but let's discuss a few things that we do know about it.

In the root of the hair there live certain cells that contain pigment. These cells have the ability to multiply, and the young cells wander upward with the growing shafts of hair and die. The pigment granules they contain are left in the hair. These pigment granules contain all shades of brown, from a reddish color to a deep black-brown.

FLAT HAIR

ROUND HAIR

OVAL HAIR

The horny substance of the hair, in which this pigment is buried, is yellow. The horny material and the pigment granules mingle, and the color of the hair is the result of the way this mixing takes place.

The hair of different peoples varies, too, in its structure. If we cut across a hair and study it under a microscope, we can see that it has a definite shape: round, flat, oval, elliptical, or even kidney-shaped. This shape has a great deal to do with whether the hair is curly or not. The flatter the hair, the curlier it is, and the rounder it is, the stiffer and lankier.

Elliptical or kidney-shaped hair is usually short and curly, sometimes called "woolly," and is characteristic of the black races. Round-shaped hair, which is the opposite extreme, produces straight, lank, and coarse hair; hair that is oval in shape produces wavy and curly, or smooth and silky hair.

What Is Equilibrium?

If you've been reading about space ships with human passengers, you've probably noticed that one of the problems that scientists will have to overcome is that of loss of equilibrium as a human being moves away from the pull of the earth's gravity.

CANALS OF EQUILIBRIUM

Equilibrium is the ability to adjust ourselves in relation to the earth, which constantly pulls at everything that is near it. Without equilibrium it would be impossible for a bird to fly, a man to walk, or for any living thing to have a sense of direction.

Man has two organs of equilibrium; they are located in the head near the ear. Each organ is like a sack and is filled with a liquid called lymph. Inside the organ, growing out from the bottom, is a kind of hair that springs out of a sensory, or recording cell. When the head is kept erect, the pressure on these hairs is distributed equally. If the head is inclined to one side or the other, the pressure on these hairs changes. The sensory cells are stimulated by this pressure and send nerve impulses to the brain. The brain sets certain muscles into action, and the body readjusts itself and returns from an inclined to an upright position.

Our organs of equilibrium also enable us to know in which direction we are moving. Let's imagine we go out for a drive in an automobile. As the car starts forward, our body sinks back against the seat. The liquid, or lymph, in the "canals" of the organs of equilibrium, bends the sensory hairs back. This causes certain nerves with which they are connected to send a message to the brain, and we feel that we are moving forward.

After awhile, the lymph moves with our body, the sensory hairs are erect, and we no longer have that feeling of suddenly moving forward. Now suppose we step on the brake! Our body keeps going forward and so does the lymph in the organs. It therefore bends the hairs forward. The message goes to the brain and we feel ourselves slowing up.

There are three "canals" in each organ of equilibrium, to correspond with the three planes of space. In this way, the sensory hairs tell us whether we're going up or down, from side to side, or backward or forward.

What Makes Our Muscles Tired?

Muscles are the "movers" of the body. For every bone that can move, there are muscles to move it. Muscles are firmly anchored to the bones.

They move a bone by pulling it. A muscle pulls because it has the ability to contract; that is, to make itself shorter and fatter. When it contracts, it pulls.

When a muscle contracts, or pulls, it produces lactic acid. This acid is like a fatigue poison—it is the chief reason the muscles feel tired. For example, when lactic acid is removed from a tired muscle, that muscle is able to go to work again. So in the course of a day, by using our muscles, we "poison" ourselves with lactic acid. We become tired.

There are other substances in the body that make us feel tired. They are called fatigue toxins, and they are created in the body when we carry on muscular activity. The blood carries these toxins through the body so that not just the muscles feel tired, but the whole body does, especially the brain.

An interesting experiment shows how the lactic acid and toxins are involved with tiredness. A dog is made to work until it is so tired it falls asleep from exhaustion. The blood from that dog is then transfused into a dog that is feeling perky and fresh. The second dog will become tired and fall asleep right in the middle of the transfusion! And it works the opposite way—blood from a wide-awake dog will wake up a tired, sleeping dog.

Why does all this tiredness occur in the body? Because the cells of the body need rest. When we are tired and resting, damages to cells are repaired, nerve cells of the brain recharge their batteries, the joints are lubricated by fluids, and so on.

Sometimes a person who is involved in some athletic activity suddenly seems about to collapse. He feels weak and can hardly breathe. This is exhaustion, and is really almost like a kind of paralysis. The cause of such exhaustion is not known, but it may be produced by an excess of the lactic acid and other fatigue toxins.

LIGAMENT OF KNEE

MUSCLES

TENDON

TENDON

TENDON

BRUISE

What Are Sprains, Strains, and Bruises?

If you were to play in a rough football game, or get into a fight, you might emerge with sprains, strains, and bruises. What causes them, and what should be done about them?

A sprain is an injury to a joint, such as the ankle, knee, or wrist. In a sprain, the ligaments are stretched or torn. This is usually caused by stretching, twisting, or pressure at the joint. One symptom of a sprain is swelling over the joint, which appears very quickly. You also can't use the joint without increasing pain, and it may look discolored. Since a joint may also be fractured, it shouldn't be used until it has been properly examined. Sometimes it takes longer for a sprain to heal than a simple break in a bone!

A strain is a different kind of injury. In a strain it is the muscle

276

or tendon that is injured. This usually comes from some severe exertion, such as lifting a heavy object from an awkward position.

The symptoms of a strain are stiffness and pain in the part that is affected. The first thing to do for a person who has received a strain is to make him comfortable so that the injured muscles are relaxed. In some cases, heat application and gentle massage will provide some relief by stimulating the circulation. Always rub the affected part in an upward direction. Rubbing alcohol may help in the gentle massage to "loosen up" the tightened muscles.

A bruise is still another kind of injury. It is caused by a blow to some part of the body that breaks the small blood vessels under the skin. As the blood collects in the tissues, it causes swelling and discoloration. A cold cloth may help to prevent discoloration, reduce the swelling, and relieve pain. But usually no treatment is needed for minor bruises. If the skin is broken, a bruise should be treated as any other open wound.

Maybe the best idea of all is simply to be careful when you play or exercise so that you can avoid sprains, strains, and bruises!

What Is Arthritis?

The word arthritis is used to describe a great variety of diseases, all of which affect adversely the joints of the body.

The two most common types of arthritis are degenerative arthritis and rheumatoid arthritis. In degenerative arthritis the aging process of the body is involved. In rheumatoid arthritis there is inflammation, and usually some crippling of the body occurs.

In degenerative arthritis there is no fever, no loss of weight, no general stiffening of the joints or deformity of the body. The joint does not become inflamed. It is a disease of advancing years, and usually begins after forty. The cartilage of the bones becomes worn away and broken, so that surfaces of the bone come in direct contact with each other. This is because cartilage acts as a sort of shock absorber of the joints.

The symptoms are either stiffness or pain when there is movement. Knobs begin to appear at the end joints of the first and second fingers. There is also usually pain and stiffness of the knee.

Rheumatoid arthritis is popularly known as rheumatism. What happens here is that the joints become inflamed. The membrane that lines the joint becomes enlarged, and this eats into the cartilage underneath.

At the same time, the bone below the cartilage begins to change. It loses its mineral substances, and the joint becomes stiff. In time, this can end in loss of motion altogether in the joint, so that the person becomes crippled.

What brings on this type of arthritis is still not fully understood by medical science. There are many theories about it, and one is that it is caused by infection. Victims of arthritis have long been hoping for some cure or magic "pill" that would end their suffering. But none has yet been found. Medical authorities want people to realize that the cause of this arthritis is still unknown, and that even some of the drugs that seem to help only give relief while the drugs are being used. When they are stopped, the symptoms return. And the damaged tissue is not repaired.

BLOODHOUND TRACKING

How Many Odors Can We Smell?

Compared to many animals, man's ability to smell is not very good at all. In fact, it is probable that as man developed, his sense of smell became less and less keen, until today he is chiefly a "visual animal."

REGISTER IN BRAIN

NERVES OF SMELL

The dog, to take an example at the other extreme, is almost completely an "olfactory animal," meaning he lives by his sense of smell. Here are some comparisons that will show how inferior man is in this respect. In our nose, the area devoted to smelling is actually about the size of a fingernail on each side. In a dog, this area, if the membrane were spread out, would cover more than half the animal's skin!

In the human brain, where the sensations of smell "register," about a twentieth of the brain is concerned with smell. One-third of a dog's brain is concerned with the sense of smell! Man, of course, has developed other senses, organs, and powers that more than make up for his weakness in smelling.

In our nose, smells are picked up by delicate hairs that are in the olfactory membrane. But the tips of these "antennae" don't stick out in the air; they are embedded in a special layer that covers the membrane. This membrane is always moist. If it becomes dry, we no longer can smell! In addition, in ordinary breathing, the stream of air does not pass over this membrane, so we really have to sniff—pull air in over this membrane—when we want to smell something.

Before we can smell anything, that substance has to dissolve in the fatty layer that covers the delicate hairs that pick up the smell. So these substances have to be volatile oils (as those from flowers), or be carried by such oils (as from coffee).

There are five important types of such substances that our sense of smell can detect. One is flowery (violet, rose, etc.). The second is spicy (lemon, apple, etc.). The third is burnt (coffee, tobacco). The fourth is putrescent (cheese, rotten eggs). And the fifth is ethereal (alcohol, camphor, etc.).

Can We Control Our Hunger and Thirst?

When you feel thirsty, you have a dry sensation in your throat. And when you feel hungry, you may have the sensation that your stomach is empty. But the truth is that neither that feeling in your throat, nor the one in your stomach, is responsible for your hunger or thirst.

Your blood should normally contain a certain amount of water and salt. This is also true of the tissues. Now, suppose this balance is upset for some reason. Your blood draws water from the tissues of your body in order to keep its balance constant. As this water is being removed, it registers in a "thirst center" in your brain. The thirst center sends an impulse to the pharynx, or throat, making it contract. This contraction makes you feel your throat is "dry," and you experience thirst.

The feeling of hunger originates in the brain, too. There is a hunger center that acts as a sort of brake on the activities of the stomach and intestines. When there is enough food in the blood, the hunger center slows up the action of the stomach and intestines. But if the blood doesn't have enough nourishment, the hunger center responds by releasing the brakes. The intestines become active, and we experience a feeling of hunger. Our stomach "growls."

To a certain degree we can control hunger by controlling the rate at which we use up our food supplies. In nature, the smaller and more active animals use up their food supply fastest. For example, a small bird may starve to death in five days, but it may take a dog twenty. When a person is calm, the protein stores of the body last longer than when he is excited or afraid.

There are people who can train themselves to go without food for long periods of time. They do this by a deliberate form of concentration, just as people can make themselves perform some exceptional athletic feat. It seems to be more difficult to control thirst, but people can make themselves able to endure it better by conscious efforts.

What Happens to the Water We Drink?

You may think that when you drink a glass of water it goes bubbling through your body and out as if it were going through a pipe. But water and your body are involved in a much more complicated way.

An adult man takes in about two quarts of water a day as fluids, and he takes in another quart from what we call "solid" foods. Fruit, vegetables, bread, and meat are really 30 to 90 percent water! Besides these three quarts he takes in from the outside, in his body about ten quarts of water pass back and forth between the different systems and organs. For example, every time you swallow, you swallow some saliva. In the next few moments, a quantity of water equal to that saliva will pass from the blood vessels into the salivary glands to replace the water you swallowed! The swallowed water returns from the stomach and the intestines to the blood. And so the ten quarts of water in your body are circulating between the blood and the organs every day!

A man has about five quarts of blood in his blood vessels, and three of them are water. His blood vessels will continue to have these three quarts of water no matter what he does. He may be "dried out" after a long hike, or he may have drunk four quarts of beer at a party —there will still be three quarts of water in his blood! And even if a man could drink ten quarts of water at a time, he could not dilute his blood; it keeps that balance of water and solids all the time.

What happens when you drink a certain quantity of water? One-fourth of it goes to the intestine; one-fourth goes into the liver; one-fourth goes into the muscles; and the last fourth goes to the kidneys and bladder. The muscles are the largest water reservoir you have in your body. In a grown man, the muscles can take in and hold up to thirty quarts of water!

When the liver gives up water to the blood, it stimulates the kidney to excrete water. This fills up the bladder, and we get rid of the excess water.

How Do Calories Make Us Fat?

Calories don't make us fat—for the simple reason that calories have nothing to do with food! Calories are a way of measuring something. That something they measure is energy or heat.

One calorie is the amount of heat it takes to raise the temperature of one gram of water one degree centigrade. When we apply this form of measure to the energy in food, we use a large, or kilogram, calorie. The kilogram calorie equals one thousand regular calories.

But what about all this talk about calories making us fat? Well, the food you take into your body can be considered a "fuel." The breaking down of the food in the body tissues is really a form of oxidation, or "burning." And since we want a way of measuring how much "fuel" we are taking in and how much the body needs, we use a fuel measurement—which is calories!

Every person needs a different amount of calories to maintain life. But it is possible to draw up general rules or requirements. For example, the average adult needs from two thousand to three thousand calories per day. But suppose you're a factory worker and use up a lot of energy on the job. You may need up to three thousand four hundred calories. And what about athletes or lumberjacks? They might need four thousand calories or more.

Children need more calories than adults. Older people need fewer calories because they can't "burn up" the fuel as easily as people in the prime of life. Outdoor workers need more calories than those who work in closed rooms.

Now, what happens if you take in more calories than you need; that is, more than you use up in the course of the day? The "fuels" of the body that provide the calories are transformed into fat and stored away! And that's why people worry about calories. If you do want to cut down a bit on calories, cut down on sugars, fats, and starches.

What Is Protein?

All living cells contain protein. This would suggest that protein is a substance necessary to life. And, in fact, we get our word "protein" from a Greek word meaning "first," because proteins are thought to be the most important part of living matter.

Each kind of cell has its own protein. The proteins are made up of combinations of substances called "amino acids." There are more than twenty-one different amino acids. Each amino acid group contains the chemical element nitrogen, in addition to carbon, hydrogen, and oxygen. The different amino acids can combine in different ways to form different proteins, and there are thousands of different proteins. For example, we all know that meat contains protein, but did you know that it is made up of at least twelve to fifteen different proteins?

Many of the foods that are considered important for us to eat are so because of the proteins they contain. These include milk, eggs, lean meats, fish, peas, beans, peanuts, and certain grains. They are important to man because they provide him with the amino acids that his body cannot make for itself. He must get the amino acids from the protein in the food he eats. In fact, they are called the "essential amino acids," which means the body cannot get along without them.

Certain kinds of amino acids, and definite amounts of them, are necessary so that the body tissues can use what they need. Plant proteins, such as those in peas, beans, and cereals, do not contain all the essential amino acids. But they are valuable in the diet when they are combined with some of the animal proteins.

Man cannot store amino acids in his body for later use. This means that the different kinds he needs have to be taken into the body at the same time. Bread and milk have to be eaten at the same meal, so the amino acids they provide can be used together to form new body tissue.

Moderate amounts of different kinds of protein foods should be eaten at each meal. In this way, you are sure of getting enough of the essential amino acids to meet the body's protein needs.

Do We Need to Take Extra Vitamins?

Vitamins are a group of substances found in food. The body needs them for life and health. So, naturally, a great many people are concerned with the question: Am I getting enough vitamins, and am I getting the right kind?

Even though very small amounts of each vitamin are enough for the needs of the body, the worry that people have about vitamins has some basis. And this has to do with their diet—the food they take in. A person eating a good variety of foods gets all the vitamins now known to be needed (with the possible exception of vitamin D).

The problem is that there are many people who don't choose foods wisely, don't get enough variety, and don't eat the basic foods they need to get their vitamins. So the answer to this question is: No, extra vitamins are not needed, providing you eat proper foods. In fact, many of the vitamins cannot be stored in the body, so when extra vitamins are taken in, the body simply gets rid of them.

It is even harmful to put too much of certain vitamins into the body. This has been found to be true of vitamins A and D, when large amounts are taken in capsules and liquids.

VITAMIN A

VITAMIN B-1

VITAMIN D

VITAMIN B-2

VITAMIN C

What foods supply what vitamins? Here is a quick, general idea. Vitamin A, for the health of the eyes, skin, teeth, and bones, is found in green, leafy vegetables, yellow vegetables, fruits, eggs, liver, and butter. B-1, which helps the nervous and digestive system and prevents certain diseases, is found in whole-grain bread, cereals, pork, and liver. B-2 is found in milk, eggs, greens, and lean meats.

Vitamin C, which helps tissues, bones, and teeth, is found in citrus fruits, tomatoes, and raw cabbage. Vitamin D is found in fortified milk and sunshine. These are only a few of the most important vitamins the body needs. The best thing to do is to get from your doctor a proper diet that includes the basic foods, and to be sure that you follow it.

Why Does the Body Use Up Vitamin C?

Here's a strange way to begin answering this question: Did you ever hear that sailors in the English navy are called "limeys"? The reason is that since 1795 all men in the English navy have had to drink lime water (or lemon juice) every day.

And why was this done? To prevent a horrible disease called scurvy. For hundreds of years, sailors had dreaded this disease. It attacked people when they had to live for long periods on preserved meats and foods and were unable to obtain fresh vegetables and fruits. Lime water or lemon juice prevented this disease.

Obviously there was something in this juice that the human body needed in order to function normally. Today, we know this is vitamin C, or ascorbic acid. Now if the sailors were getting plenty of food to eat, why weren't they getting vitamin C? Because vitamin C is quickly destroyed by heat, or storage, or exposure to air. And when most foods were prepared for storage in former times, the vitamin C was destroyed in them.

There is another problem connected with vitamin C. Almost all mammals are able to create their own vitamin C in the livers of their bodies, and so they can't suffer from a lack of vitamin C. But man (and apes and guinea pigs) are the only mammals that can't produce vitamin C in their own bodies. So they have to take it in with their food. And vitamin C is not stored up well by the body. It can be stored in small amounts, but not enough for our needs.

So all this adds up to the need for us to be constantly taking in vitamin C. The best sources of vitamin C are oranges, lemons, grapefruits, cantaloupes and strawberries. Of course, many people now take vitamin pills to supplement the vitamins they get from their diet.

The best thing to do, however, is to be sure you have a balanced diet so that you're getting all the vitamins you need, and to consult your doctor before you treat yourself with extra vitamins in any form.

What Is Pellagra?

Pellagra is a disease that results when a person doesn't have enough of a certain vitamin. The vitamin is nicotinic acid, or niacin, which is one of the B-complex vitamins. Most persons with pellagra also suffer from deficiencies of riboflavin and other vitamins.

Pellagra occurs in most parts of the world, but it has been especially prevalent in the southeastern United States and in South Africa. The reason for this in the United States was that many people in this area lived chiefly on a diet of corn. With better diets and the addition of vitamins to many foods, pellagra has now become less common. Drug addiction and alcoholism can also lead to pellagra, because people who are addicted to alcohol or the use of drugs often fail to follow the proper diet and generally neglect their health and physical well-being.

Among the first symptoms of the disease are loss of appetite, loss of weight and strength, headache, and stomach upset. A person is also likely to get diarrhea and outbreaks of the skin.

The sores on the skin are deep-red areas that gradually turn brown and become large, thickened, and scaly. They are strongest about the neck and backs of hands and forearms. There is also an inflammation of the gums and lining of the stomach.

An even worse sign of this disease can be a kind of mental unbalance that takes the form of sleeplessness, depression, or even violent behavior. So you see, pellagra is a rather unpleasant disease. At one time, about 65 percent of all patients who had it died from it.

But when it was discovered that nicotinic acid could cure pellagra, the death rate dropped to a low level. Usually, the giving of this vitamin must be accompanied by other vitamins, too. And the person must go on a well-rounded diet.

Following this kind of treatment, the symptoms begin to disappear within a few hours, and a person can feel complete relief within a few days. In fact, even the most severe mental symptoms of this disease disappear quickly after treatment with nicotinic acid.

What Is a Goiter?

In the front of your neck there is a very important gland of the body called the thyroid gland. It needs iodine in order to function.

While the body needs only a tiny amount of iodine, having this amount is essential. It helps in the formation of hormones, it is important in controlling the process of metabolism, and it has an effect on the nervous system.

The thyroid gland is subject to many different diseases, and the most common one is goiter. Goiter means an enlargement of the thyroid gland. The commonest form of goiter occurs in those parts of the world where the supply of iodine in the soil is low.

In mountainous areas, for example, iodine is often washed out of the soil, so the plants that grow there contain very little of it. Plant life is, directly or indirectly, the major source of food. So people in such areas soon become deficient in iodine.

What happens then is that the thyroid gland becomes enlarged in an effort to make up for the lack of iodine by producing more hormones. This enlarged gland is called a goiter. Sometimes such effort works, and sometimes not. It depends on the amount of iodine that reaches the thyroid. If there is no iodine at all reaching the body, then the enlargement of the gland doesn't solve the problem.

The amazing thing about this is the very tiny amount of iodine that is needed. The entire human body only contains about one fifteen-hundredth of an ounce of iodine. This is about two drops. And the daily requirement is even less, since iodine is used over and over again. By the way, this is why laws have been passed in many places requiring that iodine be added to table salt. Look at the box of salt in your home. It will probably have the word "Iodized" on it.

The addition of iodine to salt has done away with a good part of the goiter problem in the United States.

Why Does a Fan Make You Feel Cooler?

When you feel hot or cold, you are actually feeling the temperature of your blood! The body maintains an average temperature of 98.6 degrees Fahrenheit, regardless of what the temperature is "outside."

This doesn't mean that your internal temperature doesn't go up and down. It does. But whenever there is a change, the body makes some adjustment to get it back to "normal."

This process is regulated by a center in the brain that raises the temperature of the blood when it drops and cools it when the temperature is too high.

Let's imagine your blood temperature has dropped. Your sympathetic nervous system is told to go into action. Certain glands secrete enzymes to burn up oxygen more quickly. Oxidation in the muscles and the liver increases. The blood vessels of the skin contract, so that less heat is lost by radiation. If the temperature drops too low, the muscles are activated and you shiver. This is a reaction of the body intended to produce heat.

Now suppose the temperature of your blood rises. The oxidation process is slowed up, and the vessels of the skin are dilated to eliminate excess heat by radiation and to help the evaporation of perspiration. When a liquid evaporates—changes into a gaseous state—it draws away heat.

This is what happens when you perspire. The sweat that comes out of the pores of your skin is like a shower that washes the body from within and from without. It comes out of your body in the form of microscopic drops through millions of tiny openings.

If the air near your skin is humid, the evaporation is cut down. You can't seem to cool off. But when you use a fan to move the air that comes near your skin, the rate of evaporation is increased. Your body is losing heat in this way and you feel cooler.

Is All Human Blood the Same?

All human blood is made up of basically the same plasma, cells, and other chemical materials. But individuals differ in some of the arrangements and proportions of the chemicals in their cells and plasma.

There are four main groups, or types, of blood, and every human being can be classified under one of them. The groups are called A, B, O, and AB, based on the presence or absence of certain protein molecules in the blood.

When blood from two different groups is mixed and the blood clumps, it is because of a reaction between the protein molecules in the red cells and the plasma. Such chemical reactions make it dangerous for a person to receive a transfusion of whole blood from someone whose blood group is unknown. But if the cells are removed from blood, then the remaining plasma can be given to anyone, no matter what his blood group.

Blood can be exchanged among human beings whose groups and subgroups have been matched. However, certain large populations may have more of one particular group than another. Anthropologists who study man's physical development use blood groups as one of the ways of showing relationships among individuals and population groups.

So although human blood has many different groups and subgroups, it is basically all the same. In fact, each species of animal has its own kind of blood. For example, all cats have the same kind of blood, just as all dogs have the same kind of blood. The blood of one species cannot be exchanged for the blood of another.

What Is the Rh Factor?

When a person loses a great deal of blood for one reason or another, his life can often be saved by a blood transfusion. The blood of another person is put into the circulatory system and replaces his lost blood.

The first recorded blood transfusion was performed in 1677, when the blood of a lamb was injected into the veins of a dying boy. That boy was lucky and recovered. We now know that the blood of lower animals is different from human blood and cannot be used for transfusions with safety.

In 1940, it was found that there was still another way of dividing blood into groups, and this was according to the Rh factor. This discovery was made in the course of experiments on rhesus monkeys, and that's why it came to have the name "Rh."

It was found that when certain combinations of blood were made, the red blood cells broke apart. The cause was traced to certain differences in the Rh factor.

The blood of human beings in this case is divided into Rh positive and Rh negative. When blood from an Rh-positive person is transfused to a person who is Rh negative, the latter will develop a blood disease when he receives Rh-positive blood again.

In rare cases (one in forty or fifty), an Rh-positive father and Rh-negative mother will produce an infant with a blood disease if certain other conditions exist.

How Do Blood Banks Work?

Many hospitals have blood banks. In these banks, blood of all types is stored. When a unit of blood is needed, it is taken from the bank. Healthy people then give blood to the bank to replace the blood that is used. Blood can be kept refrigerated for about three weeks. A chemical such as sodium citrate is added to prevent clotting of the blood.

Transfusions are given mainly to replace blood that has been lost through severe bleeding. Such bleeding may occur as the result of illness, surgery, or accident.

Sometimes only a part of the blood is used for transfusions. Plasma, the liquid part of the blood, may be given alone. Transfusions of plasma are often given when people have been badly burned. In cases of severe burns, large amounts of plasma are lost from the bloodstream.

Transfusions of red blood cells alone may be used to treat certain cases of anemia. Anemia is a condition in which a person has too few red blood cells or his red blood cells contain too little hemoglobin.

When a person gets a transfusion, he gets blood of the same type as his. Otherwise there may be a bad reaction. For additional safety, the blood that is to be used in a transfusion is tested with the blood of the person who is to receive it. This testing is called cross matching of the blood.

Giving transfusions of blood that had been stored for some time was started by an American doctor, Oswald Robertson. He used it to treat wounded soldiers in 1918 in World War I.

PLASMA 55%

WHITE CELLS 2%

RED CELLS 43%

WHOLE BLOOD
FROM DONOR

DEHYDRATED PLASMA READY FOR
SHIPMENT TO DISASTER AREA

ANEMIC CHILD GETTING BLOOD TRANSFUSION

BLOOD BEFORE CLOTTING

FIBRIN THREADS

BLOOD AFTER CLOTTING

SERUM

(PLASMA)

BLOOD CELLS

What Is Hemophilia?

Did you know that you carry about an invisible first-aid kit in your blood? When a blood vessel is ruptured, nature applies "absorbent cotton" to stop the flow of blood. It isn't really absorbent cotton, of course, but it's something very much like it. It is a process known as clotting of the blood, and what makes it possible is the appearance of firm and very elastic fibrin threads that act as a sort of plug to stop the blood flow.

In every person's body the speed with which the blood clots form is different. There are some people whose blood clots very slowly or not at all. They are known as "bleeders," and their condition is called hemophilia.

Luckily, hemophilia is very rare. But, unfortunately, it is a condition that is inherited. It is transmitted in a peculiar way. Hemophilia appears only in men, but it is never transmitted directly from father to son.

It is transmitted from a father to a daughter, who herself remains healthy. She in turn gives it to her son, the grandchild of the sick father. So the rule for this disease goes like this: The son of a bleeder is always healthy and does not transmit the disease. The daughters of a bleeder are also healthy. Among their sons, however, the grandfather's disease reappears!

When the tragedy of this disease strikes it may be in a rich family or a poor one. In fact, this disease appeared in three of the most famous families in the world: in the Spanish royal family, in the Russian royal family, and in the children of Queen Victoria of England. In two of these cases, that of the Russian and the Spanish, the uncrowned successors to the throne were bleeders.

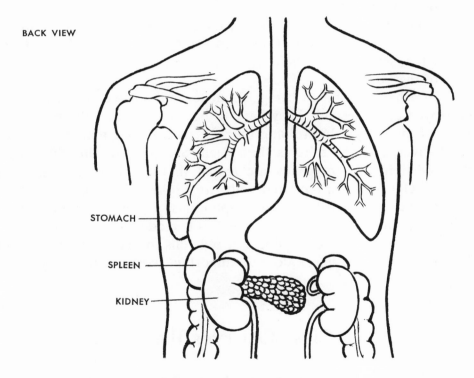

BACK VIEW

STOMACH

SPLEEN

KIDNEY

What Is the Spleen?

It is hard to believe that there is an organ in the body about which we still know little, and that what it does still cannot be fully explained. But such an organ is the spleen.

There is a well-known story about the spleen. A professor giving a medical exam asked a student to name the functions of the spleen. The student said: "I knew them all yesterday, but now I've forgotten everything." The professor said: "Too bad! We finally had someone who knew something about the spleen, and now this one person forgets it!" It's a joke, of course, but it indicates how much of a mystery the spleen is.

It is known, for example, that the spleen plays a part in making blood during childhood. It fights diseases of the blood and the bone marrow, such as malaria and anemia. Yet the amazing thing is that the spleen can be removed from the body and these vital processes will go on being performed! It seems that other parts of the body can then take over the work of the spleen.

The spleen is a large organ in the abdomen and lies next to the stomach, but it is not part of the digestive system. It is really attached to the bloodstream and could actually have been located in any other part of the body.

In a healthy human being, about ten million red blood cells are destroyed every second. They have to be replaced, and three different parts of the body help in doing this. One is the bone marrow, another is the liver, and the third is the spleen. Surplus red cells that might be needed in an emergency are stored in the spleen, among other organs. Old and worn-out red cells are broken down in the spleen.

Certain white cells, called lymphocytes, are manufactured in the spleen and in the marrow. When there is a sudden loss of much blood, the spleen releases large numbers of red cells to make up for the loss. So you see that the spleen does do important work for the body.

What Gives Our Eyes Their Color?

The eye is one of the most remarkable organs in our body. It is really a form of camera, with an adjustable opening to admit light, a lens that focuses the light waves to form an image, and a sensitive film on which the image is recorded.

Here we are not going to discuss "how we see," but rather the structure of the eye itself. The shape of the eye is round, except for a little bulge that sticks out in front where the light enters. This bulge, which curves outward in front, is called the cornea. The cornea is transparent. It helps bend the light rays as they enter the eye, and since it guards the opening into the eye, it is very sensitive. Any dust or dirt that alights on it is quickly felt so it can be removed.

The "camera film" of the eye is the retina. It is made up of ten very thin layers of cells and lines the entire inside of the eye. So now we have the opening to the eye, and the "film" which the light must reach inside.

To regulate the light coming in, we have the iris and the pupil of the eye. The iris is the circle of color, and the pupil is the little black dot in the center. By the way, the reason the pupil appears black is because it opens into the dark interior of the eye.

The size of the pupil is regulated by the iris, which closes the opening to a pinhole in bright light and expands the opening in dim light. Directly behind the iris and the pupil lies the lens, which is just like the lens of a magnifying glass. The lens is elastic and adjusts itself to long- or short-distance vision. It is the lens that bends the waves of light so that they will all come to a focus on the retina.

When we look into someone's eyes, the color we see is in the iris. The reason for this is that the fibers of the iris have pigments in them to protect the iris against light. The back part of the iris has most of the pigments, the front part almost none. Since the front part is very transparent and absorbs the red and yellow light waves as they pass through it, the light reflected from the pigmented part appears blue. The blue color is just a reflection of pigments from the back part of the iris.

If pigments don't develop in the front part of the iris in later years, the iris continues to look blue all through life. But if pigments do develop in the front of the iris, then it becomes brown.

Why Can't We See Colors in the Dark?

Light from the sun or from any very hot source is called white light. But, as Newton was the first to show, white light is really a mixture of light of all colors.

When a beam of light is made to go through a glass prism, we see all the colors of the rainbow—red, orange, yellow, green, blue, and violet. Each shade blends gradually into the next without a break. This spread of color is called a spectrum.

These colors are present in sunlight to begin with, but show up only after being spread out by refraction in the prism. Each color is refracted a slightly different amount, red least and violet most. This spreading out is called dispersion. Without dispersion, the mixture gives the appearance of white to the eye.

Color is determined by the wavelength of the light (like the distance between one crest and the next in a wave traveling on water). The shortest visible light waves are violet; the longest are red.

Most of the colors we see in our surroundings are not of a single wavelength, but are mixtures of many wavelengths. When white light falls on an object, some wavelengths are reflected, and the rest are absorbed by the material. A piece of red cloth, for example, absorbs almost all wavelengths except a certain range of red ones. These are the only ones that are reflected to your eye, so you see the cloth as red.

So color is a quality of light. It does not exist apart from light. All our color sensations are caused by light rays entering our eyes. All objects are seen by reflected light, and the colors that they show exist in the light and not in the object.

What Causes Blindness?

Did you know that there are at least fourteen million blind people in the world? There are many degrees of blindness, so it is hard to define blindness. Some people cannot even see light. Others can only tell light from dark. Still others have a small amount of vision.

Of all the blind people in the world, only a small percentage were born blind. Blindness at birth is called congenital blindness. The causes of it are not all known.

Blindness that occurs after birth is caused mainly by diseases of the eyes. A general disease of the body, such as diabetes or meningitis, rather than a disease of the eye itself, may also cause blindness. Accidents and explosions are two other causes of blindness.

In countries where people live longer because of good medical care and a high standard of living, old age often brings on certain eye conditions. Two of these eye conditions are cataracts and glaucoma. Cataracts are the leading cause of blindness in the United States.

A cataract is a clouding of the lens of the eye. The lens, the transparent part of the eye through which light rays pass, becomes cloudy, and only strong light rays can pass through it. There is consequently a loss of vision. Cataracts can be removed by surgery.

SPECIAL CATARACT LENS TO EXTEND VISION

With glaucoma, there is a hardening of the eyeball and great pressure inside the eye. Today there are medicines to control glaucoma if it is discovered in time.

The greatest single cause of loss of sight is trachoma. It is a contagious disease of the eyes caused by a virus. It affects the inner linings of the eyelids. Also, blood vessels grow over the cornea. This can destroy the vision.

Antibiotics can now control trachoma, but it is still common in some parts of Europe, Africa, and Asia.

SPECIAL LENSES TO GIVE SIGHT TO PERSON OF VERY LIMITED VISION

How Do Antibiotics Work?

Antibiotics are chemicals. When these chemicals are put into the body, they kill or stop the growth of certain kinds of germs. They help your body fight disease.

The name "antibiotics" was first applied to these medicines in 1942. It comes from two Greek words meaning "against life." Antibiotics work against the forms of life that we call germs.

Many antibiotics are made from microbes. Microbes are tiny living things. For example, bacteria and molds are microbes. The microbes used in making antibiotics are chosen for their ability to produce chemicals that wage war on the microbes of disease. In other words, man takes advantage of the struggle that goes on in nature among microbes.

Microbes are engaged in a constant struggle for survival. In the course of this struggle, microbes produce complex chemicals in their bodies. By investigating the chemical products of microbes, scientists have discovered many chemicals that kill disease germs. If these chemicals can be made in laboratories—and made in large enough quantities—they may be used to make antibiotics.

How do antibiotics cure diseases? How do they get to the right part of the body to go to work there? Strangely enough, science still doesn't know the answer. How does an antibiotic stop the growth of certain germs?

Some scientists believe that antibiotics cut off the germs' supply of oxygen. Without oxygen, germs cannot go on dividing. Others think that an antibiotic prevents germs from taking in food from the patient's body, so the germ starves to death. Still others believe that the germ mistakes the antibiotic for part of its usual diet. The germ "eats" the antibiotic and is poisoned.

Probably antibiotics work in various ways. One antibiotic may act in different ways against different germs. It may kill the germs in one case. In another, it may only weaken the germs and let the body's natural defenses take over.

What Is Chicken Pox?

The word "pox" means a disease with eruptions, and in chicken pox there are eruptions on the skin that may sometimes make it look like the skin of a chicken.

Chicken pox is also called "varicella," and is a contagious disease. While it is considered a childhood disease, adults may get it, too.

The specific organism that causes chicken pox has not yet been identified by medical science, but it is agreed that it is a virus. Chicken pox is passed on from one person to another by direct contact. It is rarely, if ever, passed on by contact with clothing or other articles touched by the infected person.

Here are the symptoms of chicken pox: a slight rise in temperature, loss of appetite, headache, and backache. Quite often, before any of these symptoms appear, a person breaks out in a rash or there are skin eruptions. The first skin eruptions are reddened spots about the size of a pinhead. They first show up in patches on the trunk of the body.

A few hours later, they enlarge and form blisters (vesicles) in the center of each spot. There is a clear fluid in the blister that later turns yellow, and then a crust or scab forms.

Most of the patches of eruptions appear on the back and chest. In severe cases almost all of the body may be covered.

Chicken pox is not considered a serious disease and usually requires little special treatment. But a doctor should be called to diagnose it and make sure there will be no complications.

The patient is usually made to stay in bed as long as new eruptions appear or there is some fever. Scratching the skin must be avoided to prevent infection or scars. One attack of chicken pox usually makes the person immune to the disease.

What Is Plague?

The first definite record we have of an outbreak of the plague is in the Old Testament. The Philistines were overcome by plague after they defeated the Israelites.

Plague is an acute infection that first attacks rats and other rodents, and then man. It is caused by an organism called *Bacillus pestis*. Fleas that live as parasites on the rodents transmit the disease by biting human beings.

When a person has plague, he has fever, chills, and swollen nodes in the groin. Spots also appear on the skin, and because these spots have a dark color, and because many people die of this disease, it was called the Black Death in the Middle Ages. It has also been called bubonic plague, and here is the reason: The swelling of nodes in the groin has been called a bubo, which comes from the Greek word

boubon, meaning "groin." A serious epidemic of any kind is sometimes called a plague; but there is a definite disease called the plague.

One of the greatest outbreaks of the plague in history was the Black Death of the fourteenth century. It originated in Central Asia, reached the shores of the Black Sea, was brought into many European ports, and within five years had spread over the whole continent.

When plague appeared, the first reaction was usually panic, and people would try to leave the region. But not everyone could. All kinds of steps were taken to prevent the spread of the disease. People were isolated in their homes and couldn't leave, and no one could visit them. Food was provided by special messengers. When a plague patient died, everything he owned was burned.

Bubonic plague returned to Europe in the seventeenth century. Almost half the population of Lyons, France, died. Some eighty-six thousand people died in Milan, and almost five hundred thousand perished in the Venetian Republic.

Today all kinds of preventive measures are taken to stop the rise and spread of plague, and most of them deal with the control of rats.

Why Do We Awaken from Sleep?

Everybody has strange experiences with sleep. Sometimes we want very much to sleep and we just can't seem to. We stay awake or wake up early. And sometimes we feel we could sleep for hours and hours more when that darn alarm clock goes off!

What wakes us up is something that scientists still can't explain fully. There are two theories about it, and let's take a look at both of them. One theory says that sleep and fatigue are pretty much the same. The nerve cells become tired because their reserve of energy is used up faster than it can be renewed.

Nerve cells can also become tired because waste materials accumulate faster than they can be eliminated. When we go about thinking and seeing and feeling and carrying on mental activities of all sorts, we use up energy. So the brain and other nerve centers need a rest. Sleep clears away our tiredness, and when we wake up we are rested and able to function again.

Some scientists believe that what really happens when we fall asleep is that one particular nervous center, called the vasoconstrictor center, becomes tired. This causes the blood vessels to cut off some supply of blood, and we go to sleep. When this center has its blood supply restored to normal, we wake up.

The other theory about sleep and waking up is quite different. According to this theory, we have a "wakefulness center" in the lower portion of the brain. Our mental activities and emotions during daily living stimulate this center. Now, if we can't shut off messages from the brain to this center, we remain awake. When we finally do it, by sending no more messages, we go to sleep.

Then suppose we get hungry while we're asleep, or feel cold or damp, or experience some emotion, such as fear. The wakefulness center is stimulated again and we wake up.

But don't forget that every adult person needs a different amount of sleep. It depends on your age, your body, your work, and even your sleep habits. An adult really needs only enough sleep so that when he wakes up he feels rested and well and can carry on his work during the day.

Do Dreams Foretell the Future?

If we tried to assemble all the superstitious beliefs that have existed about dreams since the beginning of time, we could fill a library! Most of these superstitions have to do with the "meaning" of dreams, and the "meaning" usually has something to do with the future.

It isn't just primitive peoples who believed that dreams foretold the future. In Europe there were soothsayers who claimed they could read a person's future from his dreams. In fact, divining the future from dreams was a recognized art in ancient times and was called "oneiromancy." This is taken from the Greek word *oneiros,* which means "dream."

Of course, we are all familiar with the story in the Old Testament of how Joseph interpreted the Pharaoh's dreams. And we know that even today there are people who buy "dream books" that are supposed to help them foretell their futures from their dreams.

What does science today believe about the content of our dreams? Why do we dream what we dream, and what does it mean? For one thing, science does not accept the idea that dreams are a "message" to us from any source, foretelling the future.

The subject of our dreams comes from any of several sources. It may come from some stimulus that affects us at the very moment we are dreaming, such as a sound, or the fact that our feet are cold, or a breeze blowing over us.

The subject may also come from our store of past experiences, or something we are interested in, or some strong urge we feel. Sometimes in the dream we repeat past experiences almost exactly as they happened. At other times the events are rearranged in our dream. But the subject of our dream is a result of our past experience, and not a foreshadowing of the future.

What Makes Us Daydream?

Is there anyone who doesn't daydream sometimes? It's rather nice in fact to daydream. We find ourselves doing some pleasant thing, or enjoying a great triumph, or accomplishing something we want very much, or getting something we strongly desire.

Daydreaming is actually a form of dreaming, only it is done while we are awake. Night dreaming is done while we are asleep. That is the only difference between them, since both are done when the dreamer is so relaxed that he pays no attention to what goes on around him. Then his thoughts can wander wherever they want.

For this reason, both sorts of dreams are often about strange persons, animals, or situations that could not possibly exist in real life. Night dreams are even more unusual and unrealistic than daydreams, because in sleep people have almost no control over what they think.

It is interesting to note that there are two kinds of daydreams that children have but adults do not: the daydream of the "imaginary playmate," and the daydream of the "adopted child." A child, if he has few friends to play with, may daydream that he has a playmate. Another child likes to imagine that he is "special"—that he is really a prince or princess and that his parents are a king and queen. Such a child then daydreams that he has been adopted, and that his real parents are royalty.

From this you can see that in daydreams we usually express something we need or want. In night dreams, we often express not only such things, but also things that frighten us. In either case, the dream is not something that comes from "outside," but is an expression from inside the person of needs, wants, fears, desires, and so on. The dream provides the opportunity for these to express themselves. Daydreams may give a person what he wants but cannot have in real life. In some cases they help the dreamer to plan ways of doing things in reality. Night dreams, in disguising the dreamer's feelings and granting his wishes, may help him to remain asleep and to get his rest.

A dream is something you tell yourself. A dream has special meaning for the person who creates it.

What Are Psychic Happenings?

There are certain things that people do, or that happen to them, that are considered to be "supernormal." This doesn't mean "supernatural." It means things that science doesn't recognize. They are called psychic phenomena.

There are several kinds of such happenings, and many people are very interested in studying them, many people believe in them, and many people don't believe in them at all. Let us see what some of these psychic phenomena are.

One is called "poltergeists." This concerns strange noises, movements of furniture, and breaking of dishes in situations where the people in the house can't explain how it is happening. However, where such things seem to happen, it is almost always necessary for a particular person to be present.

The more interesting psychic phenomena are the mental kind. In these cases a person seems to have knowledge of certain matters that he has no normal way of knowing. For example, a person may know another person's thoughts, or know about events that happened far away or long ago. Knowing what another person is thinking (in a supernormal way) is called "telepathy." Knowing about distant events or scenes is called "clairvoyance."

A great deal of research has been carried on by various people to prove or to demonstrate telepathy, but there are scientists who say that these experiments are not really conducted properly.

Another interesting psychic phenomenon is called "precognition." This is where people are supposed to know about events before they happen. Those who don't believe precognition is possible ask why such people can't get rich on the stock market, or prevent crimes from happening.

All in all, psychic phenomena produce arguments on both sides: those who believe in them strongly, and on the other side, the scientific world that believes they cannot and do not happen.

Chapter 4

How Other Creatures Live

What Was the Brontosaurus?

The brontosaurus was one of the family of dinosaurs, the reptiles that lived in what is known as the Age of Reptiles.

This age began in the geological period called Triassic, which began about 230 million years ago. Dinosaurs are last found in the rocks of the late Cretaceous period, which ended about 65 million years ago. So the age of the dinosaurs lasted about 165 million years.

Dinosaurs were land-living reptiles. Although some of them went into the water, these waters were mainly rivers, lakes, or swamps, rather than the sea. Dinosaurs included flesh and plant-eaters, and there were those that walked on their two hind legs as well as those that walked on all fours. They were cold-blooded, and most of them had scaly skins.

One group of large dinosaurs is called sauropod. Their "lizard feet" were huge and five-toed. The sauropods were the largest animals that ever lived. One of these was the brontosaurus, which means "thunder lizard," because it was thought that the earth must have groaned under its passing weight.

The brontosaurus had a small head (rather like that of a horse) at the end of a very long neck. The body was elephantine, and the tail was very long. It is believed that these animals must have weighed thirty or forty tons! Yet somehow they must have been able to move, find vegetable food, and survive many changes for years.

The brontosaurus probably lived chiefly in water, and the uplift of the water took a great deal of the burden of weight off its feet. In fairly deep water, it could float. A push with a foot would keep it on the move. And surrounded by water, it was thus protected against huge, flesh-eating rivals. For food it nibbled at the vegetation in the water or on the banks of lakes or rivers.

When the female went on land to lay her eggs, the flesh-eaters would attack; many a brontosarus died this way.

What Is a Narwhal?

A narwhal is a type of whale, one of the most interesting of this fascinating family of creatures. Most of us think a whale is a whale, but there are actually quite a few varieties.

Toothed whales generally live on various types of fish that they chase and capture. Sperm whales are the largest of the toothed whales. They may be sixty-five feet long, and their heads are huge. Another toothed whale is the bottle-nosed whale, which has strange bony crests on either side of its head.

The narwhal is one of the toothed whales. It is found chiefly in Arctic waters and has something that cannot be found on any other whale: the male narwhal has a long ivory tusk on the left side of its mouth that sticks out in front like a sword!

What Is the World's Largest Animal?

In prehistoric times there were gigantic creatures living on land and in the sea that were far larger than any animals alive today. The largest animal in existence today is the blue or sulphur-bottom whale. It may be over a hundred feet long and weigh 125 tons. And interestingly enough, about one-third of the length of this animal is taken up by its head!

Perhaps the most amazing thing about the whale is not its size, but the fact that it is a mammal and not a fish. Like all water mammals (such as dolphins and porpoises), whales are descended from ancestors that lived on land. There is evidence for this in the structure of their bodies. The skin and flesh of their paddlelike flippers cover the bones of a five-fingered "hand." Some whales even have the bones of hind legs embedded in their flesh.

Since the whale is a mammal, the baby whale is fed on its mother's milk like other little mammals. It is not hatched from an egg but is born alive, and for sometime after it is born it stays with its mother.

Whales have no gills, and breathe air through their lungs. They have horizontal tails, or flukes, which enable them to rise easily to the top of the water for air. The internal organs of the whale and the skeleton, circulatory system, and brain are also quite unlike those of the fish.

As whales developed and adapted themselves to life in the water, many changes took place; among them was the development of blubber. Mammals are warm-blooded animals, and it is very important for them to keep their body temperature within certain limits. Whales have a layer of fibrous tissue under their skin that is filled with oil and retains heat. On a larger whale, this layer of blubber may be from fourteen to twenty inches thick.

On the top of the whale's head are one or two blowholes; this makes it easier for them to breathe at the surface of the water. Underwater these nostrils are closed by little valves, and the air passages are shut off from the mouth, so there is no danger of taking water into the lungs. Whales can remain underwater for three-quarters of an hour!

What Are Pinnipeds?

Pinnipeds are fin-footed mammals with limbs that they use as paddles or flippers. The three main kinds of pinnipeds are the walrus, the sea lion, and the seal.

They are all carnivores, or flesh eaters. They are aquatic (water) carnivores with the same distant ancestors as land carnivores such as dogs, cats, and bears.

These early ancestors lived on land many millions of years ago. Eventually one branch of these early carnivores took to the sea and became adapted to life in the water. These were the ancestors of our seal, sea lion, and walrus.

Today about thirty different kinds of pinnipeds live in the world's oceans. Most of them live in the cold waters of the Arctic and Antarctic oceans and in the nearby areas of the Atlantic and the Pacific. A few kinds range into warmer waters, and several forms live in freshwater lakes.

Since pinnipeds spend most of their lives in the water, they have become very well adapted for this kind of existence. All are expert swimmers. Their bodies are tapered and streamlined, with a thick layer of blubber that gives them added buoyancy in the water and helps them keep warm. The blubber also serves as a reserve of food when needed.

Pinnipeds are expert divers. They can go two hundred or three hundred feet down in search of food. Many of them have big eyes that are useful for seeing in the dim depths. When they are underwater, their nostrils close. Most of them have sharp, backward-pointing teeth, so that they can seize prey and direct it down the throat.

Pinnipeds are sociable animals and live together much of the time in large herds. This is especially true during the mating season or when pups are born. All of them must return to land, or at least be on a cake of ice, before bearing their young. The young seals, sea lions, and walruses are born with their eyes open and with full coats of hair or fur.

What Is a Sea Elephant?

The sea elephant might be considered a fourth kind of pinniped, but it is really a giant seal.

There are two species of the giant elephant seals, or sea elephants. One, the southern elephant seal, lives in waters around Antarctica. The other, the northern elephant seal, lives in waters off the coast of lower California, and breeds in Guadaloupe and other small islands.

Both species look very much alike and grow to about the same size. Big adult males may measure nearly twenty feet long and weigh up to eight thousand pounds! The females are much smaller, usually not more than nine or ten feet long. A single ninety to one hundred-pound pup is born about fifty weeks after the mating season.

The enormous male elephant seal has a long, dangling snout. When danger threatens, a male inflates his snout and roars loudly.

Because they were hunted for their hides and oil, the northern elephant seals were almost extinct by 1890. But the Mexican government stepped in and protected the herds, which slowly increased. Now, each year at the breeding grounds, as many as eight thousand to ten thousand of these huge creatures can be seen.

What Are Otters?

Otters belong to another group of animals, the mustelids. This word comes from the Latin, and means "weasel." Other members of this family of animals include weasels, skunks, and badgers. They are all short-legged, have thick coats of fur and sharp, tearing teeth, and are meat-eating mammals.

Otters love water, and their webbed feet, thick tails, and dense fur make them well suited for life in the water. Two kinds of otters are found in and around North America. One is a fresh-water otter; the other is a sea otter.

The fresh-water otter is found in streams and lakes from Mexico to Alaska. Its coat is a rich, dark brown. This otter is a restless animal, always on the move; a male sometimes wanders fifty or sixty miles during the winter. It is a very shy animal and is seldom seen by people.

The home of the fresh-water otter is usually a hole dug into the bank of a stream or lake. The hole leads to a den lined with leaves. Here the young, usually two or three to a litter, are born in late winter or early spring. Before the young can swim, the mother sometimes carries them about on her back in the water.

But the young learn very quickly to swim themselves. Their parents teach them to dive and to catch the fish on which they feed. Soon the cubs are able to stay underwater for as long as four minutes.

The sea otter is found off the western coast of North America, from California to Alaska, and in other northern waters. Sea otters are larger and heavier than fresh-water otters. Their thick fur is dark brown and has a frosted appearance. They have white whiskers from which they get the nickname, the "old men of the sea."

When they are not in a hurry, sea otters often swim and float on their backs. They use their stomachs as tables from which they eat crabs, sea urchins, mollusks, and other sea creatures.

Sea otters were widely hunted for their valuable fur, and they almost became extinct. But they are now protected by international treaty and are coming back in great numbers.

Do Eels Ever Travel on Land?

Eels are fish—yet some fresh-water eels do travel over land!

Like all other fish, eels have backbones, live in water, and breathe through gills. Most eels live in the sea. A few kinds live in fresh water for long periods of time, but they, too, spend part of their lives in salt water.

All eels shed their eggs, or spawn, in salt water. This is why some eels have to travel on land.

Fresh-water eels often migrate a long distance to spawn. To reach salt water, some may have to travel over land to get around a dam or other barriers in the water.

While they are on land, their body mucus helps them breathe through their skins and also keeps their bodies from drying out. You probably will not see eels on land, because they travel at night. But you may find some eels in wells or ponds that are far from moving water.

The eels you see far inland are females. The male eels are smaller than the females, usually no more than one to one-and-a-half feet long. They are found closer to the sea in slightly salty water.

The females join the males, and all enter the sea. The eels are strong and fat, ready for their long migration to the waters where they themselves were born.

They leave the coast in the fall and swim hundreds of miles to the deep, quiet waters southeast of Bermuda. This area is known as the Sargasso Sea. There they spawn and die.

What is amazing is that the fresh-water eels of Europe spawn there, too. They swim across the ocean and shed their eggs there. When the eggs reach the larva stage, the Gulf Stream carries the larvae eastward. In about two-and-one-half to three years, the larvae reach the mouths of the European rivers, where they change into elvers, which means their bodies become like the bodies of adult eels.

Are Eels Dangerous?

Conger eels and moray eels live only in salt water. Most species of congers and morays live in tropical and warm temperate seas, and most live offshore. Some of these eels grow to giant size. A conger eel has been caught that weighed 160 pounds and was 9 feet long! Moray eels may grow as long as 10 feet, though most are 2 to 3 feet long.

Moray eels are the ones considered by many people to be dangerous. They live among rocks and in coral reefs, where they hide in holes and crannies. When they are hungry, they dart out and snap up prey that swims too near. Their jaws are very powerful, and they have sharp teeth.

The ancient Romans knew about moray eels and considered their bite poisonous, but people who have been bitten by them have shown no poisonous effects. The morays can, however, attack a human being under certain conditions and give a person quite a savage bite.

The eel that is really considered dangerous is not an eel at all. The electric eel belongs to the same order of fish as carp, catfish, and minnows. It has been found only in South America. About four-fifths of its body consists of electric organs, which are special muscles that contain electric cells.

When something disturbs it, the electric eel can discharge a powerful electric current that can give a human being a strong shock.

MORAY EEL

ELECTRIC EEL

How Many Kinds of Fish Are There?

There were no men on earth in the days when the first fish swam about through the oceans. There were no dinosaurs or elephants or any other highly developed forms of life. Fish were the first backboned animals to appear.

Fish, like all creatures that existed ages and ages ago, have undergone many changes in their development. In the world today there are more living species of fish than of any other class of backboned animals. There are at least thirty thousand different kinds of fish, and they live in every imaginable kind of water, from mountain torrents and tiny ponds to the depths of the ocean.

Fish are divided, however, into three general types. One is the cartilaginous fish, which includes skates, sharks, and rays. Instead of a bony skeleton, they have a cartilaginous one; that is, it is made of a firm but flexible substance. They also often have a tough, horny skin in place of scales.

The second type is the bony fish, which includes by far the greatest number of fish now living. Fish of this group have a complete bony skeleton and are covered with bony scales.

The third group consists of lungfish, or fish having both gills and lungs. All the lungfish live in fresh water. Their fins bear a faint resemblance to legs, and sometimes they come out on land. The climbing perch is an example of this kind.

Most fish, however, breathe by means of gills through which water is constantly passing from the mouth. The blood of fish is cold, but they have a nervous system like other animals and suffer pain and discomfort.

Their sense of touch is very keen, and they taste, as well as feel, with their skin. Two small organs of smell are located in nostrils on the head, and they have ears that are internal, which means inside the body.

Some fish are great wanderers and have no particular home, but mostly they live in little communities, much as land animals do. Most fish are predacious, which means they eat other fish or aquatic animals, and insects.

What Is the Largest Fish?

Compared to some other creatures that are now found on earth or once existed, man is very small indeed. Let's consider some of the biggest ones.

Next to the blue whale, the largest living creatures are the whale shark and the basking shark. They are classified as fish, so they are the largest fish known to man. They may reach a length of fifty to sixty feet!

Some people think of sharks as man-eaters, and since this is such a huge fish, you might imagine the whale shark capable of gobbling up a man. But it couldn't do it even if it wanted to. It has very small teeth, about an eighth of an inch long, and its throat is only about four inches in diameter. So this enormous fish actually feeds on some of the smallest creatures in the ocean, such as sardines and small squids.

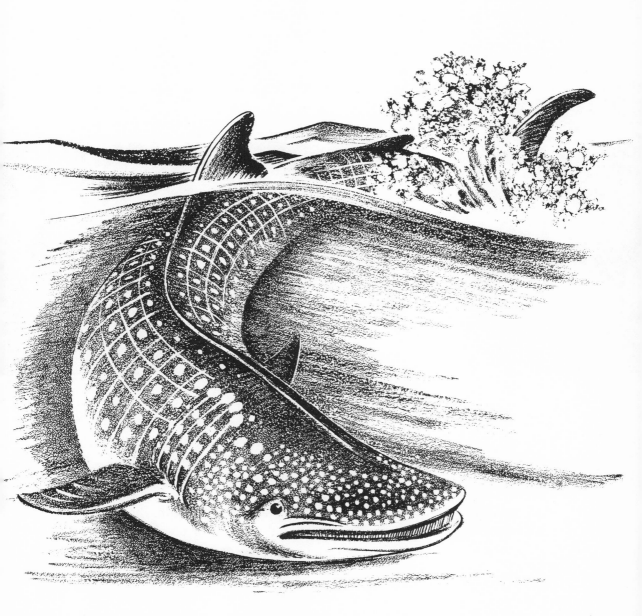

When it comes to fresh-water fish, the largest is believed to be the arapaima or piraruca, which is found in the waters of South America. This fish is said to reach a length of fifteen feet and a weight of five hundred pounds. If we consider the sturgeon a fresh-water fish, since some sturgeons spend much time in fresh water, then we have even larger fish. There have been sturgeons that measured twenty-six feet and weighed about 3,220 pounds.

What about the smallest known fish? They are found in lakes in the Philippine Islands. The smallest one is called *Pandaka pygmaea* and measures about one-quarter of an inch! In fact, they are the smallest living animals with a backbone.

How Are Guppies Born?

If you have an aquarium at home, you want fish that are beautiful, easily fed, have interesting life habits, and that are pretty sure to live. One fish that meets all these requirements is the guppy, sometimes called the "rainbow fish."

The guppy has very unusual and interesting breeding habits. You can actually see much of the process in your aquarium. Instead of the female dropping or scattering her eggs as most fish do, they hatch within her body. When fully developed, the eggs are delivered through her vent into their watery world as small but perfect fish.

They are ready to swim, eat, and to avoid the larger fish that would like to eat them. As a matter of fact, the mother herself is apt to gobble up a few of the babies, especially if she happens to be very hungry.

But there are easy ways to save the babies. The first instinct of the newly-born young is to swim toward the light. If the light side of the aquarium is thickly-planted with aquatic grasses, there will be few babies eaten. If the babies have a chance to hide, they'll outwit the adult fish.

The guppy comes from the northern part of South America, in and near Venezuela. Specimens were long ago collected by a gentleman from Trinidad named Lachmere Guppy, and were sent to the British Museum to be identified. The fish received different names at the hands of several scientists, but the one now used is *Lebistes reticulatus*. It was once named *Girardinus guppyi,* which was shortened to "guppy," and this is the name that has become famous in many parts of the world.

The male guppy has greater brilliance than the female, and every male is different. No matter how much you try, you can't seem to find two that are marked exactly alike!

What Is a Newt?

Newts are a certain kind of salamander. They belong to the class of animals known as amphibians, which includes frogs and toads as well as salamanders. Most amphibians spend part of their lives in water and part on land.

Today there are only three main groups of amphibians: frogs and toads, which have no tails as adults; salamanders and newts, which do have tails; and caecilians, which have tails but no legs.

Because newts have long bodies, people sometimes mistake them for lizards. But there is a way to tell them from lizards: lizards have scales, salamanders do not; lizards have claws, and salamanders do not.

Newts like to keep their bodies cool. Most of them live in the temperate zones of North America and Europe, where the winters are cold. Here they have adapted in various ways to the world around them. They may live entirely in the water or in underground caves. They may live in rotting trees or in cracks in rocks. On land they crawl or walk on small, weak legs. In water a salamander or newt swims or wriggles, helped by its long tail.

Newts are usually smaller than most other salamanders and have a thicker, drier skin. They are found in Asia, North Africa, Europe, and North America.

One kind of newt common in the United States leads a triple life. The eastern or red-spotted newt starts life in the water. In two or three months the tiny, light-green tadpole completes its metamorphosis and is ready for life on land. The newt turns coral-red, with two rows of black-bordered red spots on its back. It is now about one-and-a-half to three inches long, and is called the red eft.

After two or three years on land, the eft returns to water to lay its eggs. Its skin changes again, turning olive green on top. The skin becomes smooth. The round tail grows new fins. And the newt lives the third stage of its life in the water.

What Are Lizards?

Lizards are reptiles, a class of animals that also includes crocodiles, turtles, and snakes. There are about three thousand kinds of lizards.

A typical lizard is four-legged, short-bodied, and long-tailed. All lizards shed their scaly skins. They may do this several times a year. Lizards are found in all parts of the world except the polar regions. They thrive in tropical regions, but are also found in the temperate regions. Lizards of the temperate regions must hibernate in the winter.

Most lizards are small, usually less than two feet in length. The largest lizards are the Komodo monitors of Indonesia, which may grow to ten feet in length and weigh three hundred pounds. A lizard like that looks pretty much like the dragons of fairy tales.

As a rule, lizards have short life spans. Some live only two or three years. The record for a lizard in captivity is about twenty-five years.

Most lizards eat insects that they catch with their tongues or snap out of the air. They usually eat food that can be swallowed whole. Lizards have teeth that help hold their food, but they rarely use these teeth to bite off food.

Some lizards have quite specialized diets. The horned lizard usually eats only ants. Other lizards eat plants or perhaps only fruit. The large monitor lizard is one of the few meat-eating lizards. It eats dead animals and sometimes catches small wild pigs, which it swallows whole.

Most kinds of lizards are hatched from eggs, although many are born alive. The eggs are buried in the soil or hidden in decaying logs. Often the female guards the eggs against animals that might feed on them. The young have a special "egg tooth" that grows up from the tip of the upper jaw. The tooth is used to cut through the eggshell at the time of hatching, and then the tooth disappears.

Many lizards live in deserts. They can withstand the heat and dryness that make it impossible for most other animals to stay alive there.

What Is a Horseshoe Crab?

A horseshoe crab is a rather fascinating creature. To begin with, it isn't a crab, and it doesn't look much like a horseshoe. It is, however, related to crabs and spiders.

Its scientific name, *Limulus polyphemus,* describes its eyes. The animal has four eyes. One pair bulges from the sides; the other two are set close together at the front of the head and look like one eye.

A horseshoe crab is what scientists call a living fossil. Its body form has changed very little during millions of years. In fact, it has existed in its present form for almost 200 million years!

The entire body is armored by a thick shell. The tail is sword-shaped, long and pointed. It is also barbed. If the horseshoe crab is overturned by a wave, it uses the tail to right itself.

A horseshoe crab has six pairs of legs. Four pairs are used for walking along the sandy bottom of the ocean. A stronger back pair is used in pushing and swimming. A short front pair helps hold and push food toward the mouth. This mouth is practically hidden by the walking legs, so it's hard to find when you look for it.

The "shoulders," or inner joints, bear spikes. These grind and tear food and stuff it into the mouth. A horseshoe crab eats almost anything, from small clams, worms, and fish eggs to seaweed and decaying matter.

A horseshoe crab breathes by means of gill books. Each gill book has about 150 thin leaves, which take oxygen from the water. As long as these leaves stay moist, the animal can breathe.

Baby horseshoe crabs hatch from very tiny eggs. They are born without a tail and with a very soft shell. In about four weeks it is too large for its shell. The shell does not grow, so the animal must shed its shell, or molt.

Before a horseshoe crab reaches its full length of one to two feet, it may molt as many as twenty times!

What Are Mussels?

If you ever get a chance to walk along practically any shore of the Atlantic Ocean during low tide, you'll see an interesting sight. Lying exposed on the shore will be thousands of black shellfish, which we call mussels.

Mussels are in many ways similar to clams and oysters. Mussels have one unusual feature: They can anchor themselves to such things as sand, rocks, or even other shellfish. This is done by a structure mussels have called a "byssus." The byssus is composed of threads produced by a gland in the foot, or narrow end of the mussel.

Mussels are bivalves; that is, they have two shells. But unlike the oyster, they have no muscular hinge holding the shells together. The surface of mussels is smooth, also unlike the oyster's, which is rough-surfaced.

Fresh-water mussels do not have a byssus, so they cannot cling to rocks. Mussels breathe and eat by means of a tube called the siphon. This is divided into upper and lower parts by a partition. As water is drawn through the siphon, the gills take oxygen from it so the mussel can breathe. A small mouth in the tube captures the food as it goes by.

In the breeding season, the female mussel discharges millions of eggs. These small black eggs are carried under its gills until the young are hatched. When the larvae hatch from the eggs, they swim about for a few days. But soon the growing shell becomes so heavy that the mussel sinks to the bottom.

There are many hundreds of species of mussels, but the two chief divisions are salt-water and fresh-water mussels. The salt-water kind are about two inches long, and the fresh-water kind, somewhat bigger.

In the United States mussels are eaten, but they are much more popular in Europe. The shell inside is a delicate pearly-blue color, and is used for making buttons. Sometimes pearls are found in fresh-water mussels, but they are usually imperfect.

GILLS

MANTLE

STOMACH

HEART

YOUNG OYSTERS GROWING ON OLD SHELLS

What's the Difference Between Oysters and Clams?

There is a large group of animals that scientists call mollusks. The name comes from a Latin word meaning "soft." All mollusks are alike in that they have soft bodies that are covered by a thin envelope of flesh. The envelope is called a mantle. Oysters and clams belong to the mollusk family of animals.

Some mollusks have two shells. They are called bivalves (meaning "two shells"). Oysters, mussels, clams, and scallops are bivalves.

Oysters generally live in shallow waters, where they may be found cemented to rocks and shells near river mouths or along shores. The shells of an oyster open a little when it is feeding and close tightly when it is disturbed. An oyster withdraws into its shell when an enemy approaches or when the tide goes down.

The main body parts of an oyster—including heart, stomach, kidneys, and gills—lie inside the mantle. An oyster has no head, but it does have a mouth. It feeds by straining food out of the water. Food particles are drawn into a space between the soft body and the mantle. They stick to mucus that is produced by the gills. Then the food is passed along from the gills to the mouth folds and, finally, into the mouth.

Clams are usually found buried in sand or mud anywhere from just below the level of low tide out to depths of several hundred feet. Clams burrow into the sand or mud to protect themselves from various enemies and to secure firm anchorage.

A clam has a large foot that it uses for burrowing and for withdrawing quickly into the sand. When the clam wants to move from place to place, the first thing it does is extend this foot. There is a cavity in the foot, and when the clam extends it, blood rushes into the cavity. This makes the tip of the foot swell up, and it provides a kind of anchor. Then the clam contracts the muscles in the foot. Since the foot is anchored, it stays in place, and the clam's body moves forward. The clam's tough shell prevents sand or mud from pressing in on the soft body and smothering it.

No matter how deep a clam may be in the sand or mud, it gets food and oxygen from the water. It can do this because its mantle has a necklike portion that can stretch upward to the surface of the sand. This neck is called a siphon. It has two tubes. Through one tube, water is sucked in, and food and oxygen dissolved in the water are used by the animal. Water passes out again through the second tube.

How Do Oysters Eat?

When you examine an oyster in its shell you can easily wonder how it does anything but just lie there! How does it breathe, eat, protect itself?

The oyster, however, is not just a glob of living matter; it is quite a complicated creature that carries on many complex activities. It has various organs, blood, a nervous system, and so on. But here we will only concern ourselves with how the oyster eats.

First of all, what does it eat? The food of an oyster consists of tiny algae and other micro-organisms. This means organisms so small that they can only be seen under a microscope. These tiny food particles enter into the body of the oyster with the water that constantly "flows" through the oyster when its shell is open.

The food is strained from the water and becomes entangled in the mucus secreted by the gills of the oyster. The oyster actually selects certain food and rejects other organisms that are unsuitable or too big or the wrong shape, but we don't know how it is able to do this.

The oyster has an alimentary canal that begins at its mouth, and four feelers that guard the mouth's opening. These feelers receive and sort out the food.

There is a narrow esophagus that opens into the stomach, which is a large, saclike structure. A sort of rod about half an inch long projects into the stomach. This rod rotates in the stomach, mixing and grinding the small food particles. This rod also contains the enzymes that digest the food. There is also a large digestive gland surrounding the stomach.

In this gland there are blood cells that surround the food and digest it inside their bodies. Of course, this is only a rough idea of the whole eating process—but you can see that an oyster does eat!

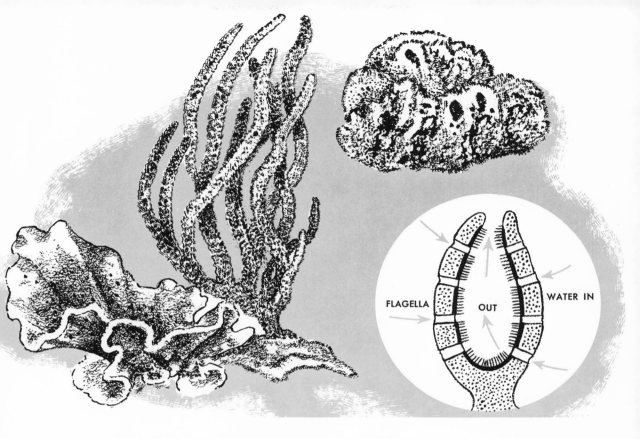

FLAGELLA OUT WATER IN

How Does a Sponge Eat?

It may seem hard to believe, but sponges are animals! They are among the strangest members of the animal kingdom, and they look much more like plants than animals.

There are more than five thousand different kinds of sponges. They range in color from green, brown, yellow, red, and orange to white. They may be shaped like fans, domes, vases, bowls, or trumpets.

Some sponges branch out like trees. Others are flattened masses of spongy tissue spread out on the surface of underwater rocks, shells, or wood. Some are small, less than an inch long. Others are big, measuring two or three feet in height or width.

Adult sponges never move about. And even though a sponge is a living animal, when you touch one it doesn't react. A sponge does not have a head or mouth. It has no eyes, ears, feelers, or other sense organs. And a sponge has no heart, stomach, muscles, or nervous system. If a living sponge is cut in two, all you see is a slimy mass with holes or channels running through it.

This doesn't make it seem much like an animal, does it? And you can understand why even scientists didn't realize for a long time that sponges actually were animals.

Then what does make a sponge an animal?—The way it feeds, chiefly. A sponge captures its food. It does not make its own food, as green plants do. It captures tiny plants and animals from the water around it.

How does it do this? The tube wall of a sponge is like a sieve, or filter, that strains tiny plants and animals out of the water. Water is forced in and out of the sponge by the beating action of tiny, whip-like threads (called flagella). The cells with flagella capture the food. Around the bottom of the flagella, there is a sticky surface that catches the food. Some of the food is digested there and some is passed on to the rest of the sponge by cells that wander through the sponge.

What Do Turtles Eat?

Turtles have many very interesting and unusual attributes, but their food habits are rather ordinary. The fact is, most turtles eat just about anything.

It depends, of course, on the particular kind of turtle. The snapping turtle, which is not a very pleasant creature to meet, is quite a good hunter. It feeds under water chiefly on fish, frogs, and even ducks!

The terrapin turtle, which people themselves like to eat, can eat its food best under water. It eats insects, tadpoles, and fish. The box turtle, which is a sort of connecting link between the land and the water turtles, likes to spend most of its time on land. But in the hot summer months it enjoys cooling off in the water. When it is on land, it likes to wander through the woods in search of berries and fungi.

Gopher turtles dig burrows in dry, barren places in which they rest during the day. In the early evening they come out and search for their favorite foods—fruit and vegetation.

And what do turtles do in the winter, when their food supply disappears? Like all reptiles, turtles who live in temperate climates go to sleep during the winter months. The length of their sleep depends on the climate. But many turtles can go without food and sleep away the time from October until March! Turtles that live in the water usually bury themselves in the bottoms of rivers and ponds. Land turtles hide themselves in the ground to spend the winter.

Land turtles breathe air through lungs, and have shells made up of a "bony box" covered with horny plates or with soft skin. These shells are divided into two parts. One part covers the back; the other covers the underpart of the turtle's body. Through the openings between the two parts the turtle can thrust out its head, neck, tail, and legs.

Turtles have a good sense of sight, taste, and touch, but their hearing is poorly developed.

How Do Frogs Croak?

If you've ever lived near a pond, then you were sure to wonder about the croaking of frogs. The noises they sometimes make at night can be enough to keep you from sleeping!

While some female frogs may make certain sounds when they are injured, the familiar singing or croaking we hear is limited to the male. The chief reason he sings his throaty song is to attract the female. But he doesn't limit his croaking to the mating season. His voice can be heard at night long after the mating season is past.

This is the way a frog makes that croaking sound. He inhales, closes his nostrils and mouth, and forces the air back and forth between the mouth and lungs. The sound is produced when the air passes over the vocal cords and causes them to vibrate.

Many kinds of frogs have vocal sacs that open into the mouth. When the frog is singing, these sacs become filled with air and enlarge. These enlarged sacs act as resonators and help give the frog's croaking that peculiar sound. By the way, the American bullfrog's voice may sometimes be heard from a distance of a mile or more!

While the adult frog has lungs, it does not breathe air into them as we do. It sucks air into its mouth through two nostrils, at the same time lowering its throat. Then the nostrils are closed, and the frog lifts its throat and pushes the air into its lungs.

Did you know that the frog uses its eyes in swallowing food? As you know, frogs catch their prey with sticky tongues. When an insect sticks to the tongue, it is folded back into the mouth. The large, bulging eyes of the frog are separated from the mouth cavity by only a thin skin. When closed, they bulge inward. So the frog closes its eyes when it has an insect in its mouth, and the inner bulging helps to push the food down its throat! Frogs are useful to man because they are insect eaters and help keep the insect population down.

How Many Kinds of Insects Are There?

What do most people think of when you mention "insects"? Well, they may think of pests, such as flies, mosquitos, moths, and beetles. Or, they may think of ants and bees and wasps; and attractive insects like butterflies. And then if you ask if they can think of any more insects, they might be able to think of a few more.

But do you know how many different kinds of insects there actually are? Get ready for a surprise. There are somewhere between two and four million different kinds of insects! Scientists have actually described in scientific language as many as 625,000 different kinds. They practically have no hope of ever being able to classify every single kind of insect that exists. There is no other class of animals on earth that even comes close to having as many kinds as do insects.

When it comes to trying to estimate how many insects are living in the world today, the number is so vast that the human mind cannot even imagine it! The only way scientists can even begin to count the insect population in any one area is to count all the insects that can be found in and on a square yard of rich, moist soil. That can be any-where from five hundred to two thousand. So it can be said that in a single acre of good soil, about four million insects live in cozy comfort!

Remember that if you, who are untrained in observing insects, were to go over this same acre and count insects, you would see only an occasional butterfly, bumblebee, or beetle. But the majority of insects are so small that the human eye does not readily notice them. Many are microscopic. And there are only a few thousand insects of all those that exist that become annoying enough to man for him to try to control them.

When you think of it this way, you realize that man really moves about in a world of insects—but he has no idea that most of them exist or how many there are!

By the way, there are two things most insects have in common: Their body is divided into three parts; and they usually have six legs. This is true of most, but not all of them.

What Are Fleas?

Most of us think of fleas as the tiny creatures that live on dogs and cause them to be constantly scratching. But did you know that there are more than nine hundred different species of fleas?

Fleas are parasitic insects, which means they live on other creatures. They live on all mammals (including man), as well as on birds and many other animals. In fact, next to flies, fleas are the insects with which people all over the world are most familiar. This is because they infect domestic animals and man, and have done so since the earliest times.

The bite of a flea can cause quite a bit of discomfort, but that is not the chief reason they are troublesome. Fleas can carry serious diseases, like typhus fever and bubonic plague, which may result in death.

Fleas lay their tiny eggs right on the host animal on whom they are living, or in the places where the host sleeps. The eggs are scattered widely by the movement of the host.

Larvae come out of the eggs, and when these are mature, they spin a tiny cocoon, and out of this the adult flea eventually comes. It only takes twenty-eight to forty-eight days for the human flea to develop from an egg stage to an adult. The rat flea in the tropics takes only twenty-one days.

An adult flea has no wings. But it has well-developed legs that it uses for leaping, and some species of fleas are quite remarkable leapers. Some can jump as high as eight inches straight up and thirteen inches horizontally!

The mouth parts of a flea are adapted to pierce the skin of other animals and to suck blood, on which they live. The body itself is flat.

Fleas are most abundant in the tropics and warmer regions, but they also exist in the polar regions and in deserts. In North America, the most important species of fleas are the human flea, the dog flea, and the cat flea. All three kinds, however, attack humans, dogs, and cats, among other animals.

ARMY ANT CARRYING COCOON

LEAF-CUTTER ANT

COMPOUND EYE

SIMPLE EYE

ANTENNA

HONEYPOT ANT

Do Ants Have a Sense of Smell?

Ants are such amazing insects that it would take much more space than we have here to tell their fascinating story. So let's just consider a few facts about them for now.

To begin with, you'll find ants in desert sands, prairies, seashores, mountain slopes, forests—practically anywhere in the world, except perhaps on the very summit of the highest mountains! They can endure almost all kinds of climates.

There are thousands of different species of ants, but they all are related to bees and wasps; that is, they belong to the same order of insects. All ants are social. This means that ants live in colonies. Each colony has three sorts of ants: the males; the females, or queens; and the workers.

The males and the queens of most species of ants have wings, but the workers are wingless. The queen gets rid of her wings after her mating flight. The colonies of ants vary greatly in size. Some may have only a few dozen ants living together; others may have hundreds of thousands of busy ants in the same colony!

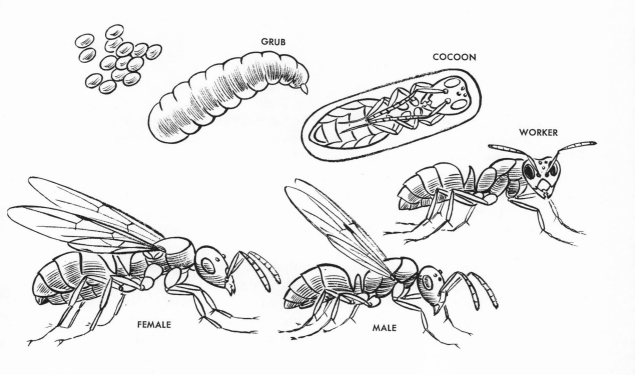

GRUB

COCOON

WORKER

FEMALE

MALE

Although ants vary greatly in size, they are all more or less alike in appearance. A pair of long feelers, or antennae, wave from the ant's head. These are constantly moving, and they serve not only as feelers, but also as organs of smell. So while the ant doesn't have a "nose" for smelling, it does have a sense of smell. The antennae also help the ant to distinguish other ants and to communicate with them.

The head of the ant also contains the brain, a pair of compound eyes, and its powerful jaws and mouth. In addition to the compound eyes, most ants have other seeing organs called simple eyes, or stemmata.

The life cycle of the ant is a fascinating one. The females of a colony fly high into the air, and the males follow them. After this mating flight, the males die almost at once, and each female, or queen, goes off by herself and starts a new colony. She digs a nest and lays some eggs. After these eggs hatch into little legless grubs, the queen mother helps each spin a cocoon. When the young ant has grown, she cracks open one end of the cocoon and pulls the ant out of its shell. Almost at once, these newborn worker ants begin their life of devotion to their mother and to the rest of the colony.

What Is an Anteater?

The anteater is an animal that feeds on white ants, the kind of ants we usually call termites. The anteater probably chooses ants rather than other foods because it has no teeth. Its very long jawbone is almost entirely covered with skin.

The anteater has a very small mouth and a wormlike tongue that is more than a foot long and is covered with a sticky substance. When the anteater sees a termite, it pushes out its tongue. The termite is trapped on the sticky substance until the anteater swallows down its prey.

Because many of the termites that the anteater hunts build large nests of hard mud, Nature has given it powerful forearms and long claws. The anteater uses its long claws to tear open the termite nest.

There are three kinds of anteaters, and each is quite different from the other. The giant anteater lives on the ground. It is about seven feet long; its head takes up about a foot of this length and its tail measures two feet. It has long, coarse hair. The claws on the front feet are so long that the anteater can't walk on them. It has to move along on the sides of its feet instead of the soles. The giant anteater feeds at night and sleeps all day.

The tamandua is another kind of anteater. It is about three feet long and has short hair. The tamandua uses its tail for many things. Without its tail, the tamandua would not be able to live in trees as it does.

The silky anteater is the smallest anteater of all. It is about a foot and a half long, half of which is the tail. So it can also live in trees. In fact, it spends the day curled up on a branch. The silky anteater lives in the area between southern Mexico and Brazil.

TAMANDUA

SILKY ANTEATER

GIANT ANTEATER

PINK BOLLWORM

What Do Moths Eat?

Most of us worry about moths in terms of destruction to our clothes. While clothes moths—in their caterpillar stage—do eat articles made from wool, fur, and other animal matter, they are not the only destructive moths in existence. Let's just go down the list of some other moths and see what they eat, or destroy.

CORN BORER   PEACH TREE BORER   SQUASH

The clearwing moth eats woody plants. There are peach, currant, and squash borers and you can guess their favorite foods. Then there is a species of moth that eats grain and potatoes. The pink bollworm, a very destructive type, eats cotton.

There are also pea moths, strawberry leaf folder moths, grapeberry moths, and bud moths. The species known as Pyralidae includes eight families of moths, all of them very destructive, including the European corn borer, the melon worm, the celery leaf tier, the meal moth (which feeds on cereals and other seeds), the oriental rice borer, and the sugarcane borer.

The larvae of the wax moth feed on wax, even going into bee-hives where they often cause serious damage. The Indian-meal moth is one of the worst destroyers of such foods as cereals, flour, nuts, and dried fruits.

Many of the tiger moths eat cultivated crops and trees. Some hawk moths feed on tobacco, tomatoes, grapes, and apples. The coddling moth is the chief pest in the apple orchard.

GRAPE HAWK MOTH

TOBACCO HAWK MOTH

But, remember, adult moths eat only nectar from flowers. It is when the moth is in the caterpillar stage that it eats all these other things.

By the way, the caterpillars of some moths have actually been used as food by some primitive peoples. For example, Indians in certain parts of the western United States ate the caterpillars of the Coloradia pandora moth.

PANDORA MOTH

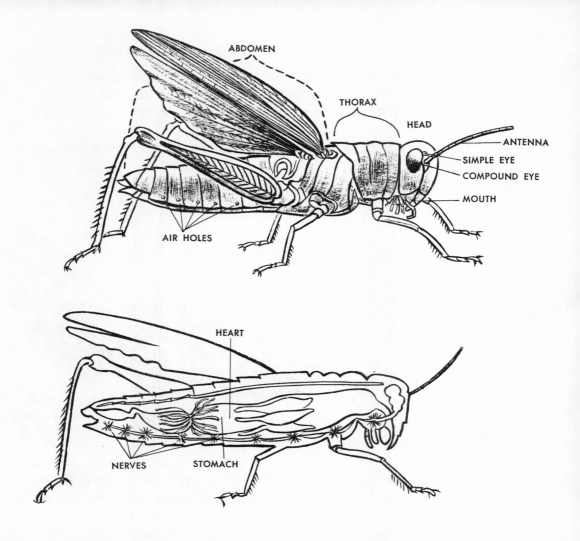

Do Insects Have Blood?

As we look at living creatures much smaller than ourselves, many of us imagine that they must lack the organs and functions that we have. How can something as tiny as an insect have a heart? How can it have a circulatory system and blood in its tiny body?

But the miracle of life is not only that these creatures have organs, but that these organs are perfect for each insect's way of life.

Adult insects have bodies with three sections: head, thorax, and abdomen. The head has a pair of antennae in front that are feelers, and that usually have some tiny organs of smell. The eyes and mouth are part of the head, too.

358

Not only does an insect have a heart, but it also has blood and a circulatory system. The blood passes into the heart by means of holes equipped with valves. When the heart contracts, these holes close, and the blood is driven out through the arteries. Insects don't have a system of capillaries and veins as we do.

The reason their circulatory system is not greatly developed is that they don't depend on the circulation of the blood for their supply of oxygen. In our bodies, as you know, the blood carries oxygen to every part and enables it to function.

But insects have a different system of breathing. They have tiny branching tubes that end in little air holes in the sides of the body. The air comes in right from the surface of the body and goes directly to the cells.

A more complicated system would be too much for their size. On the other hand, a simple system like theirs wouldn't be enough for larger animals. It's not too bad a system, though, considering that more than half of all living animals have it!

Did you know that one name for an insect is hexapod? The term is from two Greek words meaning "six" and "foot." If you count the feet of an insect, you can see why hexapod is a good way to describe most insects. The legs are usually in three pairs, and are attached to the thorax.

There are thousands and thousands of different species of insects, among them some of man's best friends as well as some of his worst enemies.

Where Do Mosquitoes Go in Winter?

We don't see mosquitoes in winter in parts of the world where winters are cold, but mosquitoes may still be there. They are alive in a different form from that of the flying insect we know.

A mosquito spends the first part of its life in water and the rest of its life on land and in the air. The life of a mosquito begins when a female lays eggs on stagnant water. Soon larvae, or "wrigglers," hatch out and begin to swim around looking for food.

In time the larvae change into pupae or "tumblers." Then each pupa becomes a grown insect and flies away. This whole process— from new egg to adult mosquito—may only take nine to fourteen days!

But when cold winter comes, the eggs lie dormant. They don't hatch. And in some species of mosquitoes, the fertile females spend the winter in a kind of sleep, too. So mosquitoes spend the winter as adults, eggs, wrigglers, or pupae.

An interesting fact is that while we think of mosquitoes as being the greatest pests in warm climates, they are actually far worse pests in the far northern regions of Canada, Alaska, and Siberia. This is because mosquito eggs are able to live through the winter in the snow. When the snow melts, the insects hatch out in such great swarms that stories have been told of men having been driven insane by them!

Of course, the danger that mosquitoes present to man is not that they are annoying pests, but that they spread diseases when they bite healthy persons after having bitten sick ones. The mosquito draws in the germs of viruses that cause diseases when it takes in blood from a sick person. Then when the mosquito bites a healthy person, it injects the germs with its saliva. The germs serve no purpose for the mosquito; it is interested only in the blood.

Do Leeches Suck Bad Blood?

Years ago, before medical sicence and knowledge were as developed as they are today, bloodletting was considered the cure for all diseases. If you could only get enough "bad blood" out of the patient, he was sure to recover!

As a matter of fact, "leech" was the name for not only the blood-sucking worm that the doctors used, but it was the name for a doctor, too! Early in the nineteenth century, leeches were so popular with doctors that some people made a business of raising them. In some countries there were even open and closed seasons for catching them!

At present, leeches are very rarely used for this purpose in Europe or America, though the practice is still carried on in some Oriental countries. One way in which leeches are still valuable to medicine is the use made of a substance extracted from their salivary glands. It is called hirudin and it keeps blood from clotting, which is sometimes necessary during surgical operations.

FRESH-WATER LEECH

UNDERSIDE   BACK   MEDICINAL LEECH

Leeches are closely related to earthworms. Most leeches are flat, and are black, green, or brown in color. They vary in size from less than one inch to almost three feet. Most of them live in fresh water, but some, especially the larger ones, live in the sea, and a few live on land. On the leech's head is a sucker-like mouth equipped with small, saw-shaped teeth.

Leeches are not especially attracted to "bad blood." Those that suck blood simply go after blood! Except for one kind of "stinging" leech, the bite of a leech is painless. In fact, sometimes the only way you can tell you've been bitten by a leech is the bleeding that continues after it has dropped off. Leeches are not poisonous. But there have been cases where people who have lain helpless in the jungle because of injury or sickness were drained of their blood until they died!

How Many Kinds of Bats Are There?

There are nearly a thousand different kinds of bats! They live in almost every part of the world except the polar regions. Each kind of bat has different habits, depending on where it lives. Yet despite all their differences the various species have many things in common.

Bats generally live in groups, but they do not make their own dwellings. They usually inhabit caves. In some caves there may be a colony of thousands of bats. But there may be bat colonies of only ten or twelve bats living in a hollow tree.

Some bats roost in trees, hanging like leaves from twigs and branches. Two kinds of tropical bats make little tents from palm leaves. There are bats living in the pyramids of Egypt and in the fruit trees of Australia. In North America and Europe, bats often live in homes of human beings. A bat can squeeze through narrow cracks and roost between layers of wall and ceiling.

While most bats are active only at night, there are some bats that venture out in bright sunlight. Most bats live on insects alone. Some eat only fruit; some eat both insects and fruit. A few kinds of bats eat meat, fish, and even flower nectar.

In India, there is one kind of bat that eats mice, birds, and lizards. The large spear-nosed bat of tropical America will eat almost anything once it is living in captivity. Such bats will eat bananas, horsemeat, liver, and hamburger. They will even eat smaller bats.

The bats with the most unusual diets are found in the tropics. The Noctilio bats of South and Middle America eat fish. Another group of jungle bats, the tiny hummingbird bats, eat chiefly the pollen and nectar of flowers.

Of course, there is the famous vampire bat of South and Middle America. It bites other animals—horses, cows, goats, or even men— laps up a small amount of blood, and flies away.

FRUIT BATS

Where Do Snakes Get Their Venom?

Scientists think there are about two thousand four hundred different kinds of snakes now living. Of these, only about 8 percent are poisonous kinds that stun or kill their prey with venom. In many poisonous snakes the venom is not strong enough or plentiful enough to be dangerous to man.

All snakes have a large amount of saliva that helps them swallow and digest prey. In the venomous snakes one of the saliva glands produces a substance that is poisonous to the snakes' prey. This substance is the snakes' venom.

Some snakes have venom that is strong enough to kill an elephant. Others have venom so mild that they can kill only small lizards. Probably only two hundred species of venomous snakes can be considered dangerous to man.

Among the venomous species of snakes known, the cobras and their relatives make up one family; the vipers, a second. And there are some venomous snakes among a kind known as the colubrids, the largest family of snakes.

The cobras and their relatives have fangs at the front of the mouth, one on each side of the upper jaw. The fangs are grooved, but in most cobras the groove is closed over, forming a hollow tube. A muscle surrounds the venom gland. When the snake bites, the muscle presses on the gland. This forces the venom down into the fang and out through the fang tip directly into the prey.

There is a spitting cobra that can spray venom from its fangs. The cobra aims at the eyes of a threatening animal, such as an antelope or buffalo. The spray reaches about eight feet and causes almost instant blindness.

In general, cobra venom affects the nervous system of the victim and makes him unable to move. When the venom reaches the nerve centers that control breathing or heartbeat, the victim dies.

Vipers have very long fangs. Their venom affects mainly the blood cells and blood vessels of the victims. It may cause great swelling and bleeding.

POISON GLAND
MUSCLE
FANGS

VIPER

366

What Do Snakes Eat?

There are no "vegetarian" snakes. They are all carnivores and eat animals of some kind.

Snakes have powerful digestive juices—and they need them, for snakes always eat their meal whole. They do not have teeth that can cut up food, such as cats have, for example. Birds and turtles have sharp beaks. All that snakes have are slender, needlelike teeth with which they can catch their prey and pull it into their mouth. But they can't chew it up.

One of the most unusual things about snakes and their eating is the construction of their jaws. The jaws are very loosely attached to the other bones of the skull. They are edged with teeth, and most snakes also have two rows of teeth in the roof of the mouth. All these rows of teeth are on bones moved by special muscles.

A snake eats by pushing one jaw over the food while the teeth of the rest of the jaw hold the prey. Then another jawbone is pushed over the food. In this way the food is pulled down into the throat of the snake.

Because of the arrangement of the jaws, a snake can eat animals that are surprisingly big. For example, pythons sometimes eat animals that are as large as deer and leopards! Of course, small snakes eat small animals. Most snakes eat animals of moderate size: grasshoppers, frogs, fish, mice, rats, and birds. Some tiny blind snakes eat only termites. And there are some snakes that eat other snakes!

Snakes tend to be particular about what they eat. A green snake may eat spiders, fish, birds and caterpillars, but not lizards or mice. And a water snake may eat fish and frogs, but not insects or mice. Garter snakes, however, seem able to eat a variety of animals, including worms, fish, frogs, rodents, and birds.

How Do Wolves Hunt?

The wolf has always had a bad reputation. It is cast as the villain of many of Aesop's fables and countless nursery rhymes and fairy tales. Little Red Riding Hood was pursued by a greedy wolf, and so were the three little pigs.

How does this creature go about getting its food? When searching for food, wolves travel regular hunting trails that may extend for a hundred miles or more. Sometimes several weeks pass before the wolves cover the entire circuit. From time to time the wolves fan out—eyes, ears, and noses alert for possible prey.

At intervals along the trail, the wolves have "scent posts." These are stumps, trees, rocks, or other landmarks upon which they urinate, just as dogs do on fireplugs or shrubbery. Each time a wolf comes to a scent post, he sniffs it carefully. In this way he learns what other wolves have passed that way.

The main food of wolves is meat, and the kind depends on what prey is most readily available. Wolves will attack and eat deer, moose, and many other large, hoofed animals. In Canada and Alaska, wolves follow herds of caribou and prey on the calves and stragglers.

In the Arctic, they sometimes attack musk oxen. And whenever domestic stock is left unguarded in wild country, it is likely to be killed and eaten. Rabbits and rodents are hunted when no easier prey is around. If wolves can't find any meat, they will eat fruit, such as berries.

Sometimes wolves track their prey for many hours. They keep up a tireless pace that is not swift, but that they can continue for mile after mile. Finally the prey is brought to bay. Several wolves may attack from the rear, others from the front. When the quarry finally goes down, the pack swarms all over it, slashing and biting until the victim is dead.

Then all the members of the pack gorge themselves, sometimes eating as much as fifteen pounds of meat each. The remainder of the meat may be hidden or buried as a supply for future meals.

Where Do Rhinoceroses Live?

There are five different kinds of rhinoceroses living today, of which two—the black rhinoceros and the white rhinoceros—are found in Africa. Both have two horns.

The other three kinds of rhinoceroses live in Asia. The Indian and the Javan rhinoceroses each have one horn. The Sumatran rhinoceros has two horns.

Rhinoceroses have huge, heavy bodies and usually move about very slowly. They pay little attention to their surroundings and do not hunt other animals for food. Rhinoceroses eat only grass and other plants.

This huge creature is usually quiet and retiring. But if it is cornered, it can become very fierce and dangerous. A rhinoceros can charge at a speed of thirty miles an hour and use its strong, pointed horns to attack its enemy.

The smallest rhinoceros, the Sumatran, usually weighs less than a ton and is about three to four-and-one-half feet high at the shoulder.

The largest rhinoceros, the African white, weighs three-and-one-half tons or more and stands six-and-one-half feet high.

The great body of the rhinoceros rests on four short legs. Each foot has three toes. Rhinoceroses are hoofed animals and are related to horses.

The horns of some kinds of rhinoceroses are often very long; the longest ever measured was sixty-two-and-one-half inches. There may be one or two horns, depending on the kind of rhinoceros. The first lies above or slightly behind the nostrils; the second is behind the first, about even with the eyes. The horns are closely-packed masses of tough hairs.

The rest of the body is usually hairless, except near the ears and at the tip of the tail. The skin of a rhinoceros is tough and thick.

Rhinoceroses usually travel alone, but they are sometimes found in small family groups.

A female bears only one young at a time. The calf is born about eighteen months after the mating season and remains with the mother for several years.

In captivity rhinoceroses may live to be about fifty years old.

How Do Elephants Live in Herds?

An elephant herd may vary from ten or twenty animals to fifty or more, most of whom are related.

The leader of the herd is usually a wise old cow, or female elephant. Most of her followers are females with young in various stages of growth. Young males also travel with the herd, but adult bulls often travel alone. Many live apart from the herd, but visit it often.

When two or more bulls join the herd at the same time, they are likely to fight each other. When one of them gains the upper hand, he may gore the other, drive him away, or even kill him.

The herd wanders far and wide, visiting favorite food areas at different times of the year. During the dry season they migrate into forests or stay close to a good supply of water. In the rainy season they wander out onto grassy plains.

The daily life of an elephant herd often follows a routine. In the early morning hours the animals may travel to a nearby river. There they drink and bathe—snorting and rolling and squirting water over themselves. Elephants are good swimmers and can cross broad rivers.

After bathing, the elephants feed on trees and other plants for several hours. Then they pause in some shady area for a midday rest. As evening comes on they sometimes go back to the river to drink again.

They may feed far into the night before taking another rest period. Some elephants lie down to sleep, but many adults—especially among the African elephants—sleep standing up.

All the adult elephants in a herd are constantly on the alert for danger. They have poor eyesight and only fair hearing, but they have a keen sense of smell. When a youngster in a herd is attacked— possibly by a lion or tiger—the rest of the herd rallies to its defense. In Asia, tigers kill about one of every four elephant calves. Adult elephants are rarely attacked by any other animal.

What Is a Gazelle?

A gazelle is a kind of antelope. There are about a hundred species of antelopes, which are members of the cattle family and which are characterized by their graceful build and upward-sweeping horns.

The graceful horns of some gazelles look like a lyre. These horns may be heavy, streamlined, or bent, varying in shape from a V or U to a bracket, depending on the species.

A gazelle is about twenty-six inches high.

The expression "swift as a gazelle" comes from the fact that they can move with great speed. A gazelle can run faster than a greyhound.

Antelopes as a whole are most abundant in Africa, where there are about ninety species. Ten species are found in India. At one time antelopes lived over most of Europe and Asia.

All male antelopes have horns, and in half the species, females have horns, too. Some kinds have only one-inch spikes, while the giant sable antelope has tremendous sixty-four-inch half-circles.

Most antelopes are graceful and shy, but certain species, such as the wildebeest, sable, roan, eland, and oryx, are dangerous when approached or wounded. The wildebeest, or gnu, looks like a horse with a beard and buffalo horns, and is especially savage. It has such great endurance and speed that it can easily outdistance a horse.

374

Many antelopes live on open plains, often in herds of hundreds. Others live singly or in small herds. Some live in marshes, near riverbanks, on cliffs, or in deserts.

Antelopes are usually tawny, reddish, or gray, often with white belly, rump, and face markings. Some are beautifully marked and colored. Antelopes walk on two-toed hoofs and, like other cattle, ruminate, or chew the cud.

Is the Duckbill a Mammal or Bird?

It would be hard to find a stranger creature in all the world than the duckbill, or platypus. The chances are that you will never see a live duckbill, because it dies in captivity. What makes this creature so odd?

For one thing, the duckbill is like a fish, like a fowl, and like a reptile, yet it is not any of them! It's a kind of in-between animal that came about by evolution.

Mammals nurse their young, and so does the duckbill. Fowl and birds lay eggs, and so does the duckbill. The body temperature of a reptile changes with the heat or cold of its surroundings, and this also happens to the duckbill! Actually, however, the duckbill is a mammal, one of the only two mammals that lay eggs (the other is the anteater).

The duckbill has webbed feet and a ducklike bill instead of a mouth. It swims in the water somewhat like a fish. It is found only in the eastern portion of Australia and in Tasmania.

The males are about twenty-one inches long, and the females, about eighteen inches. The body is covered with a fine underfur hidden by a coat of long, coarse guard hairs, whose ends turn in toward the body. It has a flat tail, somewhat like a beaver's. The duckbill can hear quite well, even though it looks as if it has no ears. It hears with a set of internal ears.

The duckbill can't breathe underwater, so it must keep its bill in the air while it swims. But since the nostrils are about one-third of the distance from the tip of the bill, it has to keep only the end of its bill out of water.

On the heel of each hind foot of the male is a horny organ connected with poison glands, so this creature can take pretty good care of itself. This peculiar animal makes its home in burrows in the banks of quiet, deep pools in rivers. The duckbills stay in the burrow most of the day and come out only at night to feed in the water. They eat water insects, worms, and shellfish.

The duckbill builds a special burrow for nesting purposes, which it fills with leaves, grass, and reeds. The female lays her eggs in the nest and lies curled around them to incubate them. The young are born blind and helpless, and remain in the burrow for some time, feeding upon the mother's milk.

BACTRIAN CAMELS

FOOD AND WATER SUPPLY DEPLETED

How Long Can a Camel Go Without Water?

At one time, before automobiles and airplanes were invented, there was only one possible way to travel across the deserts of Asia and Africa. That way was by camel. That's why the camel has been called "the ship of the desert."

While there are many things about the camel that make him especially suited for living and traveling in the desert, the most important of these is the hump on his back.

When that hump is empty, it loses its firm shape and flops to one side in flabby folds. There is no bone in the hump; it is made of fat and muscle.

The purpose of the hump is to serve as a storage place for food. For days before a camel starts out on a journey, its master forces it to eat and drink. It eats so much that a hump of fat, perhaps one hundred pounds in weight, rises on its back. This fat can nourish the camel for several days if it is unable to find food on the journey.

The camel also takes its own water supply along. The camel driver forces the camel to drink about fifteen gallons of water. He does this by giving the camel salt to make it more thirsty.

The camel has three stomachs. It uses the first one to store food while it is grazing and to form it into a cud. In the second stomach are the digestive juices, and in the third stomach the chewed cud is digested.

In the walls of the first two stomachs, there are pockets for storing water. Muscle holds these pockets closed when they are filled. Whenever the camel needs some water, these muscles open and close to let out as much as it needs.

How long can a camel go without water? As you can see, it is not really without water. In fact, men who have been dying of thirst have sometimes killed a camel to obtain its precious water. If a camel travels slowly and with a light load, that water in its stomach can last from six to ten days!

How Fast Can Birds Fly?

We have horse races and we have athletic events in which men race. It's pretty easy to decide the speed in these cases because there's a starting line and a finish line; and there are accurate measuring devices being used by several observers. But how do we measure the speed of birds in flight?

Many figures have been published about the speed in flight of various birds, but there seems to be quite a bit of disagreement on the subject because not all authorities accept the records as accurate.

For example, birds called swifts are supposed to have been timed at more than 170 miles an hours in India. In Mesopotamia, someone claimed they were timed at about 100 miles an hour. A European peregrine was timed with a stop watch while making a dive at 165 to 180 miles an hour.

But most authorities doubt these figures. One expert believes that the fastest recorded flight for a bird was that of a homing pigeon going at 94.2 miles per hour.

FALCON

PLOVER

GOOSE

DUCK

MOURNING DOVE

SWIFT

HUMMINGBIRD

Here are the generally accepted figures on the speed of flight of birds. The peregrine falcon can fly at about 65 to 75 miles per hour. The next fastest birds are ducks and geese, who can go at about 65 to 70 miles per hour.

The European swift can reach 60 to 65 miles per hour, and so can the golden plover and the mourning dove. Hummingbirds, whom we all think of as very fast, do reach speeds of 55 to 60 miles an hour. Starlings can go at about 45 to 50 miles. Swallows usually fly at about 25 miles per hour, but can fly as fast as 45 to 50.

The crow usually moves along at 20 to 30 miles, but can reach 40 to 45. Herons can fly 35 to 40 miles an hour. The pheasant can fly at 35 to 40 miles. And surprisingly enough, the wild turkey can fly at 30 to 35 miles. The blue jay moves along at 25 to 30 miles.

What Is the Bald Eagle?

The bald eagle is an American bird. Despite its name, it is not what we think of as bald.

The bald eagle was named at a time when "bald" meant "white" or "streaked with white." The adult bald eagle has white feathers on its head. Its tail is white, too. Its body and wings are dark brown, and its eyes, beak, and feet are yellow.

The bald eagle is fond of fish and likes to live near water. It feeds mainly on dead or dying fish. Sometimes the eagle steals its catch from the osprey, another large fishing bird. The bald eagle also eats small animals, such as rabbits or birds.

The bald eagle is the national emblem of the United States. Like all the other eagles in North America, it is becoming rare. But eagles are among the most interesting birds known to man.

Some eagles are more than three feet long from head to tail, and their wingspread may be more than seven feet. An eagle's beak is large and hooked. Its toes end in talons, which are strong claws. An eagle has far keener eyesight than a human being.

An eagle is a bird of prey; that is, a hunter. The eagle swoops down, picks up the prey in its talons, and flies off. An eagle, which weighs eight to twelve pounds, may be able to carry off an animal weighing as much as seven-and-one-half pounds! With its beak, it tears the food to pieces. Eagles, by the way, hunt only in the daytime.

An eagle keeps the same mate for many years, perhaps for life —no one is sure. A pair of eagles build their nest at the top of a very tall tree or on a rocky ledge. The nest, called an aerie, is built of sticks. The largest aerie on record is nine-and-one-half feet wide and twenty feet deep. Many eagles use the same nests year after year. An eagle may live as long as thirty years.

Do Any Birds Hibernate?

When the cold of winter comes, we can tuck ourselves into a warm house, sit by the fire, and stay indoors until we want to go out. But even though we are a warm-blooded animal, we can't hibernate. If man did hibernate, do you know he'd be able to prolong his life by surviving freezing temperatures?

Birds, alas, cannot hibernate either. They can, however, endure very cold temperatures. Even a little canary such as you might keep in a cage could survive outdoor temperatures of minus thirty degrees, or even minus fifty degrees, providing it could obtain enough food. For birds who can obtain food and who don't migrate to warmer climates, hibernation is not necessary.

The process of hibernation is controlled by a temperature-regulating center in the brain. When it becomes cold, warm-blooded animals react by sending blood from the skin to the interior of the body, by erecting their fur or feathers to improve the insulation against cold, and then by shivering, which increases the heat production.

Hibernating animals simply "turn down" this heat regulator in their bodies when it comes time to hibernate. They become practically cold-blooded animals. The process is triggered by cold temperature, a lack of food, shorter days, and other conditions.

As an animal enters hibernation, its temperature regulator becomes poor; when the body temperature falls, it doesn't respond as it normally would to keep the animal warm. Instead, the body temperature drops to conform with that of the air. Breathing becomes slow and irregular, the heart beats irregularly and slowly, and various nervous reflexes stop functioning.

If the air temperature drops to freezing, however, many hibernators begin to breathe faster and raise their heat production a bit. Some wake up. Those that don't respond at all may freeze to death.

How Can Parrots Talk?

People are amazed and delighted to hear parrots talk. But it seems that no one can yet explain how these birds are able to imitate human speech so well!

Some people think parrots can talk because of the structure of their tongue, which is large and thick. It may be that this kind of tongue does help it to talk, but it certainly isn't necessary in order for a bird to be able to talk. Other "talking" birds, such as mynas, crows, and ravens, don't have large, thick tongues. Hawks and eagles do have such tongues—and can't talk!

Is it because parrots are more intelligent than other birds? This doesn't seem to be the reason either. As a matter of fact, most biologists think that parrots and other talking birds do not realize the meaning of their own words. They do, however, seem to form definite associations between certain expressions and actions.

It may be that parrots can "talk" because their voice mechanism and hearing work more slowly than those of other birds. And probably the sounds made by human beings resemble the sounds naturally made by parrots, so it is easy for them to imitate them.

Parrots are rather remarkable birds in other ways, too. They can adapt themselves to practically any kind of living condition. This is why, for example, sailors have long taken parrots along on their trips. And even though a parrot is a tropical bird, when it is in captivity it can get along quite comfortably in temperate and even in cold climates.

Parrots are very brave birds and loyal to their kind. If a common danger threatens a group of them, the whole flock will stand by. When searching for food, they swing from one limb of a tree to another like monkeys, using their bill as well as their feet. In fact, they can use their feet at times almost like hands, especially when eating.

RAVEN

MYNA

Do Dogs Dream?

If you have a dog in your house, you may have noticed that when he is asleep he makes little noises and moves or twitches his legs, as though chasing something. Most dog owners who have had this experience believe this to be a sign that their dog is dreaming. While they cannot say positively that dogs do not dream, scientists will tell you that dogs probably do not dream.

To understand these scientists' theory, we must remember that men and animals are the products of evolution. This means that over millions of years gradual changes have been taking place. While men and animals are alike in some ways, the mental make-up and senses of animals have evolved in ways different from ours. As a result, animals live in worlds that are different from ours.

If the senses and the working of the minds of animals are different, we cannot expect their organs and brains to produce what our organs and brains produce. The intelligence and personality of animals are not a "miniature" of the human model.

We cannot know what thoughts animals have. So when we see what we think is a dog dreaming—moving its legs or making noises in its sleep—we cannot assume we are right. The brain cells might just be repeating their messages to the muscles, and the dog might not have any vision of a dream at all.

Those animals that have brains built something like our own may have thoughts like ours, but they will be far simpler.

Where Did the Rat Originate?

Nobody likes to talk about rats, since they are unpleasant creatures. But they have had a very important effect on the life of man. In fact, the brown rat carries fleas that can spread a very dread disease: bubonic plague, or the Black Death. More people have died from this disease than from all the wars of history!

The brown rat, which is the common house rat, was originally a native of Asia. It came into Europe at about the time of the Crusades. It came partly by land, and partly on the ships that brought the Crusaders back. In a short time the brown rat was everywhere in Europe. It came to the United States during the American Revolution, and soon spread out everywhere as the pioneers moved westward.

Why has man had such a difficult time fighting against this creature? The reason is that the rat has amazing powers of adaptation. The more prosperous man gets, the better this rat lives. Because the more food there is around, the more food it gets. When times are bad for man—and we are speaking in terms of history over the centuries— rats have a way of taking care of themselves: they become cannibals and begin to eat one another.

The brown rat is also unusually cunning. It is not fooled by the same trick twice. If poison is mixed with a food, it may kill a few rats the first time, but then the other rats learn to avoid it.

Common house rats weigh about three-quarters of a pound. They vary in color from pure gray to reddish or black-brown. Their total length is sixteen to nineteen inches. When there are other types of rats around, the brown rats drive them away and take over. They are found wherever man lives, except in the Far North and in very dry lands. Most cats, by the way, are not too good as rat-catchers.

What Is a Hamster?

Many young people enjoy having hamsters and guinea pigs as pets. They are gentle and inquisitive rodents, easy to raise.

The golden hamster is five to six inches long and weighs four to five ounces. Its home is Europe and Asia. The name comes from the German word *hamstern,* which means "to hoard."

This is because when the hamster is wild it does just that. It stuffs its large cheek pouches with food, which it then hoards in burrows, or underground holes.

The cheek pouches can carry up to half the animal's weight in food. To empty its cheeks, the hamster presses on them with its forefeet and blows. It has a plump body and short limbs. The thick, soft fur is reddish-gold on its back and grayish-white on its belly.

The hamster is one of the fastest-reproducing mammals. It has four or five litters a year. Sometimes there are more than a dozen babies in each litter. The mother nurses the young for about four weeks.

An interesting thing about keeping hamsters as pets is that it is necessary to make it possible for them to exercise, or they will get a form of paralysis. So a hamster cage should be equipped with an exercise wheel. If the cage does not have a wheel, the hamster should be allowed out of the cage often to run and get its exercise.

What Is a Paramecium?

If you examine a drop of pond water under a microscope, one of the smallest creatures you may see will be longish and shaped like a slipper, rounded at one end and thin at the other. It may be hard to believe, but this tiny living thing can be classified as an animal. This is because, like all other animals, it gets food by eating plants and other organisms (plants make their own food), and it must move about to get food (plants stay in one place).

This creature is a paramecium. Its body is almost completely covered with thin, hairlike threads, which are called cilia. The cilia beat rhythmically, like thousands of tiny oars, driving the body forward or backward or in turns.

The paramecium lives in fresh water, feeding on bacteria, yeasts, and other protozoans (tiny animal-like microbes). And it seems able to control the beating of its cilia, for it can change direction rapidly to get food or avoid danger.

Like all living organisms, the paramecium can reproduce, or multiply. When it is fully grown, it may divide in two and form two new individuals. A paramecium can also reproduce by exchanging body materials with another paramecium.

The remarkable thing about the paramecium is that while it carries out many of the same living activities that humans and large animals do, it does so in a single cell. In the human body, for example, there are billions of cells, and they are organized into groups to do specific tasks.

There is a kind of specialization even in the one-celled paramecium. Inside the cell, there are two ball-shaped masses, one larger than the other. These are the nuclei. The small nucleus controls reproduction. The large one controls the other activities of the cell.

Paramecia are one of the more than one hundred thousand different kinds of micro-organisms that man has discovered and studied. (Micro-organisms are too small to be studied without a magnifying glass or microscope.) The first animals on earth may have been something like these tiny animal-like microbes.

What Are Nitrogen-Fixing Bacteria?

Can you imagine something that is absolutely necessary to life, that is all about you, and yet that has to be "captured" to be used? This is nitrogen.

About four-fifths of the air we breathe consists of nitrogen, which is a gas. But we breathe it right out again unchanged! We only use the nitrogen to dilute the oxygen of the air so that we won't get too much at one time. Protoplasm, the substance inside all living cells, requires oxygen to be formed, and proteins, the essential food materials, are built around nitrogen compounds.

So it's pretty important for us to be able to capture nitrogen from the air. The process of doing this is called nitrogen-fixation. And a good deal of this is done for us by bacteria.

There are two kinds of nitrogen-fixing bacteria. One kind lives on the roots of plants, and the other lives free in the soil. How do they "fix" nitrogen? These bacteria take nitrogen directly from the air, combine it with oxygen, and then use this combination to build proteins.

Those that live on roots live only on the roots of plants such as beans, clover, alfalfa, and peas. But they fix more nitrogen than these plants need. The plants store the surplus in their roots. When these plants die or are harvested, the surplus nitrogen passes into the soil.

When a soil area has been used continuously for long periods of time and the plants all harvested, nitrogen is not being returned to the soil. The soil is then not able to nourish new crops. This is why farmers must use fertilizers.

The fertilizers that replace nitrogen in the soil include sodium nitrate, ammonium sulphate, and the waste products of animals and birds, such as manure. Today there are also artificial methods of nitrogen-fixation to replenish the soil.

Chapter 5

How Things Are Made

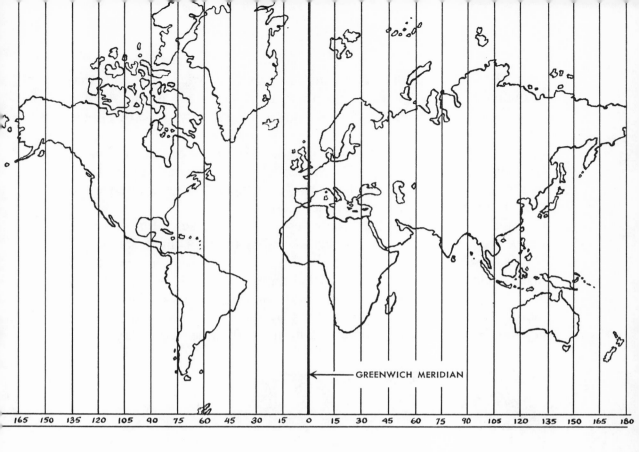

165	150	135	120	105	90	75	60	45	30	15	0	15	30	45	60	75	90	105	120	135	150	165	180

← —— GREENWICH MERIDIAN

How Is the Correct Time Decided?

The two main units of time that we have are the day and the year. They are both determined by the movement of the earth. The spinning of the earth on its axis gives us the solar (sun) day. The journey of the earth around the sun gives us the solar year.

The solar day is divided into twenty-four hours. The hour is divided into sixty minutes, and the minute into sixty seconds. Actually, the length of a solar day varies. One reason for this is changes in the earth's speed around the sun. But even though each solar day is sometimes longer or sometimes shorter than exactly twenty-four hours, we say that the mean (average) solar day is twenty-four hours.

For convenience in locating places, man has marked off the earth into meridians—circles that run through the poles. Places that are on the same meridian have the same solar time. Places that are east or west of each other have different solar times. The difference in solar time is one hour for each meridian.

There is a meridian that runs through Greenwich, England, that is numbered 0. It is called the prime meridian. This is the starting point, and all other meridians are marked off east and west of Greenwich.

Clock time the whole world over is based on mean solar time at Greenwich. Astronomers at Greenwich Observatory check their clocks against the sun or a particular star. They check the exact time when the sun or the star crosses the meridian.

Observatories in other countries also keep track of the correct time. They broadcast time signals by radio. In the United States, the Naval Observatory in Washington, D.C., determines the correct time. Special clocks are used to keep the correct time. The United States Naval Observatory uses quartz-crystal controlled clocks. The electric motors in such clocks are controlled by the vibrations of the quartz crystals. The clocks keep time to within 1/500 second per day!

What Do A.M. and P.M. Mean?

Everybody uses the expressions A.M. and P.M. to indicate before noon and after noon. But do you know exactly what they mean, and how these terms came into being?

As you know, the turning of the earth makes the sun and the stars seem to move across the sky. Daylight, of course, begins when the sun rises in the east and ends when it sets in the west. When the sun is high in the sky, between these two positions, half of the daylight hours have been spent.

Therefore, by noticing where the sun stood in the sky, early man knew he could tell the time of day. At night, the motion of the stars served the same purpose.

The important thing in keeping time is to know the exact moment of noon. For each of us, wherever we are, noon is when the sun is directly overhead. Think of an imaginary line, a meridian, drawn across the sky, stretching from the north point of your horizon down to the south point.

When the sun crosses your meridian, it is noon for you. While the sun is still east of this line or meridian, it is morning. After the sun has crossed this meridian, it is afternoon.

The Latin word for "midday" is *meridies,* from which comes our word meridian. So A.M. is an abbreviation for *ante meridiem,* or before midday. And P.M. is the abbreviation for *post meridiem,* or after midday.

Each of the world's time zones is about fifteen degrees wide in longitude, which is about the distance the sun moves through the sky in an hour. Everyone who lives in the same time zone observes noon at the same moment. In this way, the time differs by one hour as you move through each time zone.

STARRY EGYPTIAN SKY GODDESS SPANS THE EARTH

NEW MOON
EVERY 29-30 DAYS

Why Do the Number of Days in a Month Vary?

The first people to measure a year with any exactness were the ancient Egyptians. They started with a lunar (monthly) calendar based on the new moon's appearance every twenty-nine or thirty days. It was not very accurate.

The Romans also had a lunar calendar, and to make it agree with the solar year they added extra months whenever they needed to. Finally Julius Caesar adopted a new calendar based on a solar year of 365¼ days. Various changes had to be made in the months to make this calendar right. Here are the changes made by Caesar and others in the days of the month.

January was originally the eleventh month and had twenty-nine days. Caesar made it the first month and gave it thirty-one days. In Caesar's calendar February had twenty-nine days, with thirty in leap years. Emperor Augustus took one day from it and added it to August.

The number of days in March was always thirty-one. April, as a lunar month, had twenty-nine days. Caesar added a day to give it

ROMAN SOLAR CALENDAR

thirty. May always had thirty-one days and remained unchanged by Caesar. June had twenty-nine days and Caesar gave it thirty. July (named after Julius Caesar) was given thirty-one days by him.

When August was a lunar month, it had twenty-nine days. Caesar gave it thirty. Emperor Augustus, who named it after himself, added the day he took from February to make it equal to Caesar's month. September had twenty-nine days as a lunar month. Caesar gave it thirty-one, but Augustus reduced it to thirty.

October, in Caesar's calendar had thirty days, but Augustus gave it thirty-one. November also had thirty-one days under Caesar, and Augustus reduced it to thirty. December originally had twenty-nine days, Caesar gave it thirty, and then Augustus added another, giving it thirty-one.

The important thing for an accurate calendar was to have 365 days. The number of days in each month, as you can see, was decided first by Caesar and then by Augustus for whatever reasons they wished. We took our calendar from the Romans.

Why Do Watches Have Jewels?

When a watch is advertised, the number of jewels it has is often mentioned as an indication of its quality. What exactly is a "jewel" in a watch, and why is it there?

A watch (or clock) is only useful to us if it is accurate, and if it doesn't constantly break down. The average watch contains about 211 different pieces, so obviously it's quite a complicated mechanism. Let's see what makes a watch go and the part that jewels play in this.

A watch gets its power from the mainspring, which is a coiled wire about two feet long when straightened out. When you wind the watch, you tighten the coil of the mainspring.

From the mainspring, the power travels through a series of four wheels, called the train, to the balance wheel. The train moves the hands on the dial. The balance wheel acts like the pendulum on a clock. It is the heart of the watch and regulates its movement.

Inside the balance wheel is the hairspring, a coiled steel wire no thicker than a hair. One pound of the right steel will produce eight miles of this wire!

17-JEWEL WATCH

ESCAPEMENT WHEEL

LEVER

BALANCE WHEEL

HAIRSPRING

SCREWS

WHEEL 4

WHEEL 3

WHEEL 2

WHEEL 1

MAINSPRING

Around the edge of the balance wheel are adjusted tiny screws of steel or gold. Their position and weight control the speed of the watch. They are so small that an ordinary thimble will hold twenty thousand of them! Then there is the escapement wheel, which catches the balance wheel and lets it go. This regulates the movement and this is the sound that we call the "ticking" of a watch.

We've mentioned various wheels that constantly move in a watch. These wheels rest on pivots, and the constant motion creates friction. To withstand this friction, the pivots rest on tiny pieces of precious stones, such as ruby, sapphire, or garnet. These are the jewels of a watch. The more jewels, the less likely is friction to wear out or slow up the moving parts in your watch!

Can Man Make Diamonds?

The answer to this question is, "yes—but." Man can and does produce synthetic diamonds, but don't expect to be collecting them by the handful in the near future!

When you realize what it takes for nature to produce a diamond, you will see why it isn't an easy job. The production of natural diamonds started about one hundred million years ago, when the earth was beginning to cool. At that time, there was a mass of hot liquid rock beneath the ground. This liquid rock was subjected to such extreme heat and pressure that the material we know as carbon became crystallized. And that is exactly what a diamond is—highly crystallized carbon, the hardest substance known to man.

Since diamonds became so precious to man, there naturally were attempts to produce diamonds artificially; that is, to make synthetic diamonds. Strangely enough, three different men, working quite some time ago, were generally believed to have succeeded in making diamonds. One was J. B. Hannay in England in 1880, another was Henry Moissan in France in 1893, and the third was Sir William Crookes in England in 1906.

Moissan's method was to dissolve carbon in molten iron in an electric furnace. He then plunged the molten iron into a salt solution. The cooling and shrinking of the outside layer, while inside there was still molten material, created terrific pressures, and this was supposed to have produced diamonds.

The odd thing is that when the experiments of these men were duplicated by other people, no diamonds were produced! So today it is believed that the first synthetic diamonds were really produced in 1954. A special press was created in which carbon was subjected to a temperature of 2,800 degrees centigrade and a pressure of 800,000 pounds per square inch. The first such diamonds were yellow in color, and the largest measured about one-sixteenth of an inch in length.

Synthetic diamonds usually have imperfections and so are used as cutting tools rather than as gems. But someday man may be able to make perfect diamonds!

SYNTHETIC DIAMONDS

DIAMOND
POWDER

LENS

MILLING CUTTER SHOWING DIAMONDS SET IN RIDGES

INSTRUMENT FOR POLISHING LENSES

FULL SPECTRUM

VIOLET

INDIGO

BLUE

GREEN

YELLOW

ORANGE

RED

WHITE LIGHT

PRIMARY COLORS IN SHADED TONE

What Are Primary Colors?

If you hold up a glass prism to a beam of sunlight, you'll see the light form a rainbow of colors. This is called the spectrum. It consists of all the colors that make up "white" light.

Now, although you might be able to see six or seven colors in the spectrum, the white light is really made up of three basic colors. These are called the primary colors, because they cannot be made from any other colors. The primary colors of light are orange-red, green, and violet-blue. The other colors you see in the rainbow or spectrum are made by a mixture of the primary colors.

When the naked eye looks at the spectrum, it can see three mixed colors, which are called secondary colors. The secondary colors in light are green-blue, yellow, and magenta-red. You can produce these colors by mixing the primary colors in certain combinations.

But remember, we are talking about light. Paint colors are substances, and are exactly the opposite from light colors! The secondary colors in light are the primary colors in paint. This means that in paint the primary colors are yellow, green-blue, and magenta-red. And with these three colors, you can mix any colors in paint.

There are many other ways we classify colors. A color that is brilliant and has no black or white paint in it is called a hue. Yellow, red, blue, and green are hues. A color that is mixed from a hue and black is called a shade. Deep brown is a shade. A color that is made with a hue and white is a tint. Pink and ivory are tints. A color that is a mixture of pure hue, black, and white is a tone. Tan, beige, and gray are tones.

Here is an interesting fact about color. How do you think red paint looks before the can is opened? It doesn't look red. It actually looks black! That's because where there is no light, there is no color. In a dark room, there is no such thing as color.

The color of an object depends on the material of the object and the light in which the object is seen. For instance, an orange-red sweater looks orange-red because the dye in the wool reflects the orange-red part of the light. The violet-blue and green parts of light are absorbed by the sweater. Only the orange-red is reflected for you to see.

What Makes Hot and Cold?

Some things are hot to the touch, other things are cold. Sometimes the air feels hot, other times it feels cool. What makes the difference?

According to present theories, heat consists of the motion of atoms and molecules. For example, the atoms and molecules in the air are able to move about freely, bumping into each other and into objects in their path. Now, these tiny particles may move rapidly or slowly. If they move rapidly, we say the temperature of the air is high, or that the air is hot. If they move slowly (as on a cold day), we feel the air to be cool.

When it comes to liquids and solids, the atoms and molecules cannot move so freely—but they are still able to move rapidly. For example, in a block of hot iron the atoms vibrate perhaps a million times each second—and that's rapidly! If you were to touch the tip of your finger to such a block, you would feel pain because of the sudden and violent motion imparted to the molecules in your skin when they come near the fast-moving particles of the iron.

Do molecules really move about? Countless experiments prove that the molecules actually do move constantly. In fact, under the microscope tiny particles of matter in water can be seen being knocked around by millions of invisible molecules in motion.

At the temperature of melting ice, on the average, an oxygen molecule moves with a speed of about one thousand four hundred feet per second; and a hydrogen molecule about four times as fast. Even in a cubic inch of air a thousand million million collisions per second take place among the molecules!

Heat and temperature are not the same thing. The heat energy a body contains depends upon the energy of motion of its atoms and molecules. The quantity of heat may be measured in "calories." A calorie is the amount of heat energy required to raise the temperature of one gram of water one degree centigrade. But the temperature of a body indicates the level or "degree" to which the heat energy that it contains brings it. The coldest temperature possible is 273 degrees below zero centigrade. Scientists believe that at that temperature the molecules are at rest.

1 FUEL

2 OXYGEN

3 HEAT

Why Is Fire Hot?

The answer to this question is really the definition of fire itself. Fire is a chemical action that occurs very quickly and gives off heat and light.

There are several kinds of chemical actions that can result in what we call fire. The most common is the chemical action between oxygen and a fuel. If heat and light are given off, you have a fire.

To make a fire, three things are necessary. The first is a fuel; the second, oxygen. The fuel combines rapidly with oxygen. When wood burns in bonfires or gas burns in stoves, the fuel combines rapidly with oxygen in the air.

The third thing we need to make a fire is heat. Paper or wood that is simply exposed to air does not catch fire. Usually a burning match is applied to make it catch fire. When the paper becomes hot enough, oxygen can begin to combine freely with it. The paper then bursts into flames.

Every fuel has its own particular temperature at which it begins to burn. This temperature is called the kindling temperature, or flash point, of the fuel.

OXYGEN

GAS

Suppose a stick of wood is raised to its kindling temperature by a burning match. The wood as a whole does not catch on fire. The reason is that oxygen does not combine with the whole stick. Instead, the heat causes the surface layer of the wood to break up into a gas.

As the heating continues, the gas particles and the oxygen in the air move very fast. In this condition the gas and oxygen particles combine easily and quickly. Heat and light are given off—and we have a fire.

In some kinds of burning, no light is given off. If a fuel combines slowly with oxygen, heat alone is given off. That is what happens when iron rusts. Rusting is just a very slow kind of burning, so slow that you can't even feel the heat being given off. Fire is fast burning, or combustion. In combustion, both heat and light are given off.

RUSTING ANCHOR

How Do Fireworks Get Their Colors?

Fireworks have been making people say "Ahh!" and "Ohh!" for thousands of years. The magnificent displays of the Chinese delighted their people hundreds of years before fireworks appeared in western Europe.

The Greeks had some sort of fireworks known as "Greek fire," and Roman emperors put on elaborate exhibitions of fireworks to amuse the people. But fireworks didn't really develop as we know them until gunpowder came into general use and the science of chemistry had made certain advances.

In the nineteenth century the art of making fireworks was really perfected, and amazingly elaborate displays were created. For instance, certain fireworks were shot into the sky in which beautiful colored designs served as a backdrop. Other pieces were attached to frameworks against this background. When these fireworks were lit, unbelievable patterns were produced, such as waving flags, rushing trains and steamboats, and even mock battles between famous people!

The basic materials used in making fireworks are saltpeter, sulfur and charcoal. These ingredients are ground together into a fine powder and then nitrates of lead, barium, and aluminum are sometimes added in various combinations to obtain spectacular effects.

The colors in fireworks are produced by the addition of various salts of metals. Strontium produces red, barium creates green, sodium is for yellow, and copper for blue. The showers of dazzling sparks are made by using iron filings. So you see it takes quite a knowledge of chemistry to produce our modern fireworks.

Of course, there is a serious side to fireworks, too. In warfare, rockets are used for signaling, and flares can light up whole battlefields or convey messages. At sea, various colored flares and rockets have often been the means for saving hundreds of lives. And pilots in airplanes have often been able to make emergency landings, thanks to flares dropped from the plane.

Can a Thermometer Be Made Without Mercury?

We are so accustomed to thinking of a thermometer as having mercury in a thin tube that we tend to forget exactly how a thermometer works.

A thermometer is simply an instrument that measures heat. The way we measure heat is by observing what heat does to certain materials. Heat causes many materials to change. We look at what kind of change has taken place in the material, and we can say that this kind of change was caused by a certain amount of heat.

The reason mercury is used so commonly in thermometers is simply because mercury reacts quickly to a rise in temperature. It expands evenly, and it is easily seen. So in the modern mercury-in-glass thermometer, heat causes the mercury to expand; it moves up the narrow tube, and a scale on the thermometer tells us how high it has moved.

Alcohol, for example, can also be used in thermometers. But alcohol presents certain problems. It boils easily. So alcohol is not very useful for high temperatures. But alcohol makes an excellent thermometer for measuring extremely low temperatures.

There are other kinds of thermometers that use no liquid at all. Instead, two metals are used. A strip of iron and a strip of brass are fastened together in the form of a coil. One end of this coil is fastened, while the other end is connected to a pointer and is free to move.

The metals expand and contract at different rates. When heated, the free end of the coil winds or unwinds, as the case may be, and this movement positions a pointer on a dial with degrees on it.

By placing a pen on the pointer and by providing a rotating chart, we have a recording thermometer that keeps a record of the temperature for as long as we want it to!

What Is the Law of Falling Bodies?

A falling body is an unsupported object that is being pulled toward the earth's surface by the force of gravity. Gravity is the earth's force of attraction for other objects.

When there is no air resistance, all bodies fall according to a definite law. It is known as the law of falling bodies, and was first discovered by the famous Italian scientist Galileo in the 1500's.

Galileo experimented with falling bodies in his laboratory. Out of these experiments came this new law: In the absence of air, the speed of a falling body depends only on the length of the fall. The speed of the body does not depend on the body's weight.

The longer a body falls, the faster and faster it moves. When anything picks up speed, we say it accelerates. A freely-falling body has an acceleration of thirty-two feet a second during each second that it falls. This means that for each second a body falls, it gains thirty-two feet a second in downward speed.

A falling body has a speed of thirty-two feet a second after falling for just one second. It has a speed of thirty-two plus thirty-two, or sixty-four feet a second after falling for two seconds, and so on.

However, a body falling through the air does not continue to gain speed at this rate. It reaches a certain top speed. Because of air resistance, there is a limit to how fast an object falls.

This is true of even the heaviest objects. They accelerate as they begin to fall, but air resistance builds up. Soon the air resistance becomes equal to the pull of gravity on the object. Then the object can fall no faster. It has reached its final or "terminal speed," and keeps this speed as it continues to fall.

What Makes a Balloon Rise?

A balloon is really the simplest form of aircraft. It usually consists of a light spherical or cylindrical bag made of paper, rubber, silk, or rubberized fabric, containing hot air, hydrogen, or helium. To the bag may be attached (by cords or netting) a basket, or car, or gondola to carry passengers and cargo.

A balloon floats in the air for exactly the same reason that a fish floats in water. Each displaces, by its bulk, more than its own weight of the air or water that surrounds it.

As long as a balloon and all the equipment attached to it weigh less than the volume of air displaced, it will rise. If it loses some of its lifting gas, so that its volume decreases, it will sink. Hot air, hydrogen, or helium are used as lifting gases because all three are lighter than ordinary atmospheric air.

Once released, a balloon will ascend to a level where the weight of the displaced air is exactly equal to its own weight. To change flight altitude, a balloon pilot must either reduce his buoyancy to go down, or reduce his weight to go up. To go down, he must allow some of his lifting gas to escape through a valve in the top of the balloon. To go up, he must throw weights (ballasts) overboard.

Since neither gas nor ballasts can be replaced in flight, it is easy to see that the amount of control available to a balloon pilot is quite limited. At best, he can go up or down for a short time only, depending on the size of the balloon.

Once aloft, he is entirely at the mercy of the winds. A balloon cannot be steered in flight. It can only drift with the wind, and for this reason has very little use as a means of getting from place to place.

Balloons are now generally used for upper-air exploration. In warfare they are commonly used as elevated observation posts. They may form balloon barrages (like aerial fences) to protect cities from bombers.

BARRAGE BALLOONS

What Makes an Airplane Stall in the Air?

To understand this, we must first understand what enables an airplane to stay up in the air. Because an airplane weighs more than the same volume of air, it needs some force to hold it up. This force is called lift.

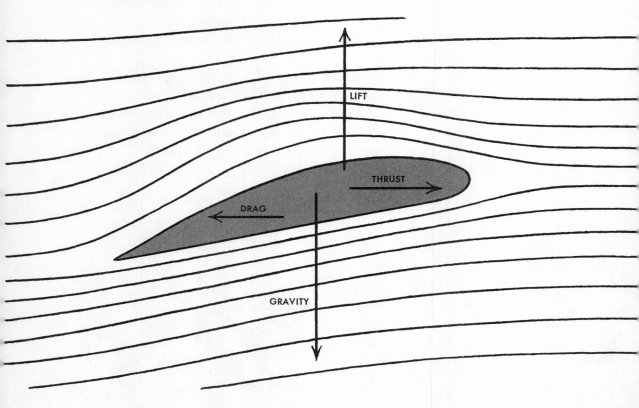

An airplane develops lift by moving forward against the air swiftly. How does this motion create lift? It has to do with the flow of air past the wings. The air flows over and under the wings as the plane moves forward. The air under the wings pushes up against the wings. The air over the wings is forced into a slight upward curve over the wings, which creates an area of decreased pressure. So we have two effects working together: the air under the wings pushes up; the decreased pressure above the wings helps draw the wings up. The result is lift.

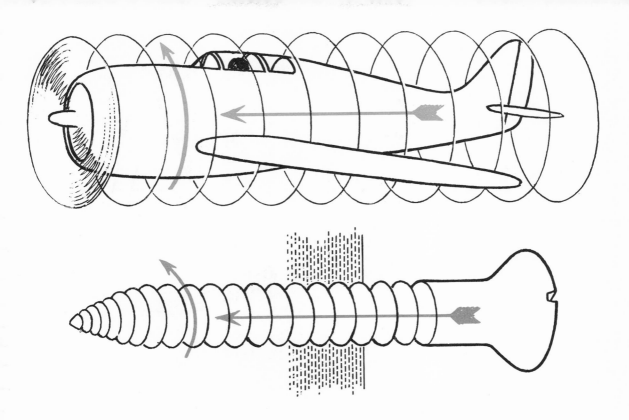

In order for the plane to move forward, it uses engine power. The propellers screw forward into the air just as a wood screw does in wood. This is possible because when air moves swiftly, or something moves swiftly into it, the air begins to act like a solid. This forward pull of the plane is called thrust. The thrust overcomes the "drag" exerted by the plane, the lift overcomes gravity, and the plane is able to stay in the air.

As long as the upward lift and the pull of gravity downward are exactly equal, the plane flies level and straight. If the speed is increased, the plane will climb because there is more lift, so the pilot must turn the plane's nose down.

When the speed is reduced, the pilot must bring the nose up. If the speed is reduced and the nose is not brought up, the air becomes "burbly," and the lift is lost. The nose drops, the plane stalls, and may go into a spin.

When a stall takes place high above the ground, there is enough altitude to enable the plane to recover and regain speed, but a stall near the ground may result in a crash.

ASTROLABE
EARLY FORM OF SEXTANT

ANOTHER EARLY
FORM OF SEXTANT

What Is a Sextant?

When you travel by land, you can usually find your way because you know where a road leads. And if you travel by ship and can see the shore, you can also find your location easily. You can recognize hills, mountains, forests, beaches, and so on.

In the earliest times, therefore, sailors kept their ships within two or three miles of the coast, so that they were never out of sight of land. The men who did venture out into the ocean were taking a great risk because there was no sure way of knowing their location.

Later, a way was found to pinpoint the location of ships at sea. This was done by finding the latitude and longitude of the place. Latitude is distance north or south of the Equator. Longitude tells how far east or west a place is, and it is measured by degrees east or west of an imaginary line that goes through Greenwich, England.

To find latitude and longitude at sea, the navigator observes the position of the stars and the sun. In the daytime, the navigator can find the latitude of his ship by measuring how high the sun is at noon. At night, he does this by measuring how high in the sky the stars seem to be. Longitude is measured by comparing the time on board the ship with the time at Greenwich, England. If his time is earlier, he is west of Greenwich; if later, he is east of Greenwich. Each hour's difference equals fifteen degrees east or west.

The sextant is an instrument used by navigators to measure the position of the sun, moon, planets, and certain stars. The sextant is shaped like the wedge of a pie, with a scale marked on its rounded edge.

One end of a swinging arm is attached to the point of the sextant. A movable mirror is fixed at that end of the arm. The other end extends to the scale. A telescope is mounted on the sextant, and a glass mirror is mounted in front of the telescope. By looking at the horizon through the telescope and a clear glass, and then moving the mirror until the reflection seems to touch the horizon, the scale end shows the height of the body observed.

How Do We Know the Height of a Mountain?

When we read of high mountains in newspapers or books, we are often told their exact height in terms of feet. How do we know exactly how high a mountain is, especially in the case of mountains that may never have been climbed by man?

It is done by means of one of the oldest techniques on earth—surveying. The science of surveying is a branch of civil engineering. It is concerned with determining the shape and size of any part of the earth's surface.

There are various kinds of surveying, but they are all based on a method known as "triangulation." When you study geometry, you will learn that if you know one side and two angles of any triangle (or two sides and one angle), you can find out the rest of its measurements.

Whether the land you want to measure is one acre, or a thousand acres, the method of measuring it is the same. You begin by measuring one distance very accurately with a chain, steel rod, or wire.

This now becomes the side of the first triangle, and is usually a level piece of ground between two landmarks. Now you select a third landmark, and make this the apex of the triangle. You then measure the angles it makes with each end of the first line you measured. You now have the requirements for measuring the area of the triangle as described above (one side and two angles of a triangle).

The instrument for measuring those angles is called a transit. Now that you have the area of one triangle, you keep on dividing the land to be measured into triangles until you have the area of the entire piece of land.

The transit doesn't just work horizontally; it also works vertically. This is called leveling, because there is a spirit level at the base of the instrument that indicates when it is level. By raising the sight to any landmark on a mountain, the same process of measuring angles can be done, and the length of one side (the height) can be measured!

How Is the Depth of an Ocean Measured?

Scientists who study the sea are called oceanographers. Since the deep ocean is cold and dark, they really know very little about it. Parts of the ocean floor have been seen through the windows of special submarines and through the eyes of deep-sea cameras, but it still adds up to very little information.

One of the things they're interested in is the depth of the ocean water. Finding the depth of water is called "sounding the depth" or "taking a sounding." In the old days, this was done by lowering a rope with a weight attached. Later on, a very light line, usually made of piano wire, was used.

Today, scientists are able to get a much better idea of what the ocean floor is like because of the invention of a device called an echo sounder. An echo sounder uses the echoes of sound to explore the ocean floor.

A device on board the ship sends out a sound signal. The sound travels through the water at nearly one mile a second. It is reflected, or echoed, back to an instrument on the ship. The deeper the water, the longer it takes for the echo to reach the ship.

In a modern echo sounder, high-frequency sound waves are beamed down from the ship. The instrument then records the echo as a dark mark on special paper. The paper is usually printed so that the depth can be read off in fathoms right away (a fathom is six feet).

The echo sounder makes it easy to find the depth of the sea. But it does much more. It provides a continuous profile, or line, showing exactly what the ocean floor is like beneath the ship. This is like having a sounding every few yards along the path of the ship.

If the ship passes over an undersea mountain, the echo sounder records the exact shape of the mountain. And if the bottom is flat, the record shows it as flat. The echo sounder doesn't miss a bump even a few feet high!

How Does an Aqualung Work?

The aqualung is a modern aid to diving. It makes it possible for a diver to go on breathing underwater without an air supply from a ship. He carries his own air supply with him, strapped to his back. He is a free diver.

For air supply the aqualung has two or more sturdy steel bottles filled with compressed air. A special valve gradually lets the air out of the bottles. A hose from the valve goes to a mouthpiece. This is made so that the diver can grip it with his teeth. Because the diver's nose is covered with his faceplate, he has to breathe through his mouth.

With the aqualung strapped to his back and a heavy belt to keep him down, a man can swim almost as freely as a fish. He uses big flippers on his feet, so he doesn't need his hands for swimming. He can hold a camera or perhaps a fishing spear. In shallow water he may be able to stay down for a half-hour or more.

But even the best free-diving outfit will not let a diver go down more than three hundred feet. At this depth the weight of the water above presses on everything ten times as heavily as on the surface. The air in the diver's bottles is used up ten times as fast. So even big bottles will let him stay there for only one minute or so.

There is another problem in deep diving. The compressed air in the aqualung bottles is about four-fifths nitrogen and about one-fifth oxygen, like ordinary air. We need the oxygen to stay alive. Ordinarily the nitrogen we breathe in is breathed right out again. But as the pressure of air increases, some of the nitrogen dissolves in the blood and tissues.

As the diver comes up, the nitrogen must leave his blood and tissues. If it cannot come out fast enough through his lungs, it turns into tiny bubbles inside his body. The bubbles squeeze nerves and block blood vessels, and the diver gets what is called the bends. The diver feels great pain. A bad case of the bends may kill him or cripple him for life.

This is why a diver must come up quite slowly when he is down to a depth of two hundred or three hundred feet. And he must stop often on the way up.

How Is Water Made Drinkable?

First of all, why does water have to be made drinkable? Why can't we drink it just as we find it? The reason is that we can almost never obtain pure water.

Probably the purest natural source of water is snow. The next purest is rain water, but rain contains dissolved gases of the air and traces of carbon dioxide, chlorides, sulfates, nitrates, and ammonia. Even the water from streams and lakes that are found in the mountains may contain dissolved inorganic salts. Water from rivers and lakes in low regions is usually quite polluted. Water from springs and wells has filtered through the ground, so it is quite pure, but it may also contain inorganic salts.

So it seems that all water we drink needs to be purified to some degree. There are many methods for doing this. One is simply by storage. When water is stored in a reservoir, certain things take place.

426

Solid impurities settle at the bottom, a process known as sedimentation. Many bacteria lose their power when water is kept in a storage reservoir.

But this method does not give complete protection. So chemicals may be added to provide better sedimentation. In addition, the water may be aerated to remove tastes and odors and dissolved gases.

Many years ago it was discovered that if water could be filtered through sand, many of the impurities and most of the bacteria could be removed. So various methods for sand-filtering were set up, including a method that forced the water through mechanically at great speed.

A commonly used method for purifying water is chlorination. This is a very cheap, quick, and effective method. From two to eight pounds of chlorine are added to a million gallons of water. This is enough to destroy most of the dangerous bacteria that may be in the water.

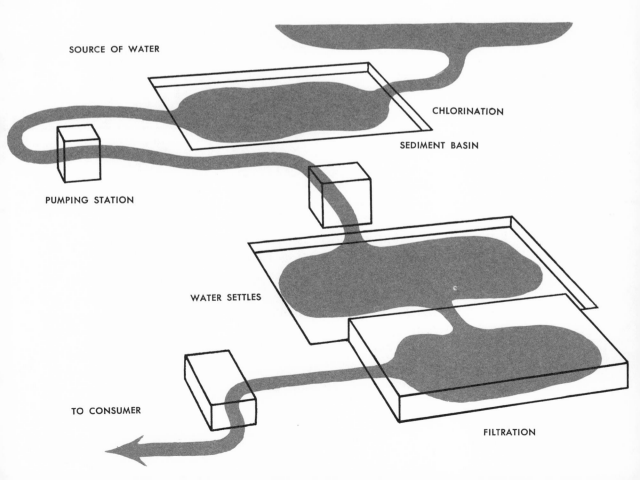

SOURCE OF WATER

CHLORINATION

SEDIMENT BASIN

PUMPING STATION

WATER SETTLES

FILTRATION

TO CONSUMER

How Can Calories Be Counted?

Nowadays millions of people watch their weight, because they realize it's not healthy in most cases to be too fat. So they "count calories." This means they find out how many calories various foods produce and try to keep their calories down. Of course, all dieting or "counting calories" should be done under a doctor's direction. But what exactly do calories have to do with a person's weight or health?

BREAD

1 SLICE—1 OZ.

76 CALORIES

1 EGG

1 4/5 OZ.

75 CALORIES

1 BANANA

3 1/2 OZ.

96 CALORIES

NUTS

1/2 OZ.

100 CALORIES

Let's find out what a calorie is. If two similar pans of water are put over two equal gas burners on a stove, the pan containing the lesser amount of water will reach boiling temperature first. Even though the final temperature of boiling is the same for both pans, the pan with less water takes less heat to reach that temperature than the pan with more water in it.

The amount of heat required to raise the temperature of a gram of water one degree centigrade is called a gram calorie. The kilogram calorie, or large calorie, is a thousand times as great.

FISH	4 OZ.	177 CAL.
BEEF	4 OZ.	369 CAL.
MILK	7 OZ.	138 CAL.
CHEESE	2/3 OZ.	89 CAL.
CHICKEN	4 OZ.	269 CAL.
VEGETABLES	3 1/2 OZ.	89 CAL.

Where does this heat come from? It comes from the burning up of a fuel. In the kitchen, for example, we might use gas as a fuel. Now the body is able to function because it also burns up "fuel." In the body, that fuel is the food we take in. When we want to measure food as a "fuel," we do it in terms of calories, which is the way to measure quantity of heat. The energy value of food is usually measured in large calories.

Different foods furnish different amounts of calories. One gram of protein, for instance, furnishes four calories. But one gram of fat furnishes nine calories! The human body doesn't care where it gets its calories, as long as it gets enough to keep functioning. How many does the body need? It is estimated that an average adult needs somewhere between two thousand and three thousand calories per day. But a lot depends on the work the person does. A housewife might need only two thousand, five hundred calories. A factory worker might need from three thousand to four thousand calories. And an athlete might need four thousand calories and more!

What happens if a person takes in more calories than he needs? The food is not burned up but is transformed into fat instead! And that's why, under a doctor's care, many people are now "counting calories."

How Is Fashion Decided?

The French word *couturier* means "dressmaker." In the world of fashion, the word has come to describe a designer of high fashion or *haute couture*. It is these designers who begin trends and create new silhouettes. The work of famous couturiers of different countries is copied all over the world.

Paris has always been the traditional center of world fashion. But recently Italian designers have had great influence in setting new styles, and so have certain designers in London.

French designers guard the secrets of their new designs until their collections are shown to the public. Then pictures of the styles are published in newspapers and magazines all over the world.

People from many countries travel to Paris to buy the clothes and to copy the newest ideas. In January they come to see the spring clothes; in July, to see the fall designs.

Many dress manufacturers from other countries buy the original clothes of the famous French designers. They take them back to their own design rooms, where the clothes are copied line-for-line to be made in great numbers. That's why you may be able to buy in your town the clothing that is in the latest style without paying a very high price for it.

Some manufacturers use the Paris styles only as a starting point for their own ideas. Others may adapt only a part of the French design into their own styles.

The United States has become one of the most important fashion centers in the world. In New York City, there are American designers who create new fashions and show their collections. Buyers from stores all over the world come to New York to buy the clothes.

After the buyers choose the designs, the dress manufacturers add up the store orders, buy fabrics, and have the dresses sewn by machines. They are then shipped to cities all over the United States and the world.

What Is Lipstick?

Like so many other cosmetics in use today, lipstick is a product of the chemist's laboratory. Every ingredient that goes into it has a definite purpose, and the combination makes quite a complicated formula.

The chief ingredients in a lipstick are castor oil and a mixture of various waxes. In addition there are cacao butter, lanolin, mineral oil, petrolatum, and different chemicals. Coloring matter to obtain the exact shade is, of course, a very important ingredient.

The oils and waxes are melted together and the colors mixed in by grinding. The whole mass is then remelted and poured into molds, where it is allowed to harden. Lipsticks are made so that they will soften under pressure, which makes it possible to apply them to the lips evenly.

The use of cosmetics by women goes back to very early times. They probably originated in the East, but in ancient times they reached their greatest development in Egypt. Almost six thousand years ago various kinds of cosmetics were already being used in Egypt.

Cleopatra carried the use of cosmetics to new heights. At that time, it was the eyes that received the most attention. Women of the court painted the under side of the eye green, and the lid, lashes, and eyebrows black! Henna was also used to dye the fingernails, palms, and soles of the feet.

In the Bible there are many references to the use of cosmetics by women—for example, "When Jehu was come to Jezreel, Jezebel heard of it; and she painted her face. . . ."

In Rome, at the time of Nero, cosmetics and perfumes were widely used. Here are some of the cosmetics they had then: white lead and chalk to whiten the skin; paint for the eyelids and lashes; a rouge for the cheeks and lips, which may be the ancestor of our lipstick; barley flour and butter as a cure for blemishes; and pumice stone for whitening the teeth. They also had a kind of soap for bleaching the hair.

In England, about four hundred years ago, women used to take all kinds of baths to make their skin beautiful. It is said that Mary, Queen of Scots, actually bathed in wine, and other women of the time took milk baths!

What Is Lace?

Lace is an airy and delicate fabric made of fine threads stitched into patterns. Lace is used to add beauty to many of the things we wear and use. It may be made by hand or by machine.

The first true hand-made lace was probably made in Italy in the middle of the 1500's. Very soon afterward, laces were being made in France. Today hand-made lace is made chiefly in Italy and Belgium. Machine-made lace is produced in England, France, and the United States.

PAPER PATTERN

Hand-made lace is usually made by one of two methods: needle-point or bobbin. Needlepoint lace is made by drawing the design on a thick piece of paper backed by linen. The outline of the pattern is stitched onto the paper. The stitching is used as a framework on which the lacemaker works with a needle and single thread, building up the pattern with looped stitches. When the work is completed, the framework stitches are clipped and the lace is lifted off the pattern.

Bobbin lace is made with a large number of threads, each fastened to a bobbin (spool). The pattern is drawn on paper, and the paper is fastened onto a cushion. Then pins are stuck into the cushion to keep the threads in position while the lace is being made. The lace is made with a pair of bobbins in each hand. These are moved from side to side to twist or interlace the threads. As the work progresses, the pins are moved farther along.

Chantilly lace is a bobbin lace that has vine or spray patterns on a mesh ground; it is often used on evening dresses and bridal veils. Cluny lace is a fairly coarse bobbin lace; it is often used to trim children's dresses and household linens.

What Is Embroidery?

Embroidery is the art of sewing decorative stitches on cloth. It is a very old art. Evidences of embroidered clothing have been found by archaeologists digging among ancient Assyrian and Persian ruins. The Old Testament describes the beauty of the embroidery done by the Jews in Biblical times.

In the Middle Ages embroidery reached a high point. Great Italian and Dutch painters designed needlework tapestries illustrating religious subjects. Noblewomen spent many hours in their castles embroidering gowns to be worn on state occasions, or altar cloths and hangings for the church.

One of the most famous medieval embroideries is the Bayeux tapestry, which illustrates the Battle of Hastings. Its warriors and horses, griffins, phoenixes, and monsters are worked in eight shades of wool on a linen strip measuring 230 feet long and nearly 20 inches wide.

During the eighteenth century embroideries became so valuable that they were worth more than their weight in gold! In the 1700's and 1800's, little girls in America had to spend a certain amount of time each day learning to embroider. They practiced different stitches on a piece of linen that was called a sampler. Houses, animals, numbers, the letters of the alphabet, and sometimes verses were embroidered on the sampler. When the stitching was finished, the little girl added her name, her age, and the date.

Each country has its own style of embroidery. The Chinese and Japanese use silk and gold threads on fine damask to embroider dragons, birds, flowers, and landscapes. Warm countries, such as Spain and Italy, produce embroideries that are gay in color and pattern.

France and Switzerland are noted for the most delicate kind of needlework, often embroidered in plain white. In the Balkan countries embroidery of fine stitches in vivid colors decorates clothing and linens that are passed on from generation to generation.

436

hIC

SAMPLER

AYEUX TAPESTRY

What Is Kapok?

Today, chemists are able to create all kinds of wonderful products in their laboratories. So many of them appear on the market under various names that we sometimes forget that Nature herself is able to turn out some pretty interesting products, too! Kapok is one of these.

Kapok is the product of a tree of the bombax family that is cultivated in Java, the Philippines, Malay, and Ceylon. The tree is native to the West Indies and other parts of tropical America.

Since this tree can be grown under widely different conditions, many varieties of it have been developed. In fact, there are now at least fifty-four different trees that produce what we call kapok, and some of these trees yield crops for fifty years or longer.

What is kapok? It looks like fine, yellowish, shiny cotton. It grows in fat pods on these tall trees. The growing kapok fibers are not attached to the seeds, so ginning (as with cotton) is not necessary.

The cleaned kapok fiber, which is called floss, is springy, slick, and odorless. It sheds water like a duck's back, and resists the passage of sound and heat. It is half as heavy as wool and just as warm. High-quality floss supports as much as thirty-eight times its own weight in water.

KAPOK PODS

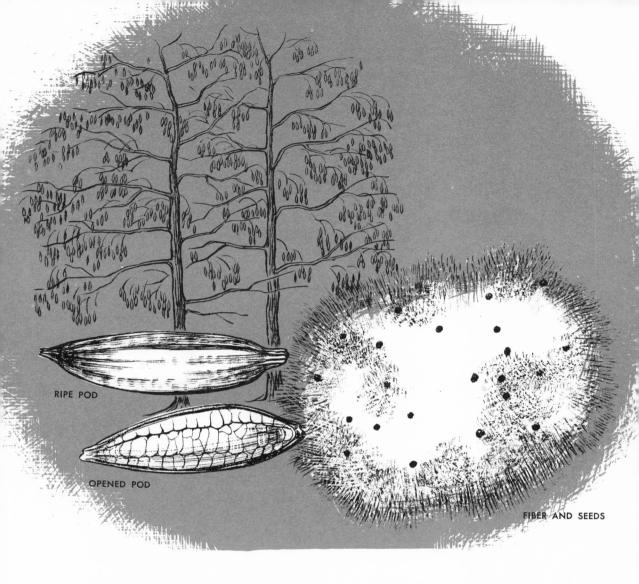

RIPE POD

OPENED POD

FIBER AND SEEDS

Each kapok fiber is a smooth closed tube coated with wax. Not having the twist that grows in cotton fibers or the hooks found in sheep's wool, kapok won't mat or felt, and cannot be spun into threads.

Kapok-stuffed life preservers support six times as much weight as those filled with cork. They last three to five times as long without getting waterlogged. In wartime, kapok is used to line tanks, trench coats, and sleeping bags. In peacetime, it is used to insulate refrigerators and airplanes, and in softballs, boxing gloves, mattresses, and upholstery. The seeds of the kapok tree yield an oil that is used in food and in making soap.

LOG WITH BARK

BARK-REMOVING DRUM

GRINDER

PAPER MACHINE

How Is Paper Processed?

Paper is made of millions of tiny fibers. The fibers are cellulose, a substance from the cell walls of plants. The cellulose used in paper today comes mostly from trees.

When the bark of a tree log has been stripped off, the wood is ready to be turned into pulp. Pulping is done either by grinding up the wood or by cooking it with chemicals. Some pulping methods use both grinding and cooking.

The wood pulp is then screened and washed to clean out impurities and chemicals. It may then be bleached to make the paper whiter, so that printing or writing shows up better on it.

In the next step, the pulp is beaten in a large mixing machine and mixed with water. The beating frays the fibers, which helps them mat together. Starch, clay, or other materials may be added to improve the surface of the paper for printing and writing.

The pulp then goes into a machine called a Jordan refiner, where the fibers are trimmed evenly. At this stage the pulp consists of 99 percent water and 1 percent fiber. It is now ready to go into the paper-making machine.

In this machine, water drains out of the pulp through a screen, and suction pumps remove more water. The screen vibrates to make the fibers interlock and mat together. The wet mat then passes under a roller that presses it down into a smoother sheet.

The sheet goes through a series of pressing rolls, which squeeze out water and make the paper dense and smooth. Then it travels through a series of heated drums called dryers. At this time a coating can be applied to make the paper slick and shiny. Paper comes off the machines in large rolls. It is trimmed to take off the rough edges and cut to the desired width.

What Is Origami?

You have probably enjoyed many, many times just sitting around and folding pieces of paper to make them look like a bird, a ship, or some animal. What you probably didn't realize is that you were practicing a very ancient "art," the art of paper folding, or origami.

The Chinese invented paper almost two thousand years ago, and origami is just as old as paper itself. It is possible that the art developed from an ancient custom: the Chinese funeral rite of making paper houses, furniture, vehicles, and servants, as well as paper money. In fact, at Buddhist funerals colored-paper symbols of all kinds of things are burned. The idea is that the dead person will enjoy all the comforts that are symbolized by the paper objects in the next world.

In the seventh century paper folding was brought to Japan. The Japanese developed many of China's arts and crafts into their own forms of expression. They found new methods of folding paper into pretty forms and images, and made origami a highly creative art.

From a few simple folds the Japanese make things of great beauty and realism. Some decorate the shrines and temples as religious symbols. Others, such as the crane, tortoise, and lobster, are good-luck symbols. These are fastened to gifts as ornaments or used as festive decorations.

Japanese magicians, traveling in Europe, introduced paper folding to the western world. The magicians were so expert that with a few quick movements they could make a bird, animal, or insect to surprise and delight the audience.

Did you know that many great men of the past not only enjoyed origami, but also became very good at it? Among these people were Leonardo da Vinci, the poet Shelley, and the writer Lewis Carroll, the author of *Alice in Wonderland*.

What Makes Glue Stick?

Glue is an adhesive. An adhesive is any substance that is used to bond (join) two or more pieces of material without mechanical fasteners.

Adhesives are made out of a great variety of materials. Some are made from animal by-products, such as hides, bones, or blood; others are prepared from various vegetable starches. The latest developments are the synthetic resins, which are made from chemical raw materials.

Glue is one of the oldest adhesives known to man. It is an impure form of gelatin, and is obtained chiefly by boiling animal hides and bones. Some glue is also made from fish.

Glue makes a very strong joint, but it is not waterproof; it dissolves easily in hot water. Glue was by far the most important adhesive until the latter part of the nineteenth century. Even today many people call all adhesives glue, which they are not, of course.

Adhesives act in three different ways to join materials. They may penetrate the tiny surface pores of the materials and hold them together physically, the way a burr sticks to clothing. This is known as mechanical bonding.

Or, an adhesive may act by means of powerful but little-understood forces of attraction between its molecules and the surface molecules of the pieces being joined. This is called intermolecular bonding.

With certain materials, however, the adhesive actually unites chemically with the surface molecules of the pieces being joined. This is chemical bonding.

Whenever adhesives are used, the surfaces to be joined must be clean and must fit each other closely. The strength of the bond depends to a great degree on the surface areas that are actually in contact with the adhesive. If the surfaces do not fit closely, the adhesive may shrink away while drying and leave only small patches firmly bonded.

How Many Kinds of Nails Are There?

Nails are usually used for joining pieces of wood or for fastening other materials to wood. Nails are simply hammered into place and are held there by friction. Some nails have roughened shanks so that they will hold better.

Most nails are made by machine from heavy steel wire. These machines can make hundreds of nails per minute. First the machine cuts the wire to the correct length. Then it flattens one end of the wire to make the head. And finally, it cuts the point at the other end.

Some types of nails, called cut nails, are stamped, or cut, from sheets of metal. Cut nails are rectangular, rather than round.

There is a tremendous variety of nails, since they are used for so many different purposes. The ordinary all-purpose nails most of us use are called common nails. Finishing nails, used in furniture and cabinetwork, have very small heads that do not show on the finished work.

Roofing nails have very large heads. They are used for nailing shingles or tar paper to a roof. The large head holds the thin material and keeps it from tearing loose.

Some nails have two heads, one above the other. The nail is driven only as far as the first head. The top head of the nail remains above the surface of the work, to make it easy to pull the nail out. Two-headed nails are used to hold scaffolding and other temporary structures together.

Most nails are made of steel. Masonry nails, used on concrete or masonry, are made of specially hardened steel. Some nails, such as roofing nails, are galvanized. That means they are coated with zinc to prevent rusting.

Nails used on boats must be extra rustproof. They are usually made of brass or bronze. Large nails are called spikes, and are usually over six inches long.

What Are Dies and Molds?

Many of the things we see and use every day are made with dies or molds.

Dies are special tools that shape and cut metal and plastic by pressure. If you have ever watched as star-shaped cookies were punched out of a sheet of dough by a cookie cutter, you have seen a very simple type of die in action.

Molds are special tools used to shape materials in liquid form. Metal, plastic, or whatever other material is used is poured or forced into the cavity of the mold and is allowed to solidify. A mold of gelatin is an example of a very simple type of mold.

Dies are used in industry to make parts with shapes that are hard to produce with other machine tools. Examples are automobile parts, such as hoods and fenders.

Molds are also used in industry to make parts, such as refrigerator-door handles, radio casings, and some automobile radiator grilles.

To make parts like these by regular machine operations of cutting, grinding, and drilling would take a great deal of time and much material would be wasted. With dies they can be stamped out like cookies. The same holds true for molds.

In addition to producing difficult shapes, dies and molds are good for fast production of large numbers of identical parts. The parts that dies and molds turn out usually need no finishing. Difficult parts may require a little grinding or polishing to remove seams on molded parts and rough edges on die-stamped parts.

Molds and dies in general are made in two halves. When brought together they will make the shape of the part. Molds form the outside shape only. Dies can form both the inside and outside shapes.

Did you know that dies were used as long ago as 650 B.C., when Greek metalworkers made silver coins with them? The coins were produced by pounding metal into a pattern cut into a harder metal block.

What Is Ceramics?

In a museum you can see vases, jars, cups, and dishes—all pieces of pottery. Pottery is clay that has been shaped when soft, then hardened by heat. The art of making such products is called ceramics.

The word "ceramics" is sometimes used for enamel and glass, as well as pottery. In all three cases the work involves applying heat to earthy materials—clay, sand, or ground rock.

Ceramics is one of the oldest of man's arts. Clay is found almost everywhere. Pieces of ceramic work have been found that date from before the beginning of recorded history. A well-hardened piece of pottery is very durable. It may break, but it will not rot or rust away.

The outstanding early potters were the Chinese. They made a very hard and translucent type of pottery known as porcelain. In the West, porcelain became known as china, after the country that first produced it.

EARTHENWARE

PORCELAIN

There are six main groups of clay that are used in ceramics. The first is called common clay, and is not used for making fine pottery. The pottery made from common clay is called earthenware.

The purest type of clay is called kaolin, or china clay. It is used to make Chinese porcelain. When fired, it turns a pure white.

Many years ago, before refrigeration was developed, ceramic jugs (called "crockery") were used to keep liquids cool. This is because crockery is a coarse type of ceramics that permits liquids to seep through its tiny pores. The liquid then evaporates on the outside. And the constant evaporation of the moisture keeps the jug and its contents cool.

Today, however, most crockery is glazed and has a shiny surface; this doesn't allow this kind of evaporation to take place.

What Is Concrete?

Concrete is one of the most useful building materials ever developed by man. It is strong, long-lasting, fairly cheap to use, and easy to handle. It is not harmed by fire, water, weather, or heavy pressures. Huge dams, bridges, and skyscrapers, as well as highways, homes, and airport runways, are built of concrete.

Concrete is made from Portland cement, water, and sand, gravel, or crushed stone. The materials are measured and mixed together to make concrete. After mixing, the concrete can be given any shape that is wanted by placing it in molds that are called forms.

The mixing turns the water and cement into a paste that coats the pieces of sand and gravel. When this paste hardens, it holds the pieces together in a solid, rock-like mass. Keeping the concrete moist after putting it in the forms makes it even harder. Because of a chemical reaction between the cement and the water, the concrete keeps getting harder as it ages.

Concrete is treated in various ways to make it suitable for special purposes. For example, when concrete is used in long, slender parts, it may snap or be pulled apart. To make concrete structures hold up under forces that would bend them or pull them apart, steel rods or mesh can be set in the concrete. This is called reinforced concrete.

Concrete can also be strengthened by casting (pouring) it around high-tension steel wires. When these wires are tightened—before the concrete hardens—they place the concrete in a squeeze that makes it stronger. Such concrete is called prestressed concrete.

A kind of concrete is now made that contains billions of tiny air bubbles in each cubic inch. It is called air-entrained concrete. Highways built of this concrete are not harmed by freezing and thawing.

So you can see how much can be done with concrete to make it serve special needs in construction.

What Is a Dredge?

The water in harbors, rivers, and lakes often contains a large amount of mud and silt, which settle on the bottom. If enough of this material builds up, the water becomes too shallow for ships to use. To keep the waterways open, the mud and silt must be scooped up and removed from time to time. The machines used for this are called dredges.

Some of these dredges are mounted on ship hulls and can sail about under their own power. Others are mounted on floating platforms that have to be towed about in the water.

Dredges use several different kinds of power. Suction dredges, which suck up mud and silt like a vacuum cleaner, are usually driven by steam turbines or diesel engines. Some dredges use electric power supplied from the shore. Dipper dredges operate by means of steam or diesel power.

A dipper dredge is a seagoing version of the common steam shovel. A dipper on the end of a dipper stick is attached to a long boom that can be raised and lowered. The steel cutting teeth of the dipper bite into the mud. When the boom is raised and swung over a barge, the hinged bottom of the dipper opens and dumps its load into the barge.

A kind of dredge known as a grab dredge has two types of buckets: the "clamshell" and the "orange peel." The clamshell bucket has two hinged parts that open to scoop up the mud. The orange-peel bucket has three hinged parts.

The ladder-type bucket dredge scoops up mud and silt with an endless chain of buckets. The buckets are mounted on a long steel frame, which is lowered to the bottom. As each bucket reaches the bottom, it fills with mud and silt. It travels back to the surface, and at the top of the frame it up-ends, spilling its load onto a barge.

Ladder bucket dredges are also used in mining operations in swampy areas in Alaska, California, South America, and many other places. They dig up the earth and feed it into huge washing cylinders that separate out the ore.

DIPPER DREDGE

SECTION OF LADDER-TYPE BUCKET DREDGE

How Do We Get Energy from Coal?

Let's start by finding out what coal is. Coal is made of the remains of ancient trees and plants that grew in great swampy jungles in warm, moist climates hundreds of millions of years ago.

When these trees and plants died, they fell into the quiet swamp waters, which protected them against rotting. Bacteria changed some parts of the wood to gases which escaped, leaving behind a black mixture, mostly carbon, which was to become a coal seam.

In time, thick layers of mud and sand were washed in on top of the vegetation. Pressure from this mud and sand gradually squeezed out most of the liquid, leaving behind a pasty mass which slowly hardened into coal. All this took place anywhere from a million to 250 million years ago.

Energy, the ability to do work, comes from matter. Everything in the world that has mass (or weight) and takes up space is made of matter. Energy and matter are the two things that make up the universe and everything in it, and also keep everything going.

Matter is made of atoms, and every atom has in it particles of energy. Energy holds the parts of an atom together. Matter can be changed into energy and energy into matter, over and over again.

The energy in coal originally came from the sun. Millions of years ago plants used this energy for chemical transformations necessary to growth, and carbon dioxide from the air was built into carbon compounds that became coal.

The way we release this energy from the coal is by means of heat. Heat makes atoms and molecules move faster and faster, until some of the electrons jump out of them. When coal is burned, it supplies heat energy. The energy was there all the time in a form we call potential energy. The heat releases the stored energy and changes it into kinetic, or working energy.

This is the energy that is used to drive the engines and generators that work for us.

OIL DRILL BITS

How Does an Oil Derrick Work?

When you think about drilling for oil, you may imagine a tall steel structure with black oil gushing out of it. But gushers are a thing of the past. Modern drilling methods have practically eliminated them.

Many kinds of oil derricks are used. Some are as tall as a twenty-story office building, others are attached to trucks, and still others are located on platforms and barges for offshore drilling.

Rotary drilling accounts for about 85 percent of the wells in the United States. Rotary drilling uses a rapidly-turning bit that bores into the earth. Different kinds of bits are used for different kinds of rock. Attached to the bit is a drilling pipe in thirty-foot sections called joints, each weighing about five hundred pounds.

A flat steel turntable grips and turns the pipe, which extends through it into the earth. As the pipe turns, the bit attached to it cuts into the earth. Section after section of pipe is added as the drill chews its way downward.

During the drilling, "drilling mud" is pumped down inside the pipe, which cools and lubricates the bit. As the hole deepens, a long steel pipe, called casing, is added from time to time.

Cutting through rock dulls the bit, so it must be replaced often. This means all the drill pipe must be pulled out of the hole. There is a lot of work involved in this, and it may take four to six hours to replace the bit and put the pipe down again.

When a well has reached a certain depth, the bit and drill are pulled up, and casing is run all the way down and filled with chemical mud. A small gun is lowered to make holes in the casing and start the oil flowing. Later, water is pumped in to get rid of the mud. Pressure begins to rise from the well, and finally oil begins to bubble out of valves into an open tank.

How Does a Geiger Counter Work?

You've probably read about a modern type of "prospector" who goes out looking for precious metals with a Geiger counter. Or perhaps, when people are talking about the danger of atom bombs, there is mention of using Geiger counters as a safety measure.

In both cases, what is involved is the matter of radiation. Certain radioactive substances give off rays, and a Geiger counter is a simple way of detecting and measuring these rays. The Geiger counter was invented by Hans Geiger, and later perfected by a man called Müller.

It is really a kind of vacuum tube. In simple terms, the tube consists of a very thin glass envelope, much like an ordinary radio tube. Inside are two metal plates and a small amount of gas, such as argon.

You're familiar with another kind of tube that contains a gas—the neon tube. In the neon tube or lamp, the gas can be made to glow by connecting the plates to a source of electrical voltage, providing this voltage is high enough. The high voltage breaks the gas down and allows a large flow of electrons to take place between the plates. And when this flow takes place, the gas inside the tube begins to glow.

In a Geiger counter, the voltage is deliberately kept too low so that the glow of the gas won't take place under normal conditions. Now, let's assume there is some radioactive substance nearby. A ray from this radioactive substance enters the tube and collides with the gas molecules. This gives them enough energy (just as higher voltage would) to cause the gas to glow.

So now there is a current surging through the tube. This current can be put through an indicating meter so that you can read the amount of radiation that has entered the tube. Or, it can be made to produce that familiar ticking sound that is associated with Geiger counters.

Since a Geiger counter is a means of detecting radiation, it obviously can't detect anything that doesn't emit rays. So its use is limited in searching for precious metals.

GLASS TUBE

WIRE ANODE

METAL CYLINDER (CATHODE)

METER

RADIOACTIVE SUBSTANCE

How Do Escalators Work?

An escalator is basically a set of moving stairs.

Each step is loosely connected to the next step by two very heavy roller chains. This is so that the steps can rise and sink easily. Each step has axles with wheels or rollers on them. The wheels rest on metal tracks inside a steel frame called a truss. The truss rests between two floors like a steeply slanted ladder. In fact, the word "escalator" was made up from a Latin word meaning ladder.

The steps lie flat at each end of the escalator. This is to make it easier for passengers to get on and off. As the steps travel up or down the escalator, they automatically rise so that they look like steps in a staircase. As the steps approach the end of the ride, they automatically flatten out again.

Under the floor at the top end of the escalator is a set of sprockets. A sprocket is a wheel with projecting teeth, like the gear wheel of a bicycle.

The teeth of the sprocket catch the links of the roller chain and drive it around and around, pulling the steps along their rails. The sprocket at the top end of the escalator is driven by an electric motor beneath the floor. The chains run over pulleys at the bottom. These pulleys steer the chains properly and keep them tight.

At each side of the moving steps is a protective wall called a balustrade to keep passengers from falling off the sides of the steps. On top of the balustrade is a moving endless belt of rubber or metal, which is the handrail passengers hold onto to keep their balance.

The first escalator was patented in the United States in 1859, but it wasn't used commercially. The first practical escalator was built in 1891.

How Are Bells Rung?

For hundreds of years bells in church towers have been rung for a variety of purposes. Bells reminded Christians of the relation of the church to their daily lives. They would be rung at daybreak to wake people up and call them to morning prayers. Through the day the bells counted the hours, the half-hours, and the quarters. They pealed for weddings and tolled for funerals, and were heard at Easter and Christmas.

A bell may be rung in two ways: the bell may be swung to hit the clapper; or the bell may be struck by the clapper or by some outside object. In the Far East some big stationary bells are rung by striking them with a log in the manner of a battering ram. One such bell in Burma weighs about ninety tons.

The Russians once cast a giant bell that weighed twice as much, but it cracked. To ring such a bell requires several men pulling a rope attached to the clapper.

In England a different method of bell-ringing was developed, called change-ringing. In change-ringing, the bells swing in complete circles in a definite order. The bells sound variations, or changes, on a descending scale. There is no melody, only a rhythmic pattern, and it can go on for hours.

There are over five thousand towers in England, each containing a set of bells for change-ringing. A set can number from three to twelve bells, and each bell is swung by one ringer using a rope and wheel.

A bell known as a clock-bell originated in the monasteries of Europe. This was because the monastic day was divided into devotional periods called canonical hours. In some monasteries the bell had to be rung seven times in twenty-four hours.

Since the first clock-bells could not ring by themselves, a man was hired for the job of striking them at the proper times of day. But in time he was replaced by machinery. With machinery it was possible to ring many bells, and it became customary to ring a short tune as a warning that the hour bell was about to strike.

VANGUARD 3

ECHO 1

PIONEER 5

How Does a Satellite Transmit TV Programs?

An artificial satellite is a man-made spacecraft circling the earth. Such satellites are sent into space for many purposes.

Satellites can be any size—from a tiny package of instruments to a huge balloon. They can weigh a few pounds or many tons. They can be any shape—balls, hatboxes, tin cans, bell buoys, and cigar boxes.

Some satellites have orbits around the earth as near as 110 miles away. Some travel 22,300 miles from earth. A satellite's orbit is chosen by scientists in advance, according to the task the satellite must perform.

TIROS

All satellites need electrical power to operate their equipment. The main source of this power is the sun. Satellites carry many solar cells on their outside surface. A solar cell is a device that uses sunlight to generate electricity; this electricity keeps the satellite's batteries charged.

Radio and television signals can be sent from one continent to another by means of communications satellites. Most communications satellites have receivers and transmitters. The receivers pick up radio and television broadcasts from a ground station.

Electronic devices then increase the strength of the broadcast signals. The transmitters send the broadcasts to a distant ground station, which may be on another continent.

TELSTAR

An example of such a satellite is Telstar. Telstar I was launched by the United States in July, 1962. Direct television transmission between the United States and Europe was first made possible by Telstar I.

One type of communications satellite has a "stationary" orbit around the earth. It is at a distance of 22,300 miles above the earth and completes one orbit in 24 hours, the same time it takes the earth to rotate on its axis. Thus the satellite is always in the same place above the earth. The Early Bird satellite is this kind of satellite. Because its orbit is so high, it can transmit signals over very great distances.

465

What Are Radio Waves?

Did you know that the space around you is filled at all times with radio waves from nearby broadcasting stations? These waves cause minute vibrations in all the metal objects in the room. You cannot hear the vibrations until they become sound waves, and they become sound waves only when you turn on your radio.

A radio wave might be called a disturbance that moves out into space. When electrons move back and forth rapidly, we have a radio wave. Heat and light also travel through space in the form of waves. The difference is that radio waves have a much longer wavelength than either heat or light waves.

Radio waves travel through space in much the same way that waves travel when a pebble is dropped into water. The waves radiate in all directions from their source. Although all radio waves travel at a speed of about 186,000 miles a second, the number of radio waves that travel past a point in one second can vary greatly. This number is called the frequency.

WAVELENGTH

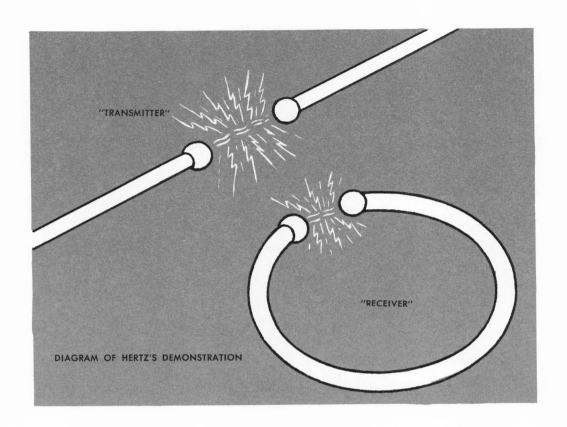

"TRANSMITTER"

"RECEIVER"

DIAGRAM OF HERTZ'S DEMONSTRATION

One complete wavelength is called a cycle. So frequency is the number of complete cycles that take place in a second. If wavelength is short, the waves are close together; the crests are close together and follow each other quickly. If wavelength is long, crests are far apart and follow one another slowly. So long waves are of low frequency, because crests do not come as frequently as those of short waves.

High-frequency waves are measured in kilocycles, or thousands of cycles per second. On your radio, from left to right, are the numbers 540, 550, 560, and so on to 1600 kilocycles. Each number refers to a wave frequency. A radio program broadcasts its programs only on its own wave frequency.

The existence of radio waves was predicted long before they were actually discovered. The prediction was made in 1864 by James Maxwell. In 1888 a German physicist, Heinrich Hertz, demonstrated that the waves actually do exist, and travel through space.

What Is a Radio Telescope?

When we look at stars and planets through a telescope, we see light waves that they send out. Light is a form of radiation. But stars send out other forms of radiation besides light.

Part of the radiation from stars is sent out as radio waves. Some of these waves can be detected by special radio receivers here on earth. The radio receivers collect and magnify the radio waves, just as ordinary telescopes collect and magnify the picture the light waves give. These radio receivers are called radio telescopes.

There are many kinds of radio telescopes, but all of them consist of two parts—an antenna and a radio receiver. The antenna is often a huge, spectacular-looking metal dish. It may be fitted on a movable stand or mounting, so that it can be pointed to any part of the sky.

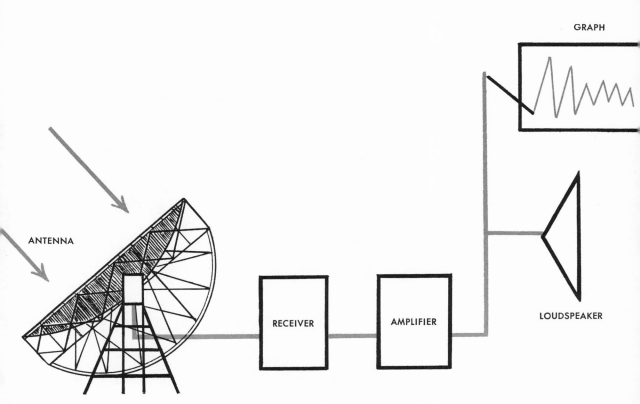

ANTENNA

RECEIVER

AMPLIFIER

GRAPH

LOUDSPEAKER

The large metal dish is what people usually think of when they think of a radio telescope. But the radio receiver is an equally important part. Without the receiver the huge antenna would be of no use.

Special kinds of radio receivers are needed to magnify, or amplify, the incoming waves. This is because the waves are often very weak. After the radio signals are amplified, they may be sent to a loudspeaker that lets the astronomer hear their hissing noise. Usually, however, a record of the radio waves is made on paper. The signals are written down in the form of a wavy line on a strip of paper.

Radio telescopes can operate in all kinds of weather, because radio waves are not affected by mist or fog or other kinds of bad weather. They can also be built in any place that is convenient, and don't have to be built on high ground or on mountains as optical telescopes must be.

Radio telescopes help astronomers learn facts about the universe that could not be learned in any other way we now have.

What Is Radio Astronomy?

In 1931, a communications engineer working for Bell Laboratories was exploring radio frequency disturbances in the atmosphere that might interfere with a transoceanic telephone. He noticed that he was picking up a noise that didn't come from thunderstorms—but from somewhere in outer space! He discovered that he was able to pick up radiation from far away in our galaxy; and a new branch of astronomy was born—radio astronomy.

Radio astronomy works in two ways. By using special types of antennae, it picks up radiations sent out by objects in space. Some of these are "thermal" radiations, the radiations that any heated body emits in radio frequency waves. But there is also noise, or "cosmic static," which is picked up from outer space and is not thermal in origin.

Another way radio astronomy works is in sending signals out to such objects as meteors and the moon, and obtaining the reflection. This is the way radar works.

So far radio astronomy has been most useful in the study of meteors, the moon, the sun, and other planets. By bouncing back beams from meteors, we learn much about their orbits. By studying the moon with radio astronomy, we learn something about its surface. For example, even before men landed on the moon, radio astronomy led scientists to believe that its surface layers consisted of powdered rocks.

Perhaps the most exciting use of radio astronomy is about to begin—the search for messages from other worlds! A radio telescope has been developed that can detect a signal almost 50 trillion miles away. What kind of signal do scientists hope to pick up? They believe that if there is some civilization somewhere in outer space, and it wants to make its presence known, it would probably send out some very simple signal such as a series of numbers. It is also thought that the signals would be of the radio frequency of 1,420 megacycles, the frequency at which natural hydrogen emits radio energy in outer space.

Index

Index

475